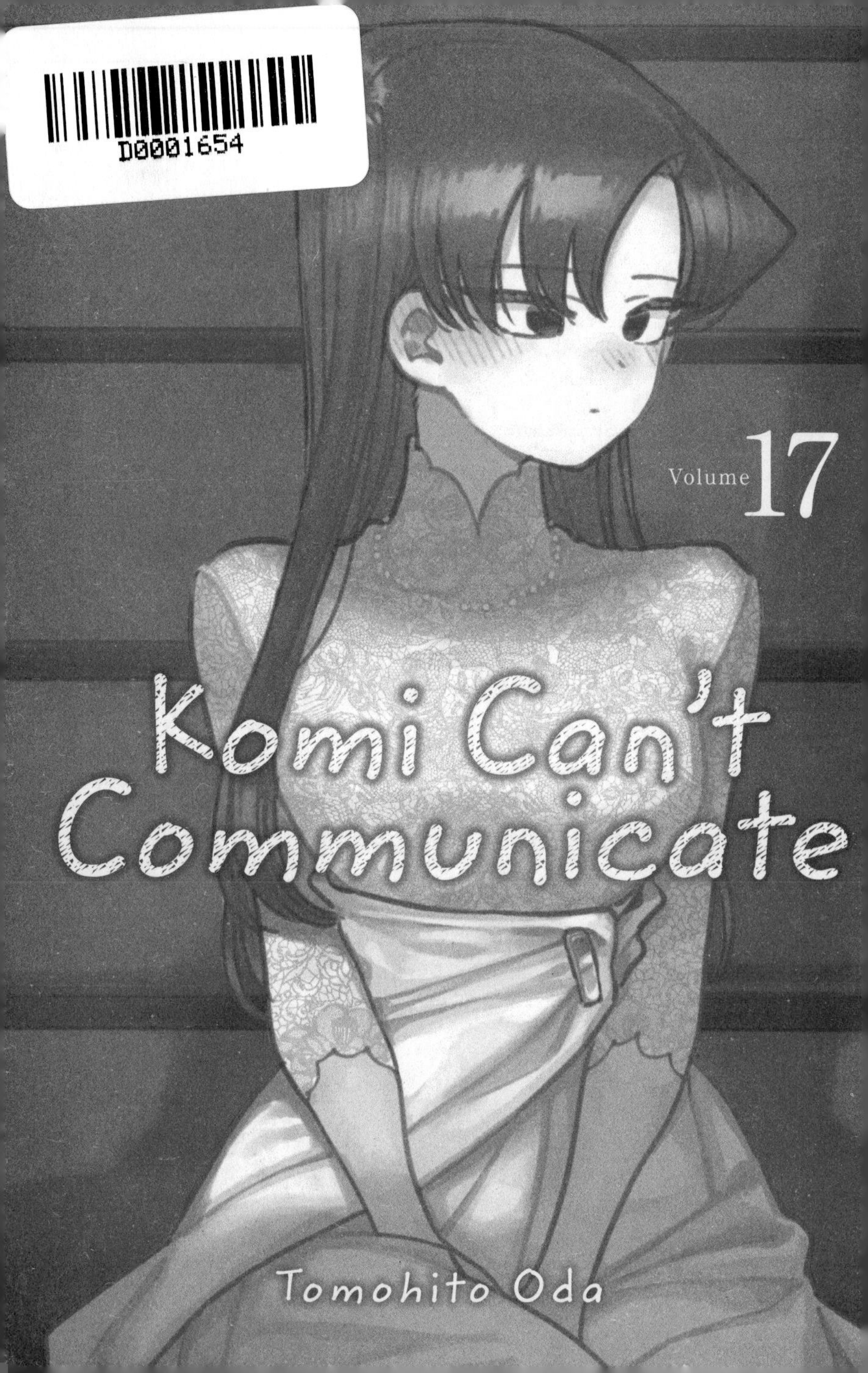

Komi Can't Communicate

Volume 17

Tomohito Oda

C o n t e n t s
17

Komi Can't Communicate

Communication disorders...

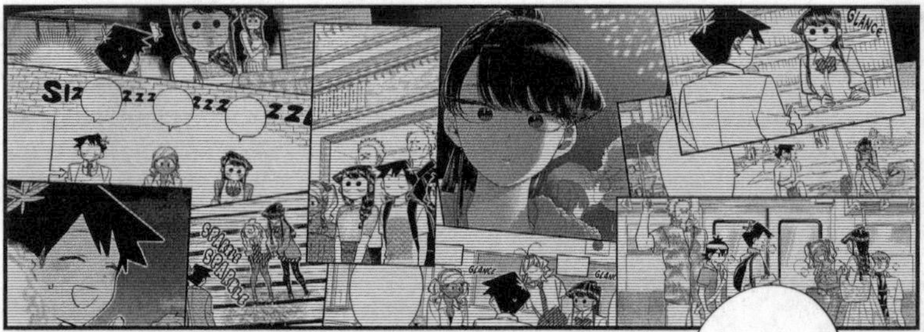
GLANCE

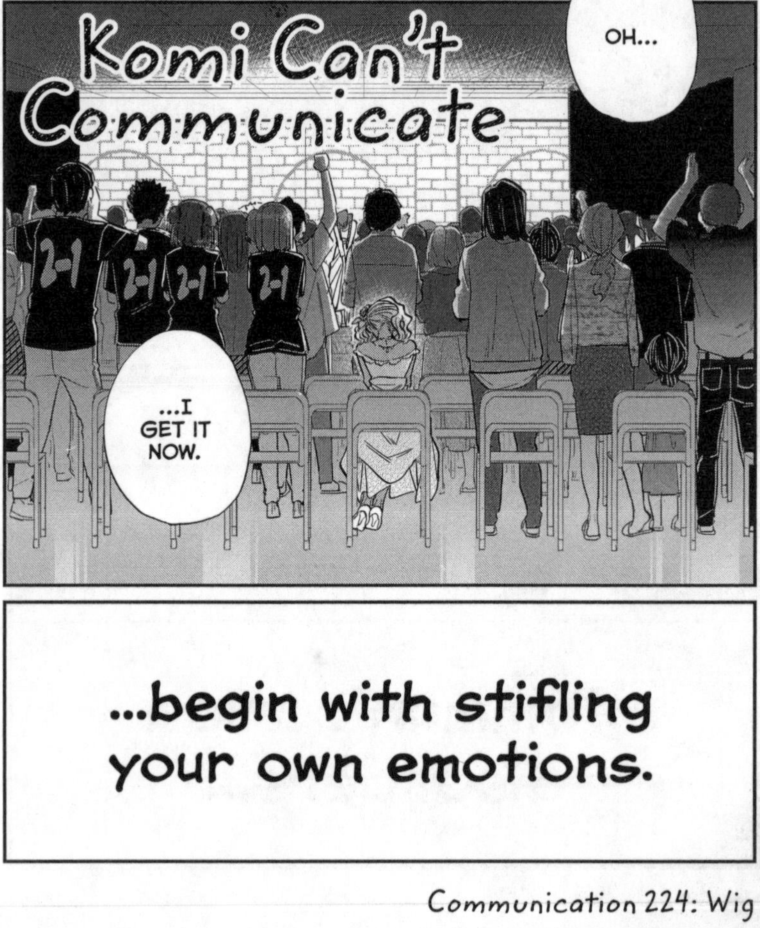
OH...
Komi Can't Communicate
...I GET IT NOW.

...begin with stifling your own emotions.

Communication 224: Wig

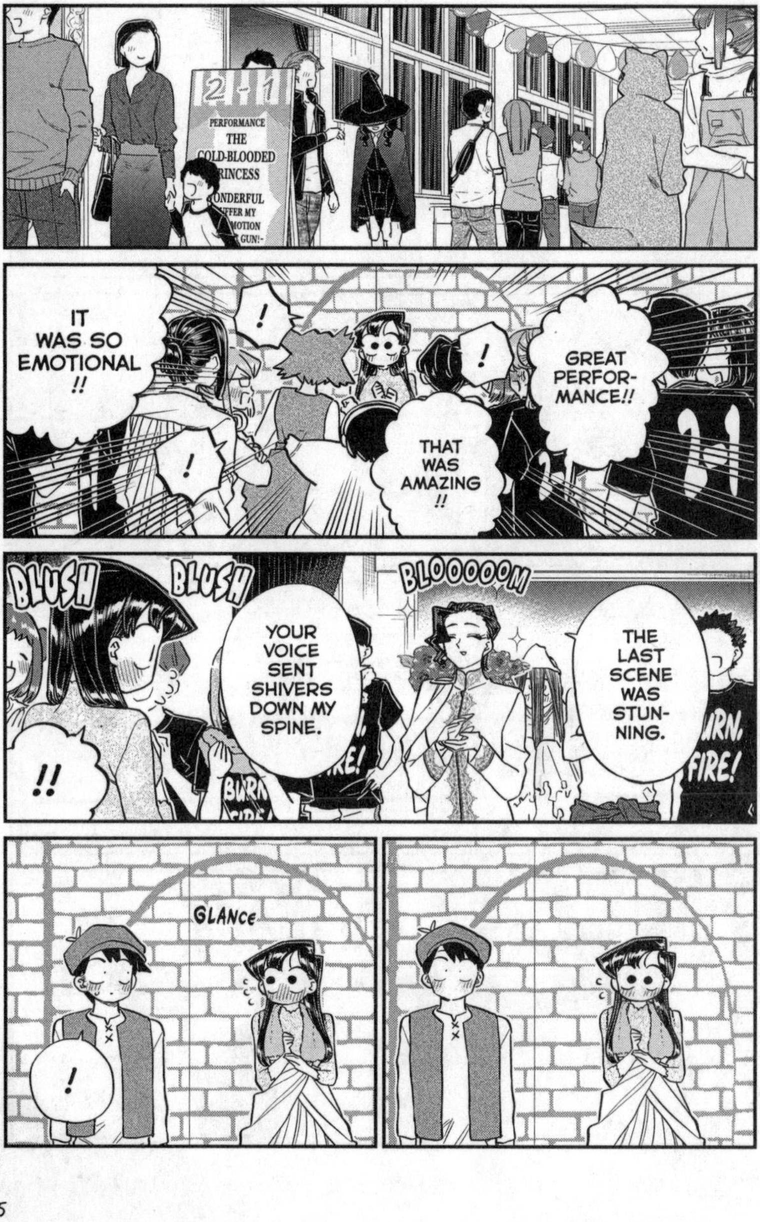
2-1
PERFORMANCE
THE COLD-BLOODED
GREAT PERFORMANCE!!
!
THAT WAS AMAZING!!
!
!
IT WAS SO EMOTIONAL!!
!
THE LAST SCENE WAS STUNNING.
BLOOOOOM
BURN, FIRE!
YOUR VOICE SENT SHIVERS DOWN MY SPINE.
BLUSH
BLUSH
!!
GLANCE
!

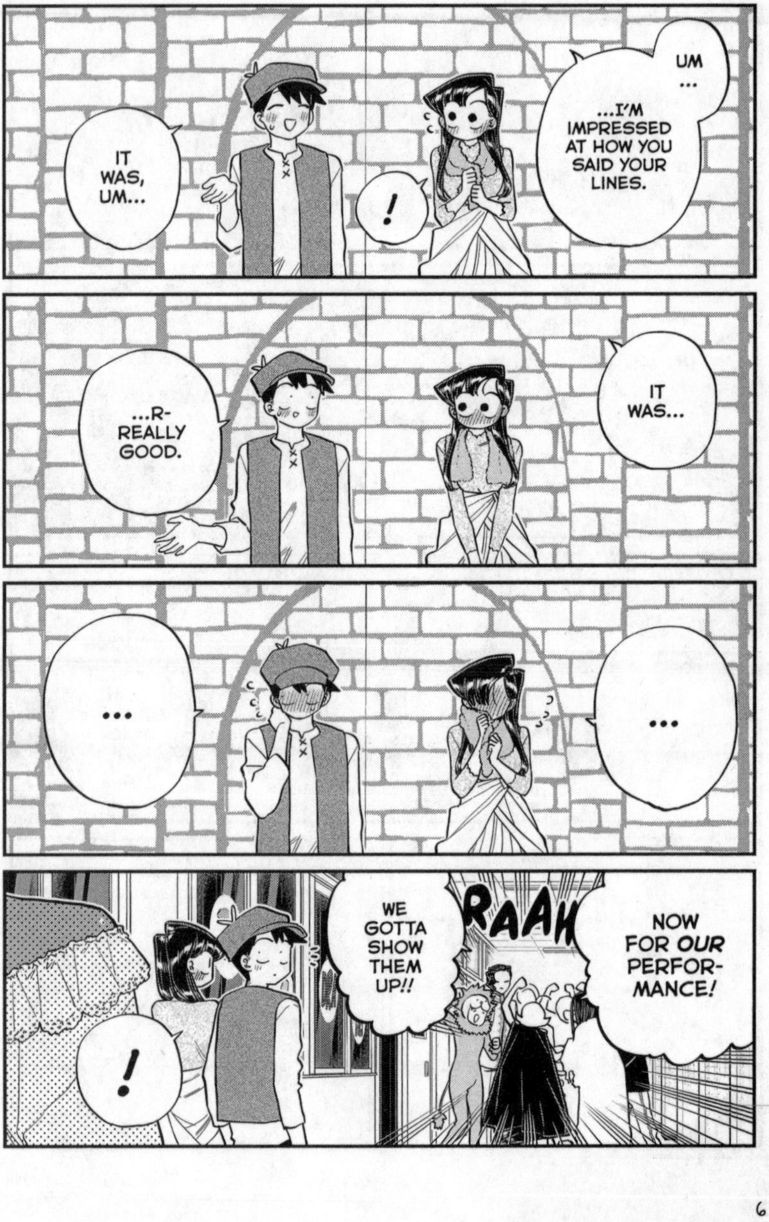
UM ... ...I'M IMPRESSED AT HOW YOU SAID YOUR LINES.
!
IT WAS, UM...
IT WAS...
...R-REALLY GOOD.
...
...
NOW FOR *OUR* PERFORMANCE!
RAAH
WE GOTTA SHOW THEM UP!!
!

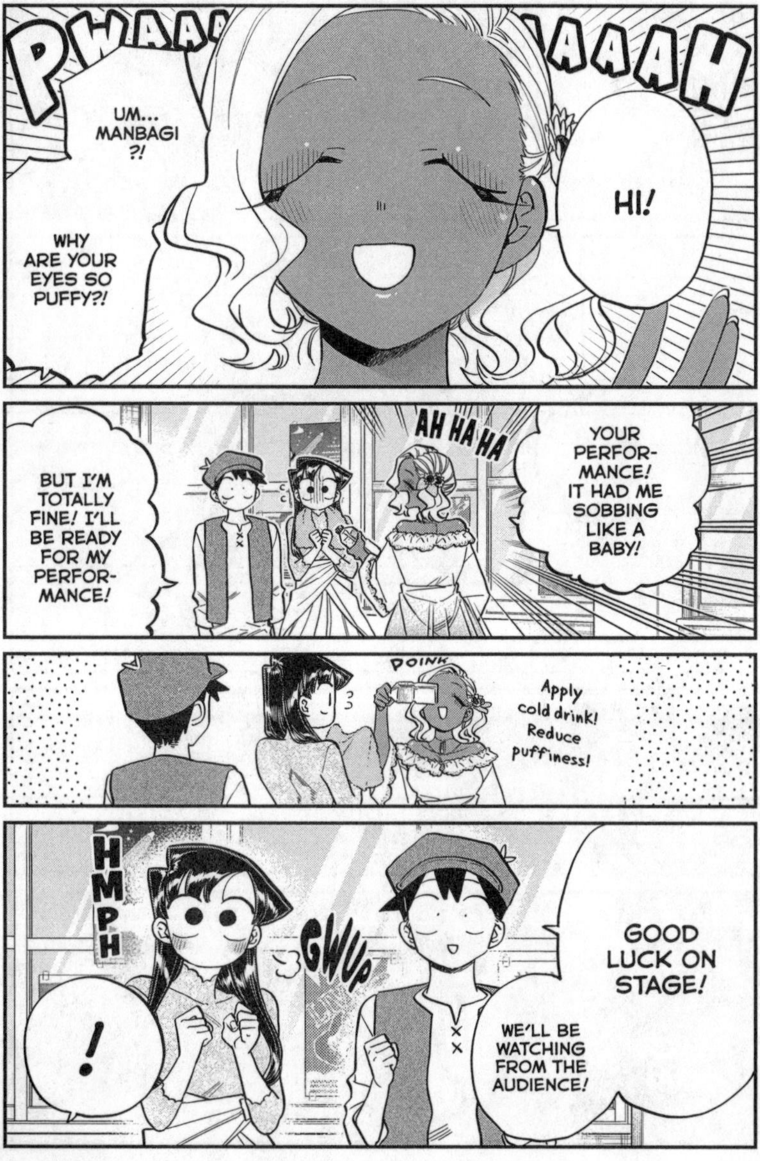
PWAAA
AAAAAH
HI!
UM... MANBAGI?!
WHY ARE YOUR EYES SO PUFFY?!
AH HA HA
YOUR PERFORMANCE! IT HAD ME SOBBING LIKE A BABY!
BUT I'M TOTALLY FINE! I'LL BE READY FOR MY PERFORMANCE!
DOINK
Apply cold drink! Reduce puffiness!
GOOD LUCK ON STAGE!
WE'LL BE WATCHING FROM THE AUDIENCE!
GWUP
HMPH
!

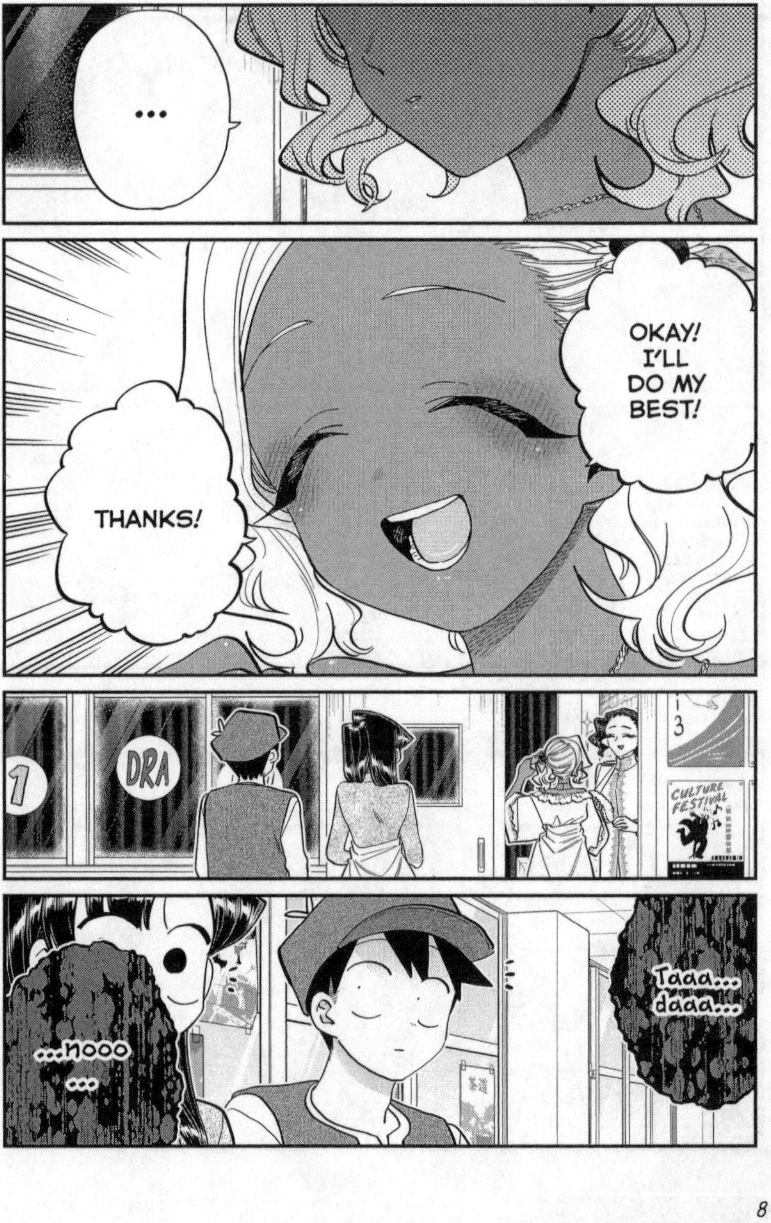
...
OKAY! I'LL DO MY BEST!
THANKS!
3
CULTURE FESTIVAL
DRA
1
Taaa... daaa...
...nooo ...

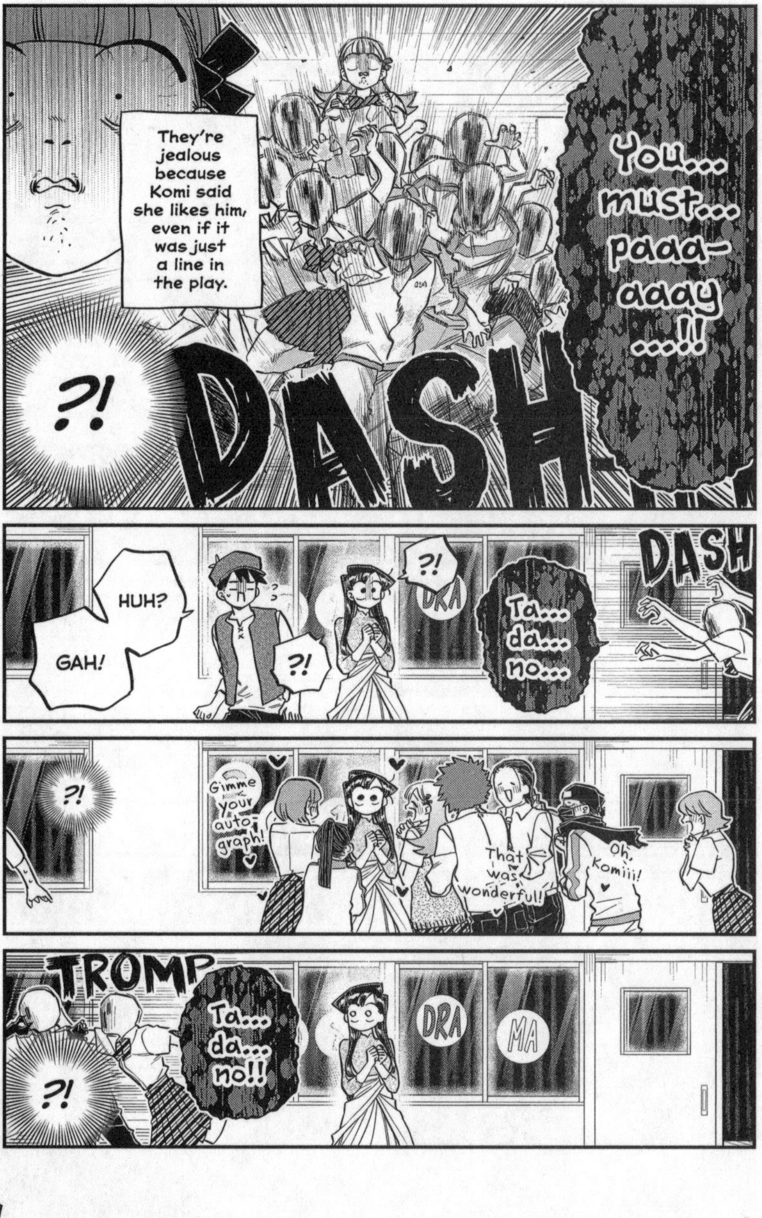
You... must... paaa-aaay ...!!
DASH
They're jealous because Komi said she likes him, even if it was just a line in the play.
?!
DASH
Ta... da... no...
?!
DRA
HUH?
?!
GAH!
Oh, Komiii!
That was wonderful!
Gimme your autograph!
?!
TROMP
MA
DRA
Ta... da... no!!
?!

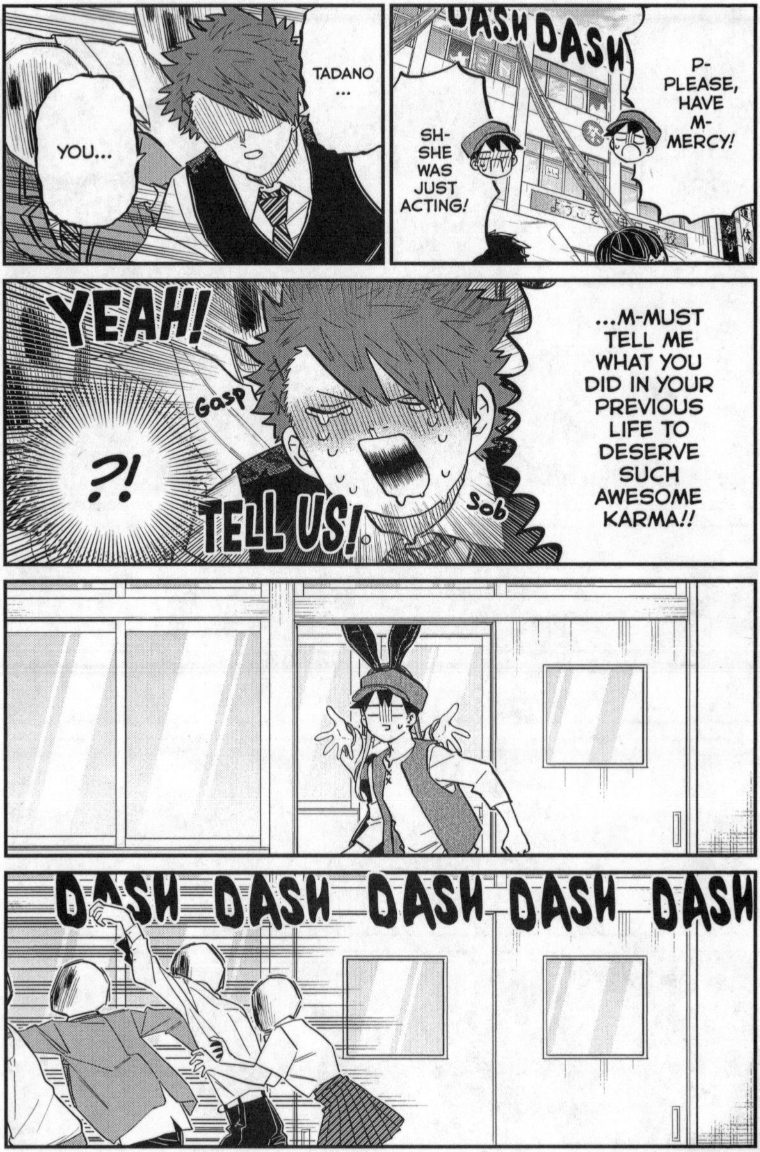
DASH DASH
P-PLEASE, HAVE M-MERCY!
SH-SHE WAS JUST ACTING!
TADANO...
YOU...
...M-MUST TELL ME WHAT YOU DID IN YOUR PREVIOUS LIFE TO DESERVE SUCH AWESOME KARMA!!
YEAH!
Gasp
Sob
?!
TELL US!
DASH DASH DASH DASH DASH

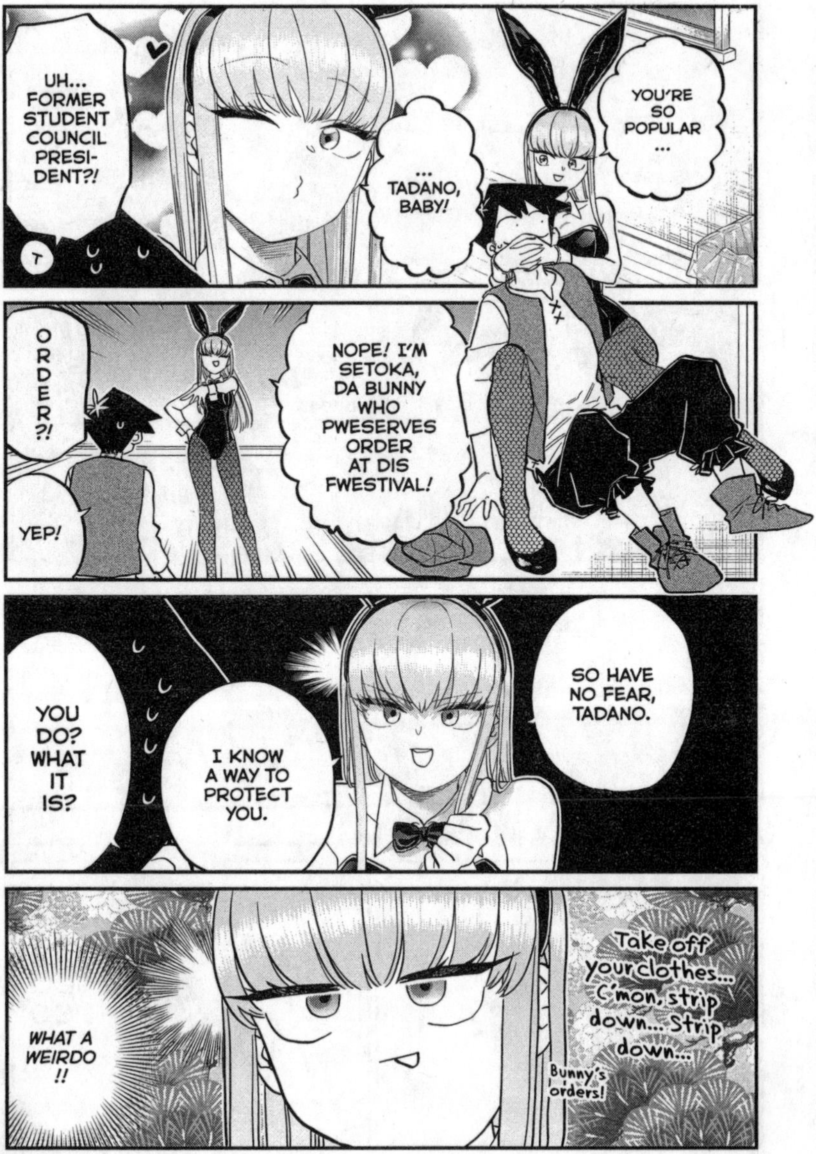
YOU'RE SO POPULAR ...
... TADANO, BABY!
UH... FORMER STUDENT COUNCIL PRESI- DENT?!
T
NOPE! I'M SETOKA, DA BUNNY WHO PWESERVES ORDER AT DIS FWESTIVAL!
ORDER?!
YEP!
SO HAVE NO FEAR, TADANO.
I KNOW A WAY TO PROTECT YOU.
YOU DO? WHAT IT IS?
Take off your clothes... C'mon, strip down... Strip down...
Bunny's orders!
WHAT A WEIRDO !!

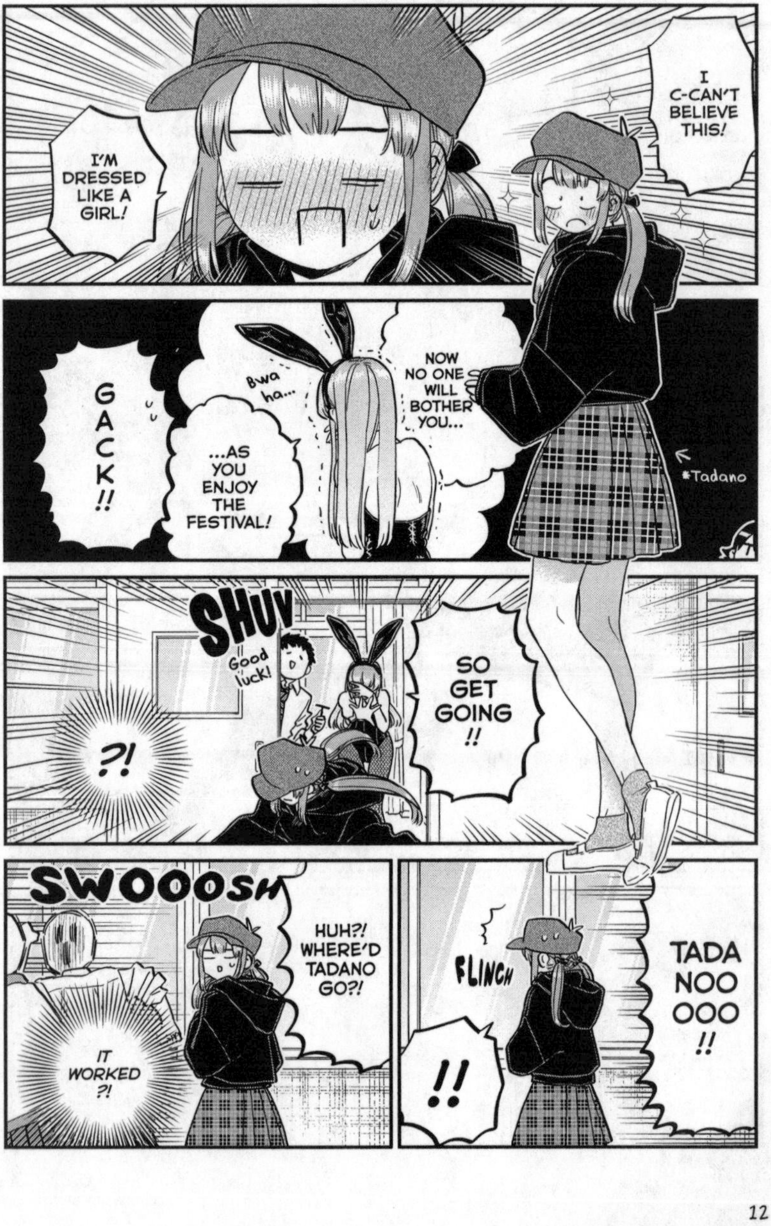
I C-CAN'T BELIEVE THIS!
I'M DRESSED LIKE A GIRL!
← *Tadano
NOW NO ONE WILL BOTHER YOU...
Bwa ha...
...AS YOU ENJOY THE FESTIVAL!
GACK!!
SO GET GOING!!
SHUV
Good luck!
?!
TADA NOO OOO!!
FLINCH
!!
SWOOOSH
HUH?! WHERE'D TADANO GO?!
IT WORKED?!

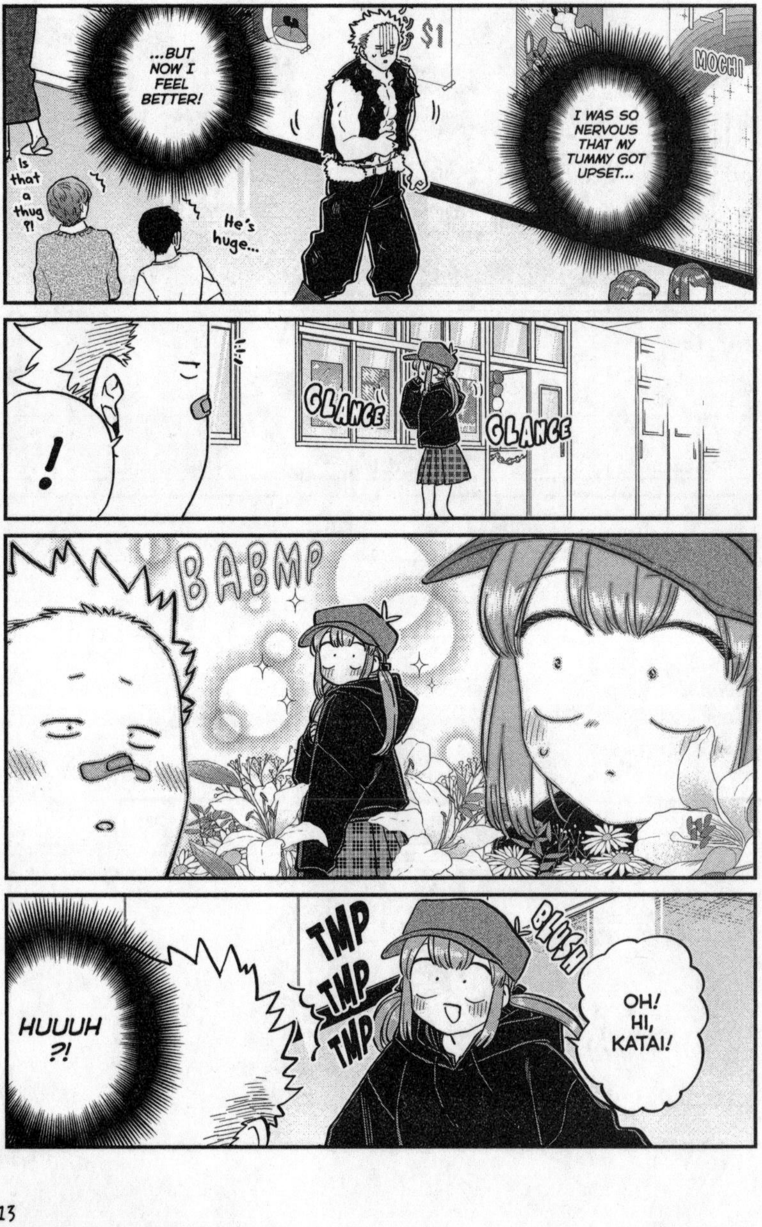
MOCHI
I WAS SO NERVOUS THAT MY TUMMY GOT UPSET...
$1
...BUT NOW I FEEL BETTER!
He's huge...
Is that a thug?!
GLANCE
GLANCE
BABMP
BLUSH
OH! HI, KATAI!
TMP TMP TMP
HUUUH?!

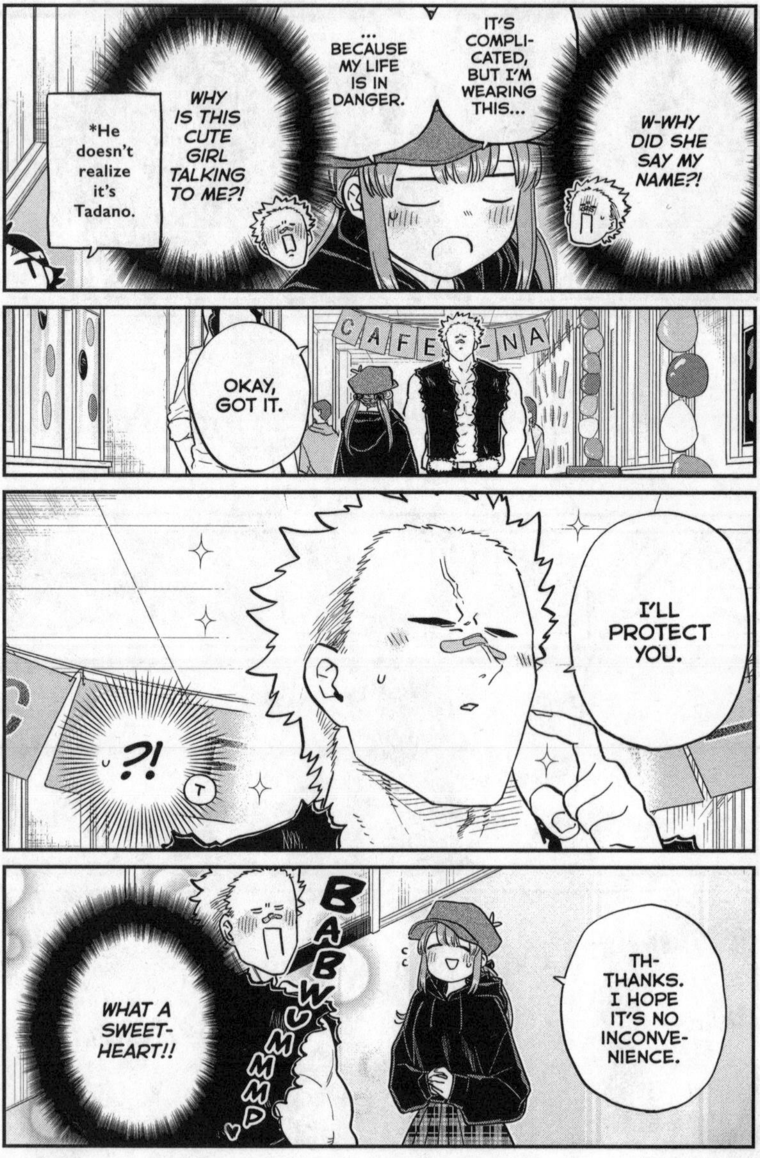
W-WHY DID SHE SAY MY NAME?!
IT'S COMPLICATED, BUT I'M WEARING THIS...
... BECAUSE MY LIFE IS IN DANGER.
WHY IS THIS CUTE GIRL TALKING TO ME?!
*He doesn't realize it's Tadano.
OKAY, GOT IT.
I'LL PROTECT YOU.
?!
TH-THANKS. I HOPE IT'S NO INCONVENIENCE.
BABWUMMMMP
WHAT A SWEET-HEART!!

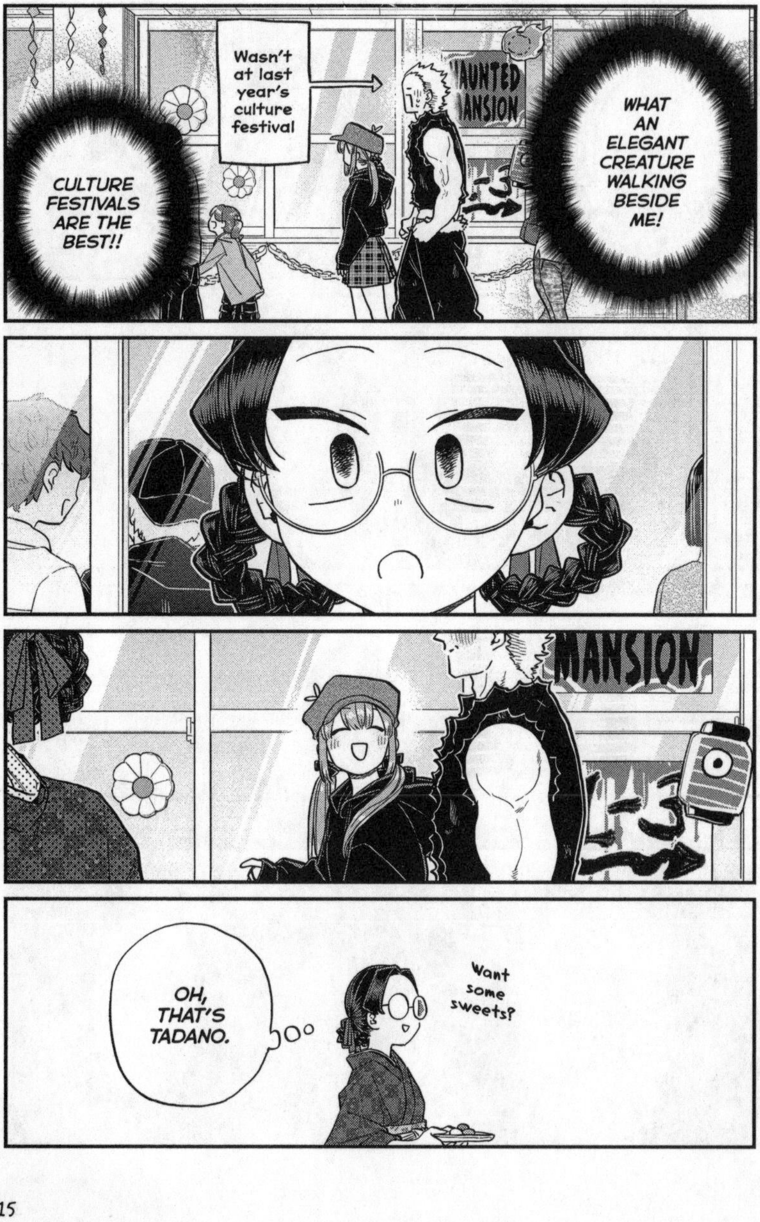

AUNTED
ANSION
WHAT AN ELEGANT CREATURE WALKING BESIDE ME!
Wasn't at last year's culture festival
CULTURE FESTIVALS ARE THE BEST!!
MANSION
Want some sweets?
OH, THAT'S TADANO.

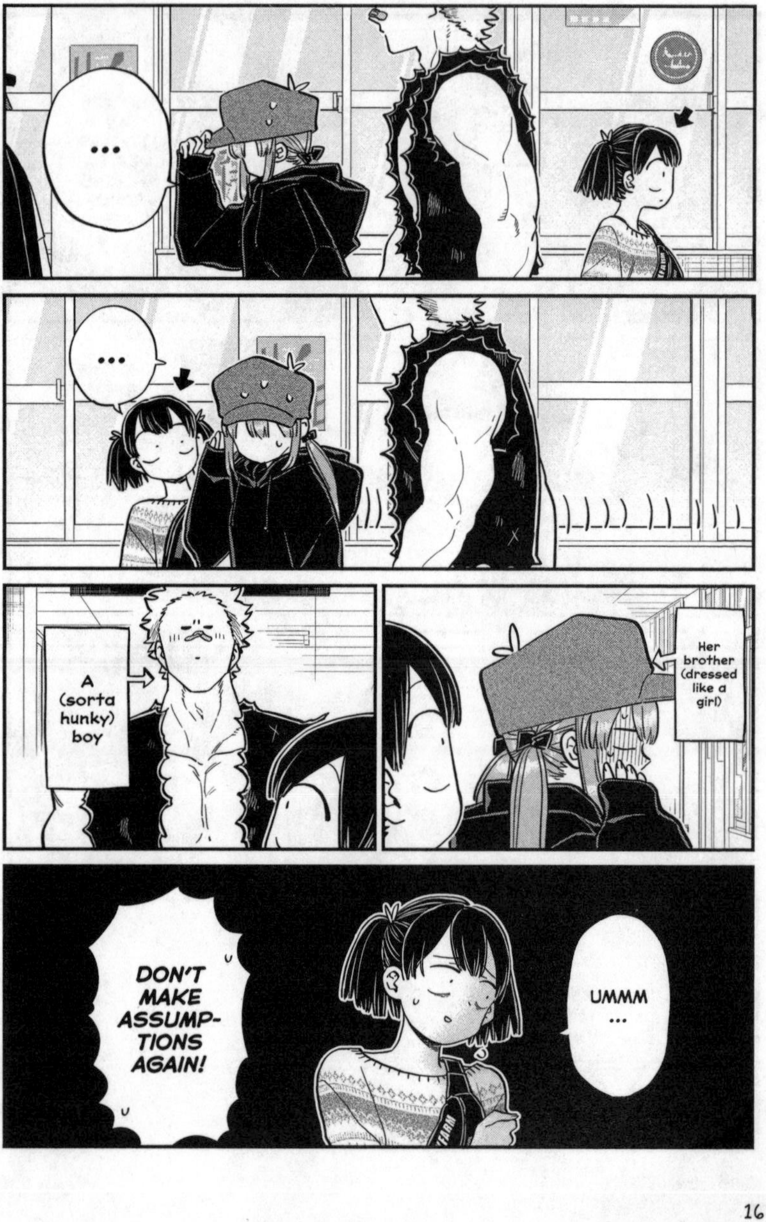
...
...
Her brother (dressed like a girl)
A (sorta hunky) boy
UMMM ...
DON'T MAKE ASSUMP-TIONS AGAIN!

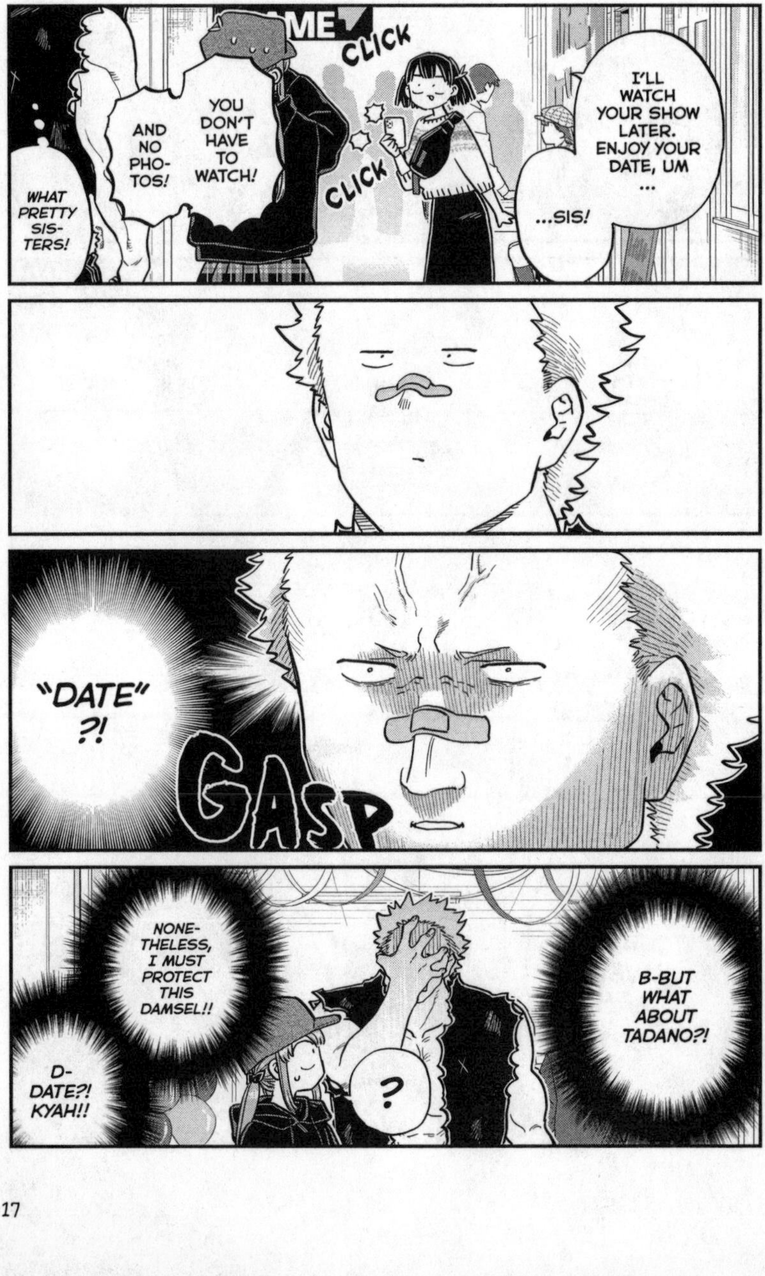
I'LL WATCH YOUR SHOW LATER. ENJOY YOUR DATE, UM ...
...SIS!
CLICK
YOU DON'T HAVE TO WATCH!
AND NO PHO-TOS!
CLICK
WHAT PRETTY SIS-TERS!
"DATE" ?!
GASP
B-BUT WHAT ABOUT TADANO?!
?
NONE-THELESS, I MUST PROTECT THIS DAMSEL!!
D-DATE?! KYAH!!

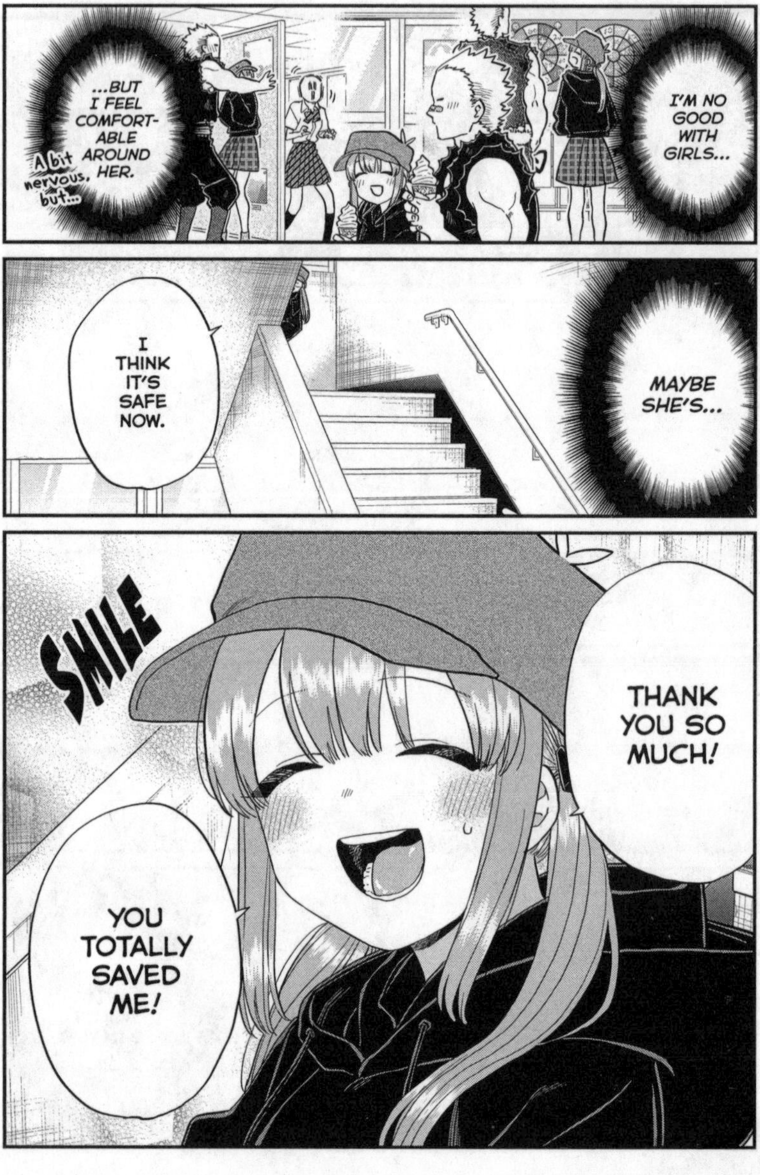
I'M NO GOOD WITH GIRLS...
...BUT I FEEL COMFORTABLE AROUND HER.
A bit nervous, but...
MAYBE SHE'S...
I THINK IT'S SAFE NOW.
THANK YOU SO MUCH!
SMILE
YOU TOTALLY SAVED ME!

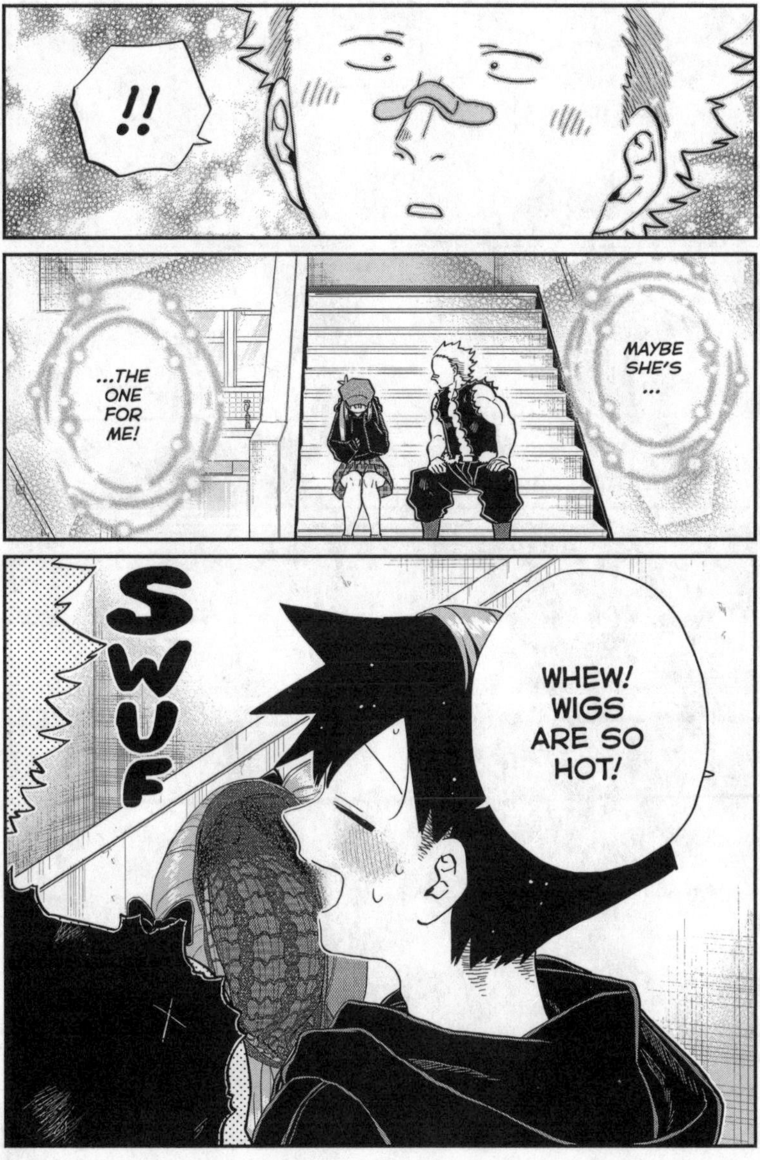
!!
MAYBE SHE'S ...
...THE ONE FOR ME!
WHEW! WIGS ARE SO HOT!
SWUF

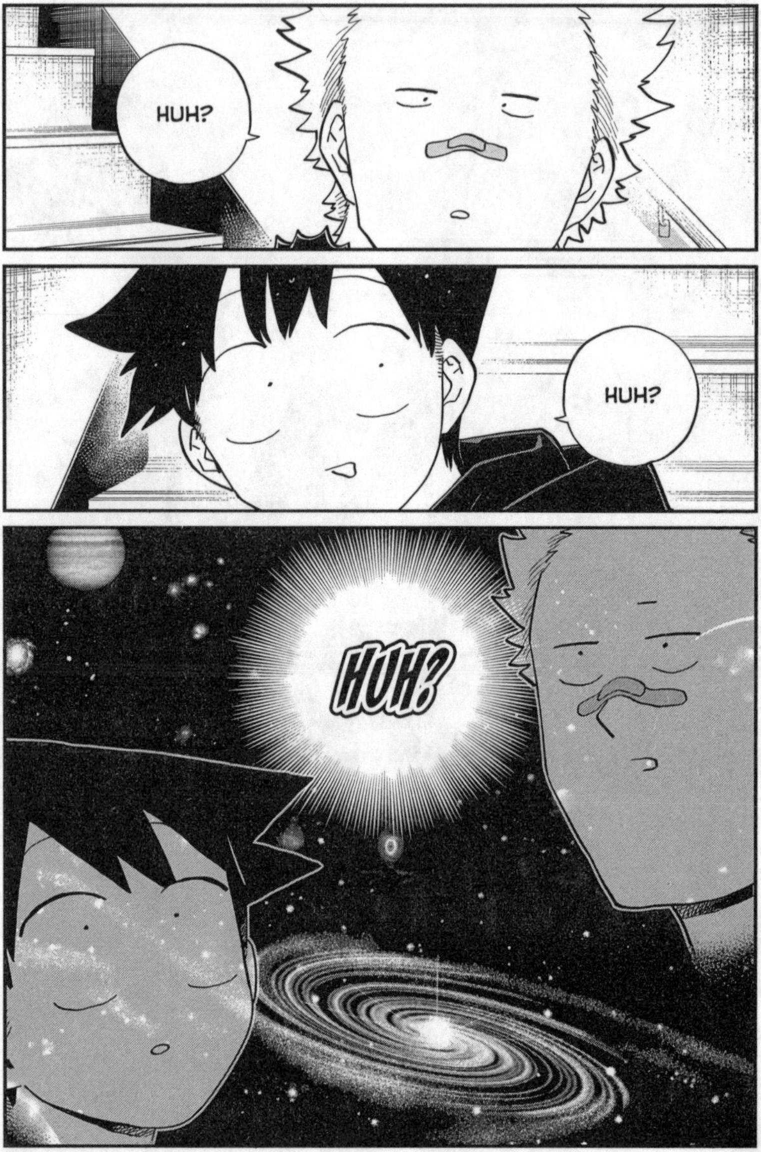
HUH?
HUH?
HUH?

Communication 224 — The End

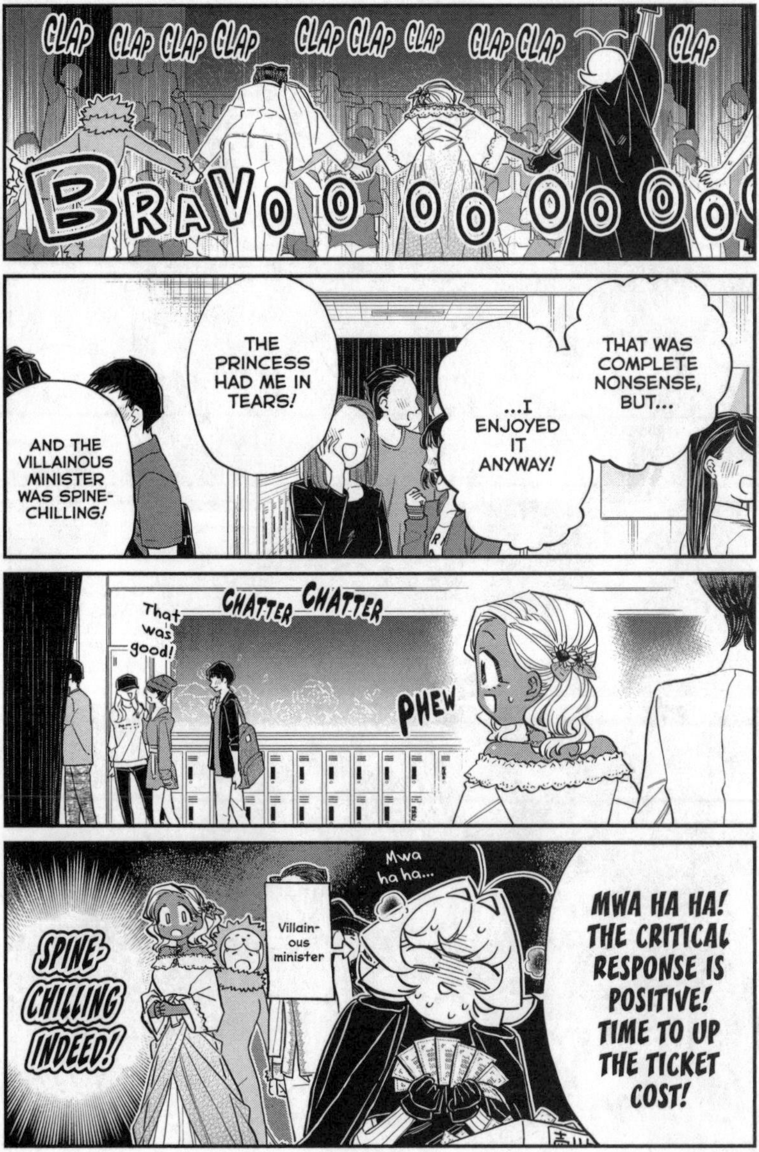
CLAP CLAP CLAP CLAP CLAP CLAP CLAP CLAP CLAP CLAP
BRAVOOOOOOOOO
THAT WAS COMPLETE NONSENSE, BUT...
...I ENJOYED IT ANYWAY!
THE PRINCESS HAD ME IN TEARS!
AND THE VILLAINOUS MINISTER WAS SPINE-CHILLING!
PHEW
CHATTER CHATTER
That was good!
MWA HA HA! THE CRITICAL RESPONSE IS POSITIVE! TIME TO UP THE TICKET COST!
Mwa ha ha...
Villain-ous minister
SPINE-CHILLING INDEED!

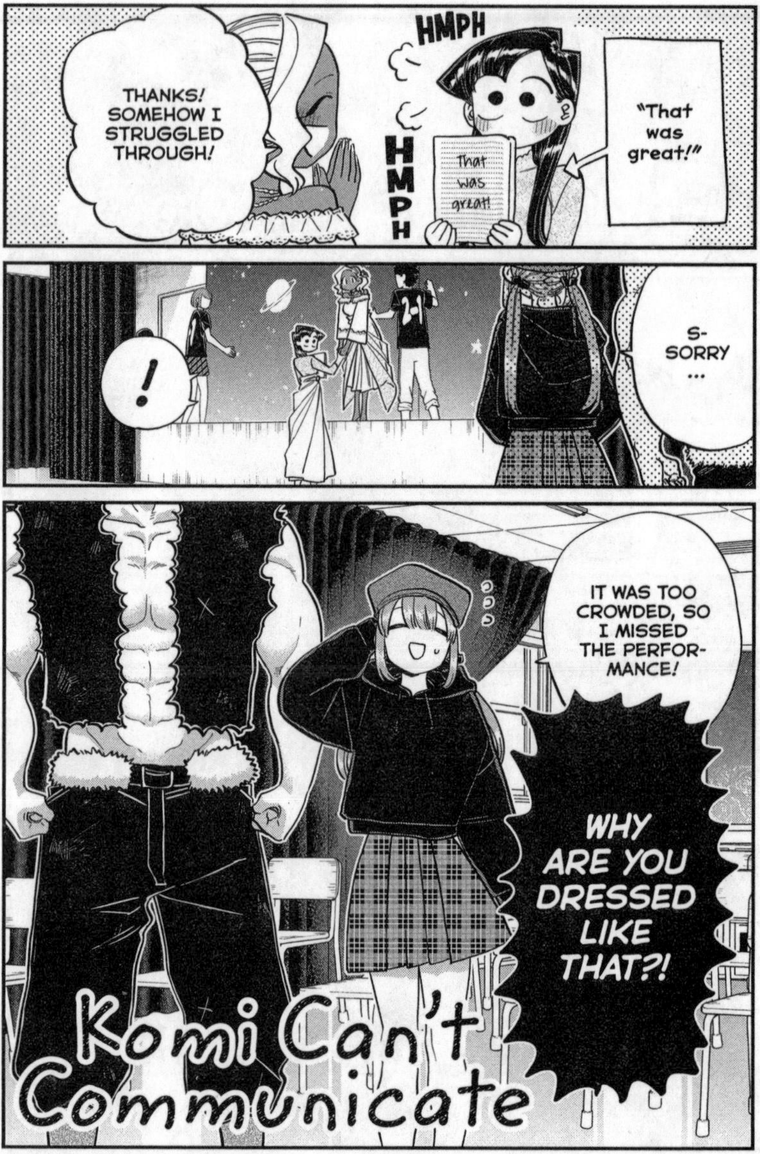
"That was great!"
HMPH
That was great!
HMPH
THANKS! SOMEHOW I STRUGGLED THROUGH!
S-SORRY ...
!
IT WAS TOO CROWDED, SO I MISSED THE PERFORMANCE!
WHY ARE YOU DRESSED LIKE THAT?!
Komi Can't Communicate

Communication 225: Feeling Okay

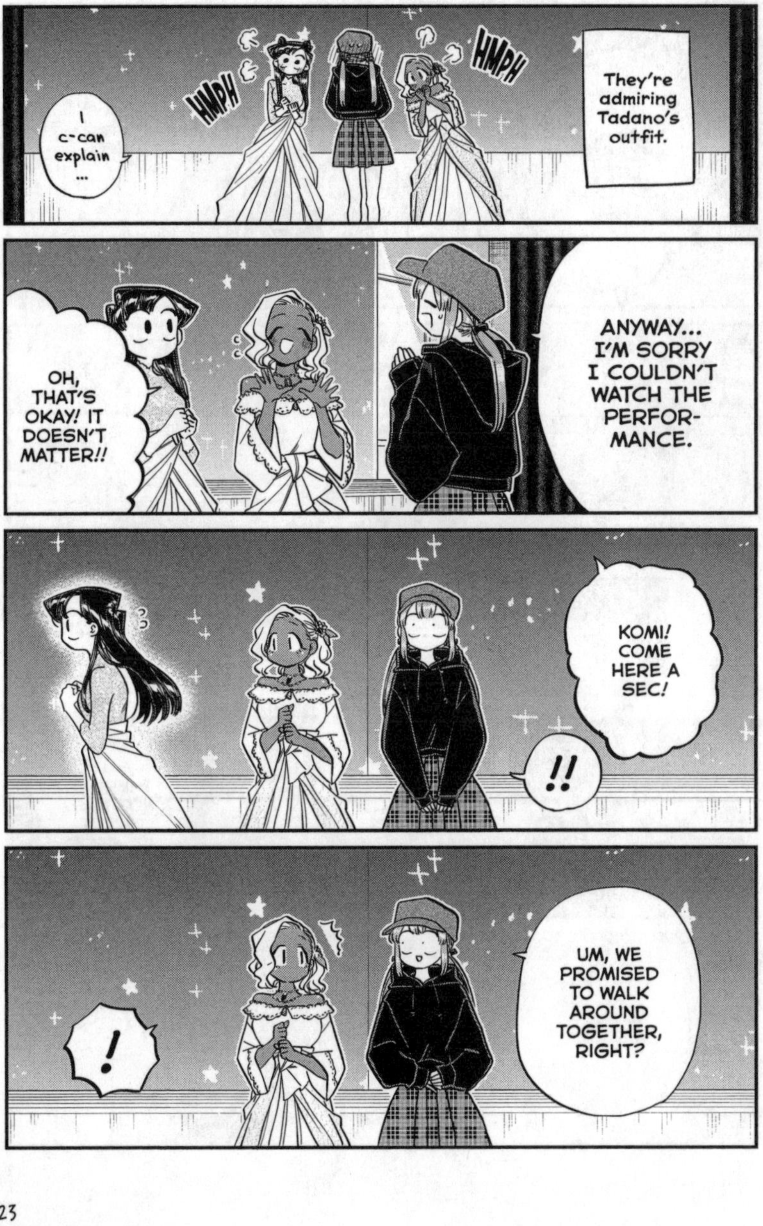
They're admiring Tadano's outfit.
HMPH
HMPH
I c-can explain ...
ANYWAY... I'M SORRY I COULDN'T WATCH THE PERFORMANCE.
OH, THAT'S OKAY! IT DOESN'T MATTER!!
KOMI! COME HERE A SEC!
!!
UM, WE PROMISED TO WALK AROUND TOGETHER, RIGHT?
!

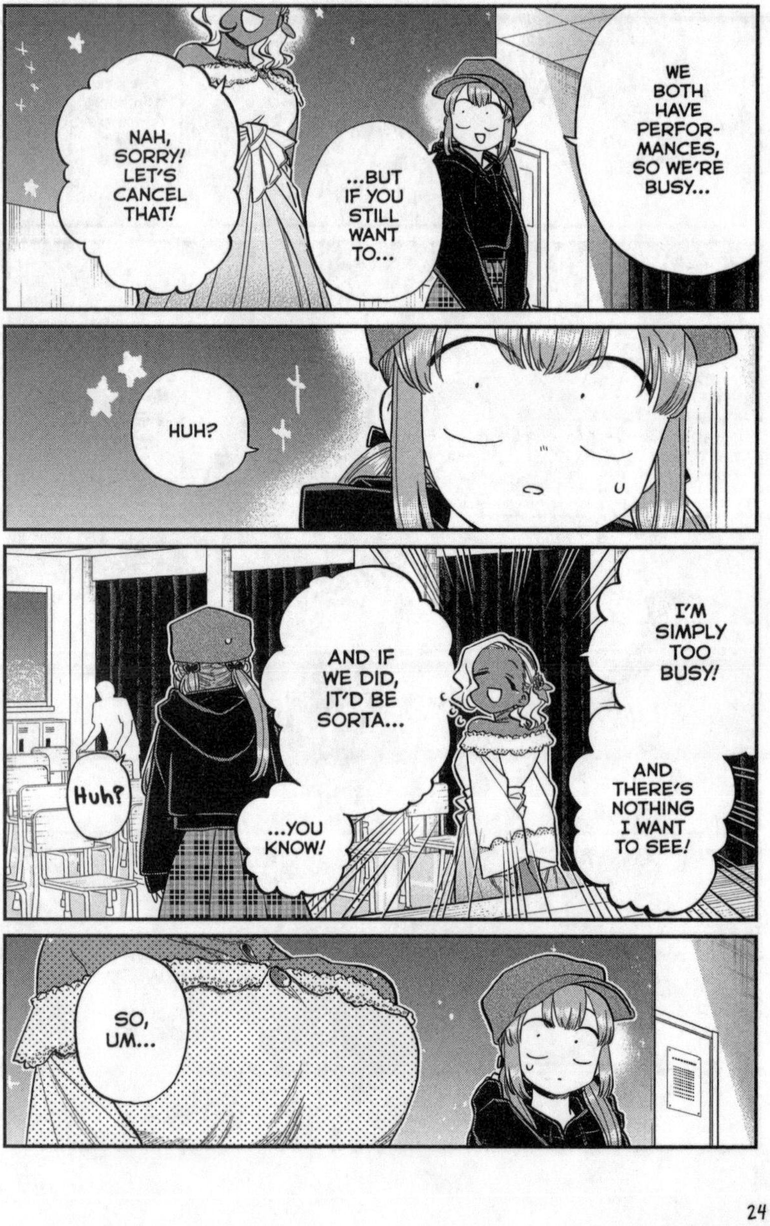
WE BOTH HAVE PERFOR- MANCES, SO WE'RE BUSY...
...BUT IF YOU STILL WANT TO...
NAH, SORRY! LET'S CANCEL THAT!
HUH?
I'M SIMPLY TOO BUSY!
AND THERE'S NOTHING I WANT TO SEE!
AND IF WE DID, IT'D BE SORTA...
...YOU KNOW!
Huh?
SO, UM...

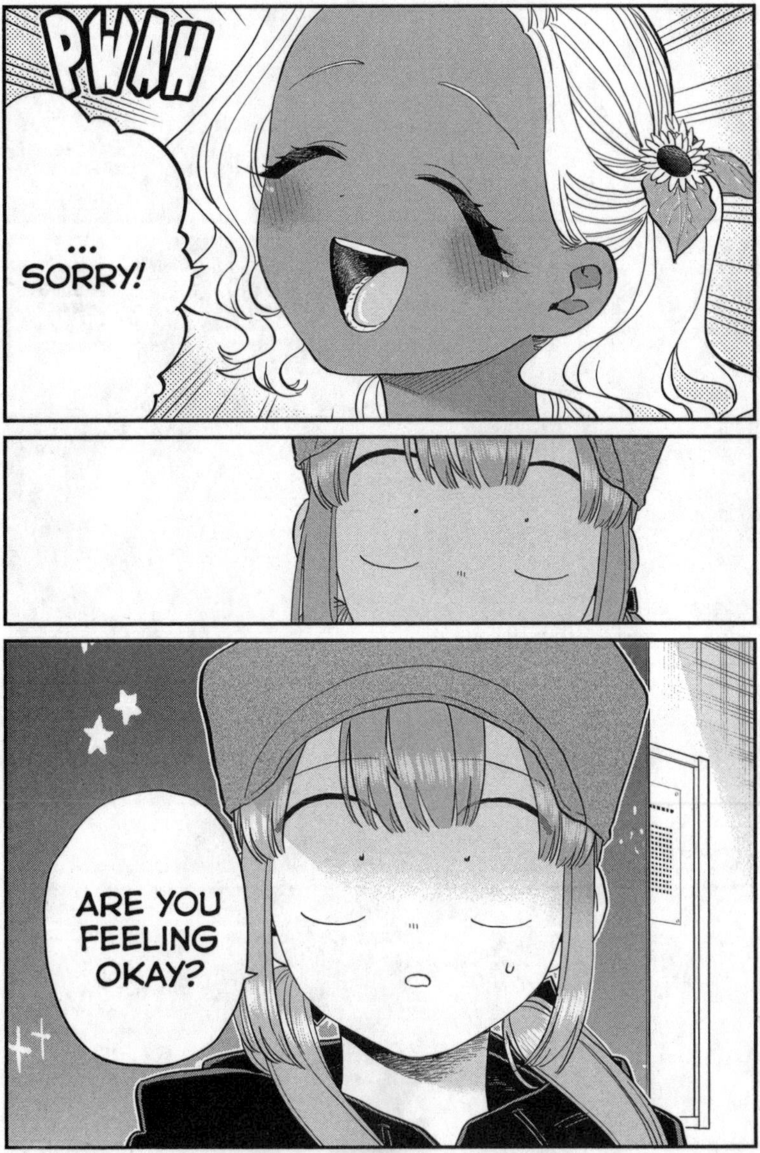
PWAH
... SORRY!
ARE YOU FEELING OKAY?

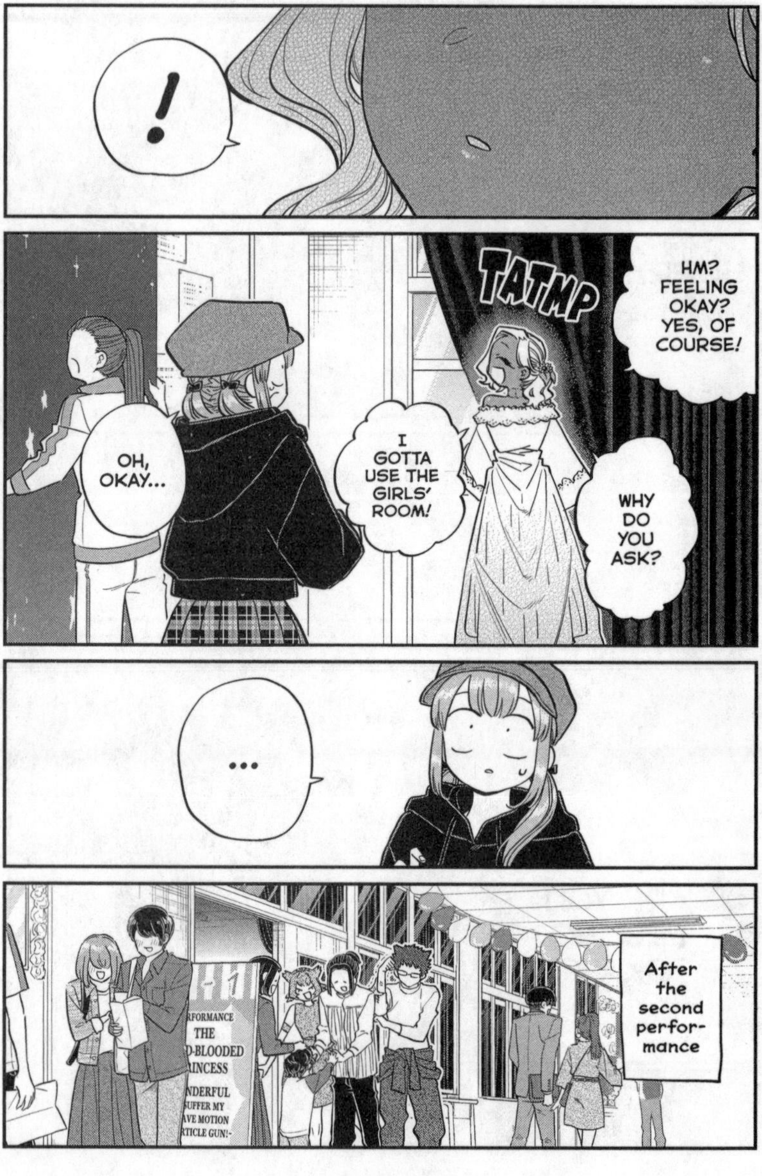
!
HM? FEELING OKAY? YES, OF COURSE!
TATMP
WHY DO YOU ASK?
I GOTTA USE THE GIRLS' ROOM!
OH, OKAY...
...
After the second perfor-mance
ERFORMANCE
THE
D-BLOODED
RINCESS
NDERFUL
SUFFER MY
AVE MOTION
RTICLE GUN!-

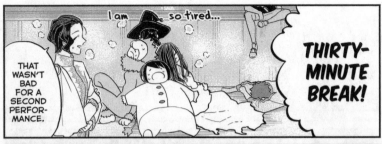

THIRTY-MINUTE BREAK!
I am so tired...
THAT WASN'T BAD FOR A SECOND PERFORMANCE.
KOMI! WANNA WALK AROUND TOGETHER?
NOD NOD
!
TEA CEREMONY
That's the princess!
OOH! LOOK, KOMI! OCTOPUS DUMPLINGS!
AND GRILLED SQUID!
ALL OF A SUDDEN, I'M SUPER HUNGRY!
!
NOD NOD

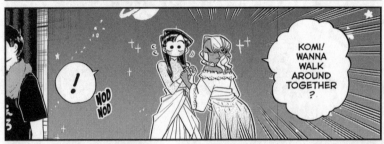

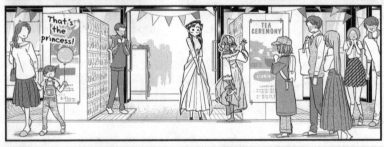

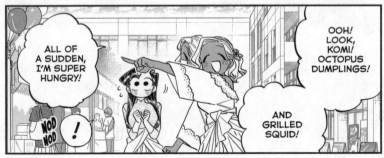

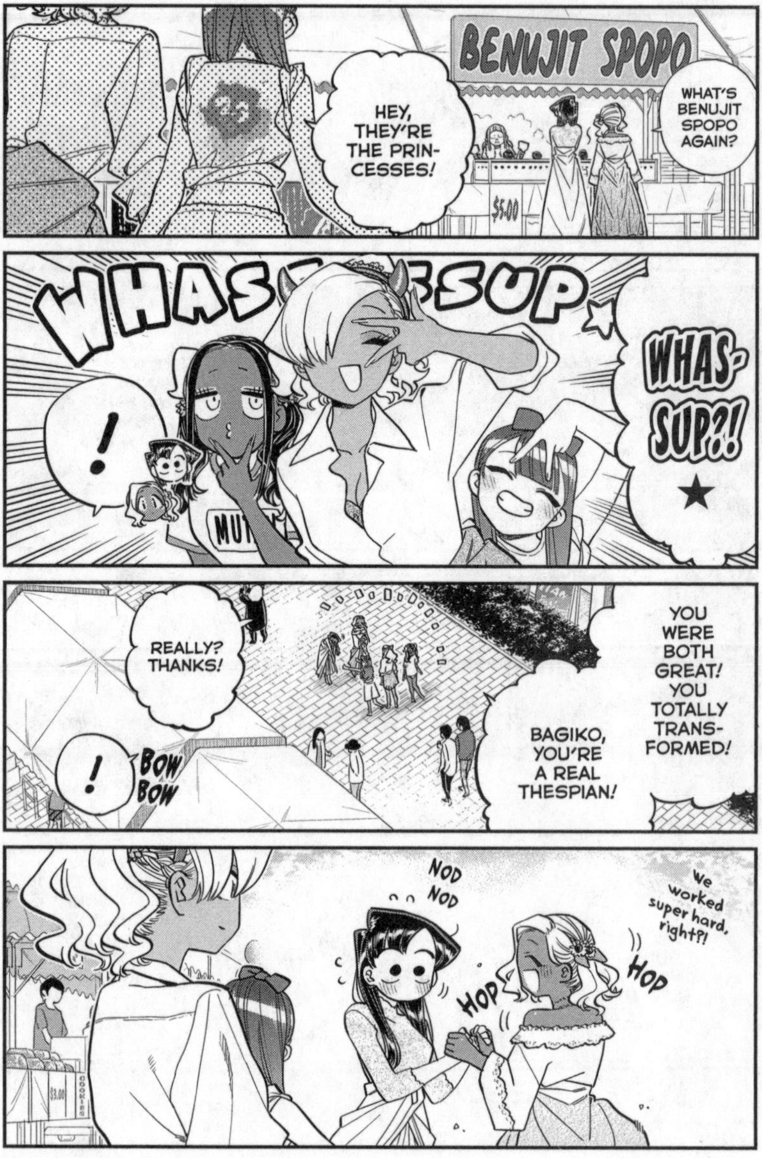
BENUJIT SPOPO
WHAT'S BENUJIT SPOPO AGAIN?
HEY, THEY'RE THE PRIN- CESSES!
$5.00
WHAS- SUP?!
★
WHAS
SUP
!
YOU WERE BOTH GREAT! YOU TOTALLY TRANS- FORMED!
BAGIKO, YOU'RE A REAL THESPIAN!
REALLY? THANKS!
!
BOW BOW
We worked super hard, right?!
HOP
HOP
NOD NOD
$3.00
COOKIES

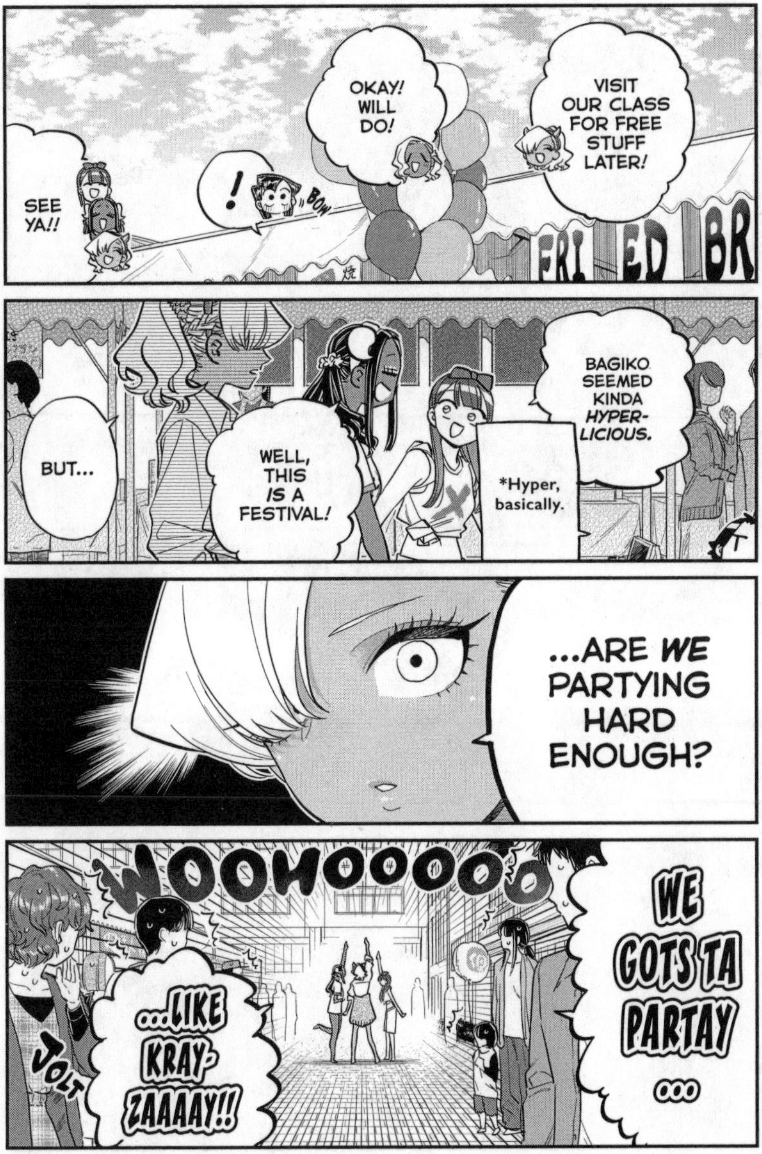
VISIT OUR CLASS FOR FREE STUFF LATER!
OKAY! WILL DO!
!
BOW
SEE YA!!
FRI ED BR
BAGIKO SEEMED KINDA HYPER-LICIOUS.
*Hyper, basically.
WELL, THIS IS A FESTIVAL!
BUT...
...ARE WE PARTYING HARD ENOUGH?
WOOHOOOOO
WE GOTS TA PARTAY ...
...LIKE KRAY-ZAAAAY!!
JOLT

TMP
YUKA'S CLASS IS DOING A "STUDENT CABARET"!
TMP
IS THAT ALL RIGHT?!
WAFFLES
CREPES
Ooh! That looks fun too!
3-4
SUMO BATTLE
...
CLUB
Are you feeling okay?
!

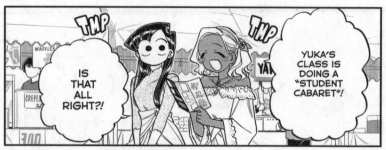

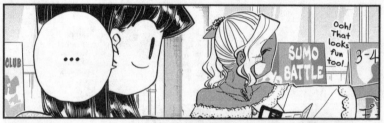

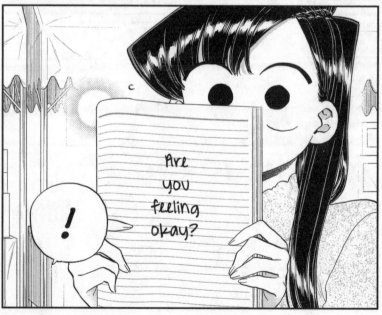

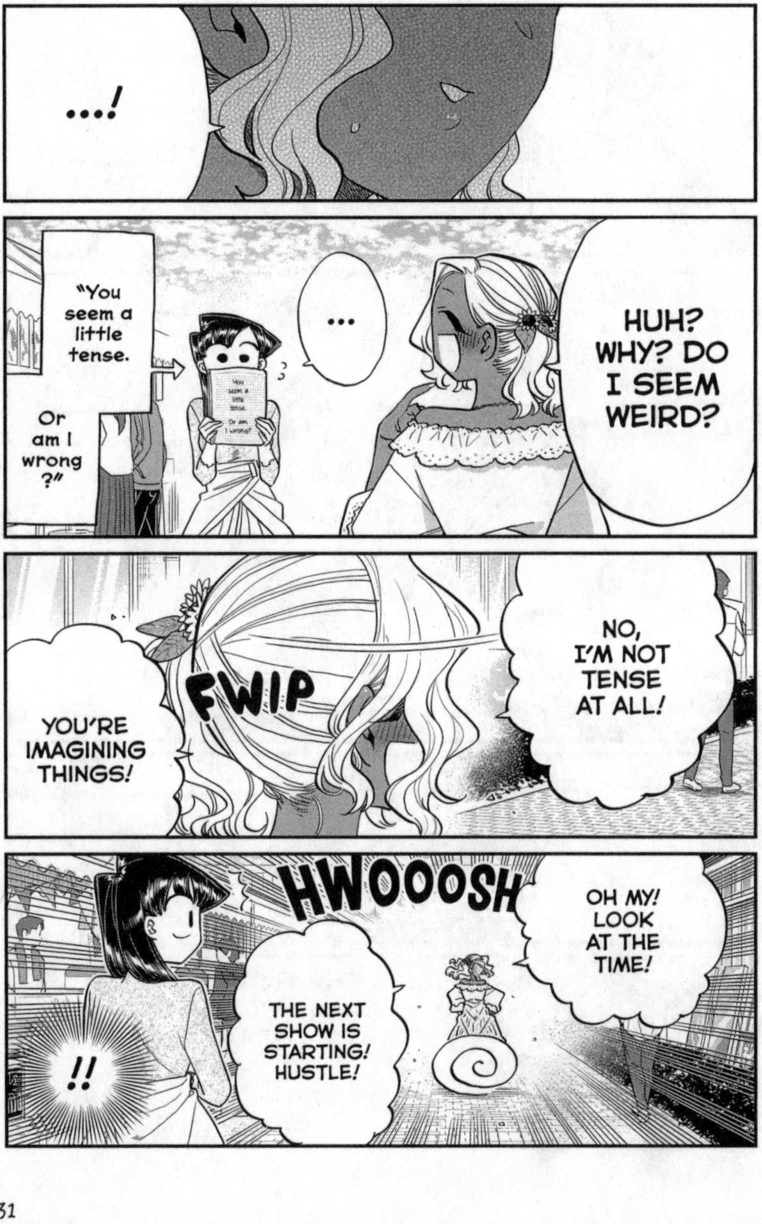
...!
HUH? WHY? DO I SEEM WEIRD?
...
“You seem a little tense. Or am I wrong?”
NO, I'M NOT TENSE AT ALL!
FWIP
YOU'RE IMAGINING THINGS!
OH MY! LOOK AT THE TIME!
HWOOOSH
THE NEXT SHOW IS STARTING! HUSTLE!
!!

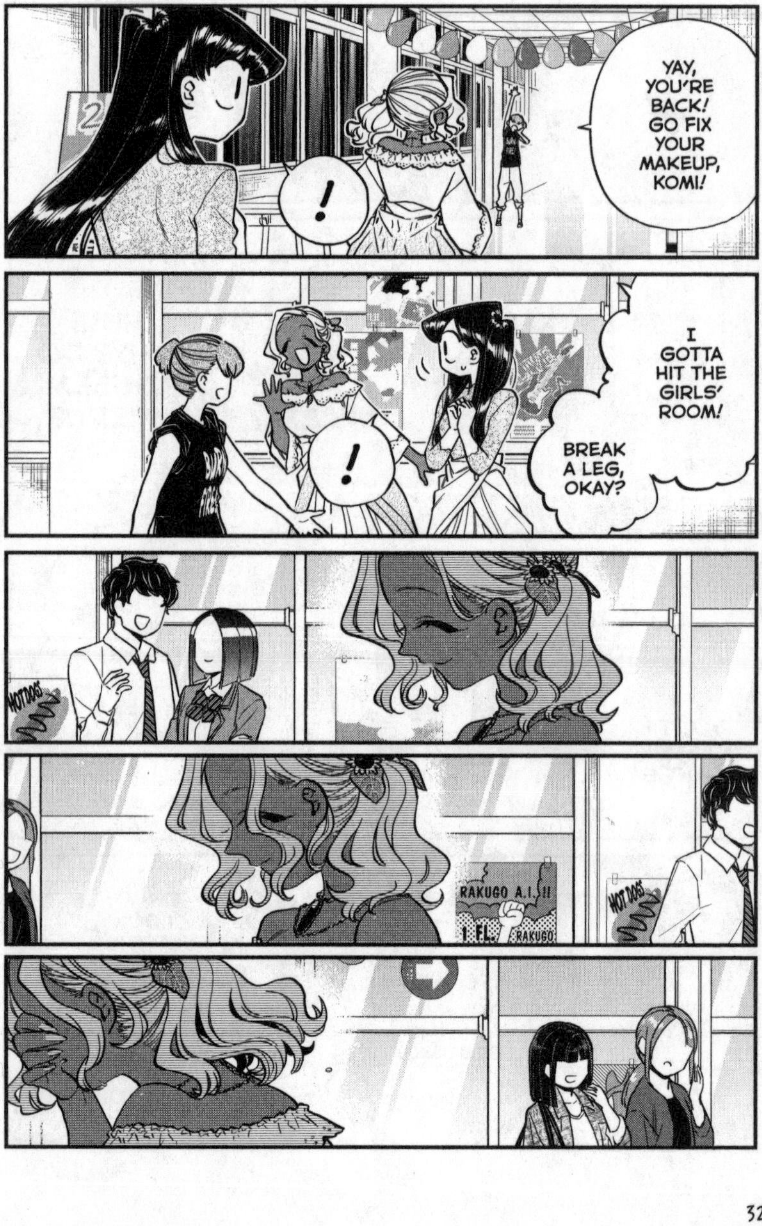
YAY, YOU'RE BACK! GO FIX YOUR MAKEUP, KOMI!
!
I GOTTA HIT THE GIRLS' ROOM!
BREAK A LEG, OKAY?
!
HOT DOGS
HOT DOGS
RAKUGO A.I.!!
1 F.L.
RAKUGO

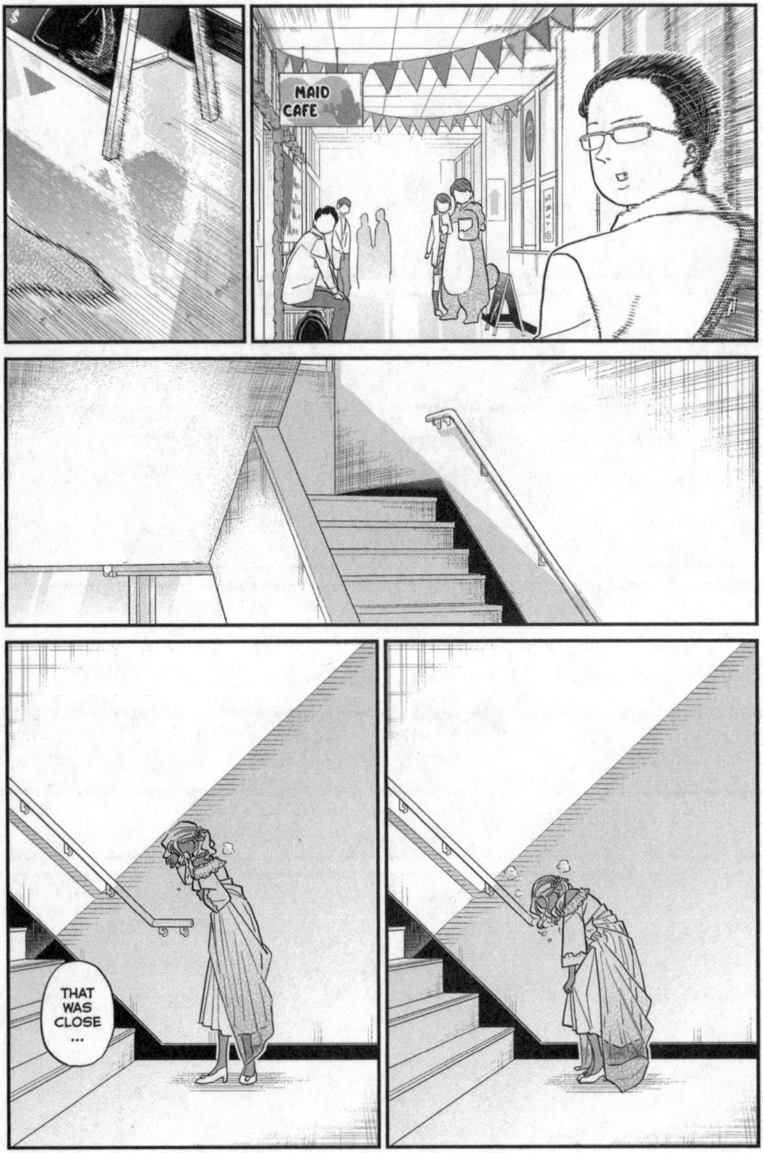
MAID CAFE
THAT WAS CLOSE ...

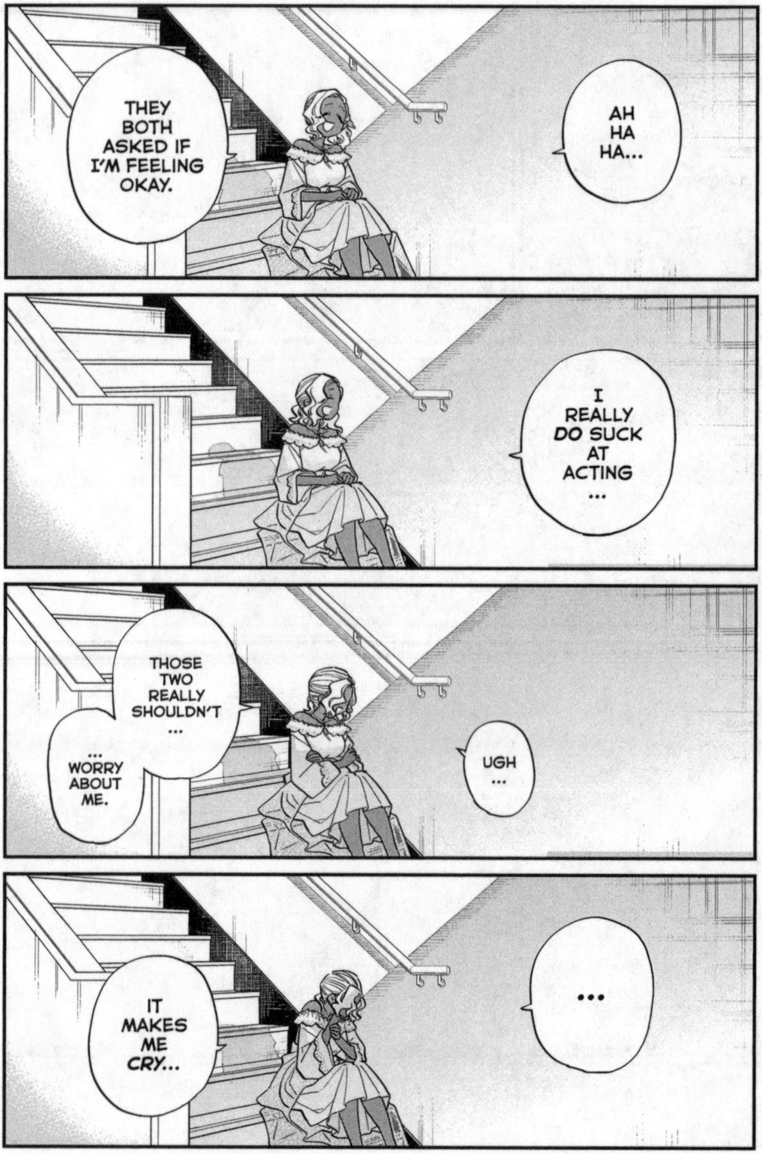
AH HA HA...
THEY BOTH ASKED IF I'M FEELING OKAY.
I REALLY *DO* SUCK AT ACTING ...
UGH ...
THOSE TWO REALLY SHOULDN'T ...
... WORRY ABOUT ME.
...
IT MAKES ME *CRY*...

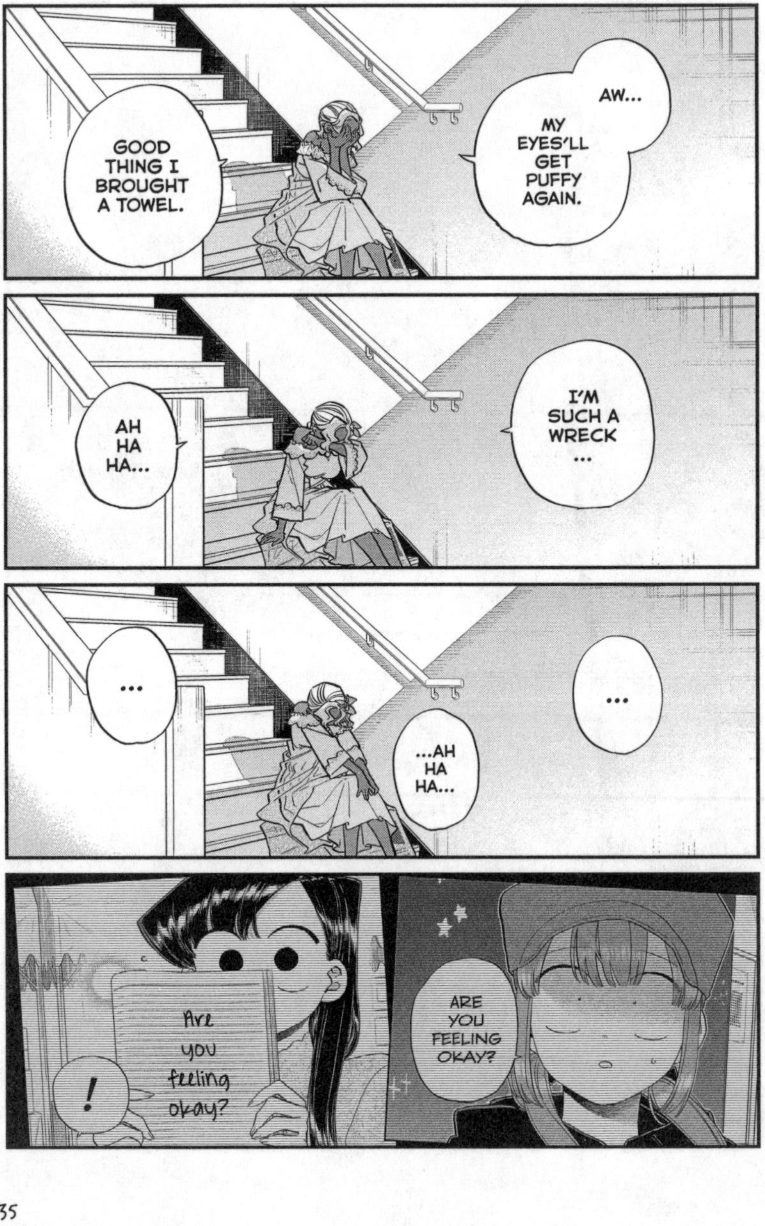
AW... MY EYES'LL GET PUFFY AGAIN.
GOOD THING I BROUGHT A TOWEL.
I'M SUCH A WRECK ...
AH HA HA...
...
...AH HA HA...
...
ARE YOU FEELING OKAY?
Are you feeling okay?
!

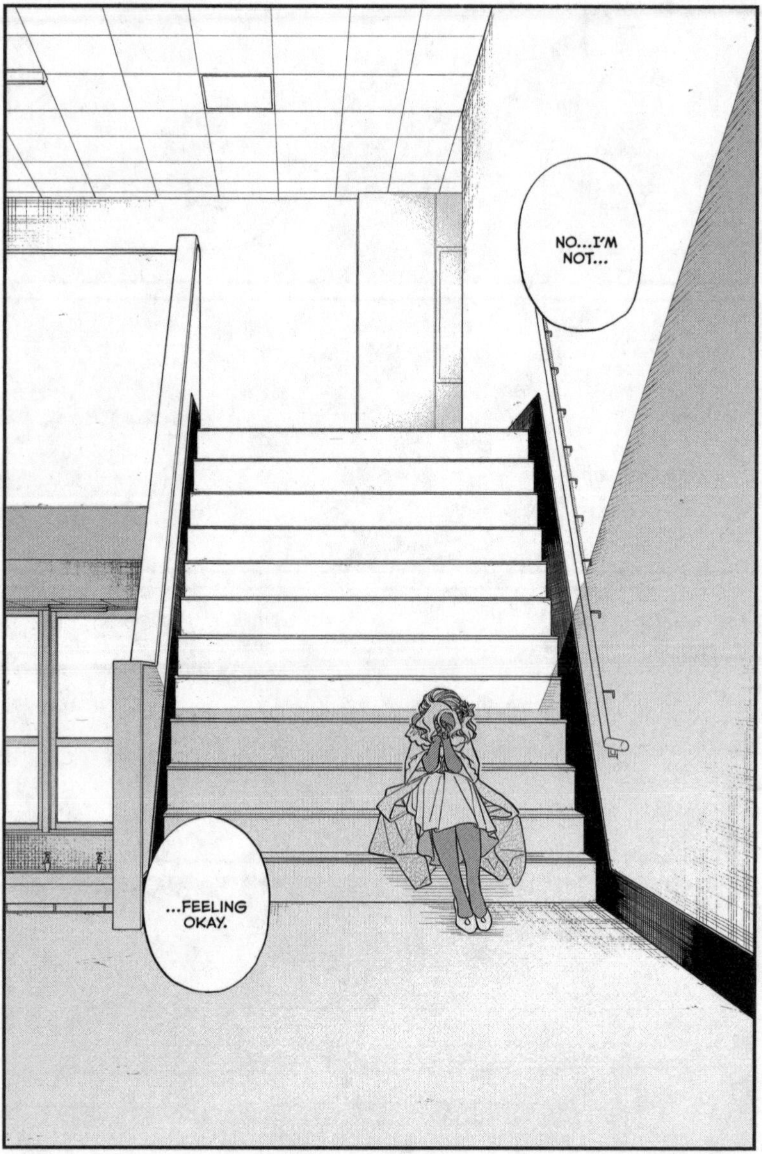
NO...I'M NOT...
...FEELING OKAY.

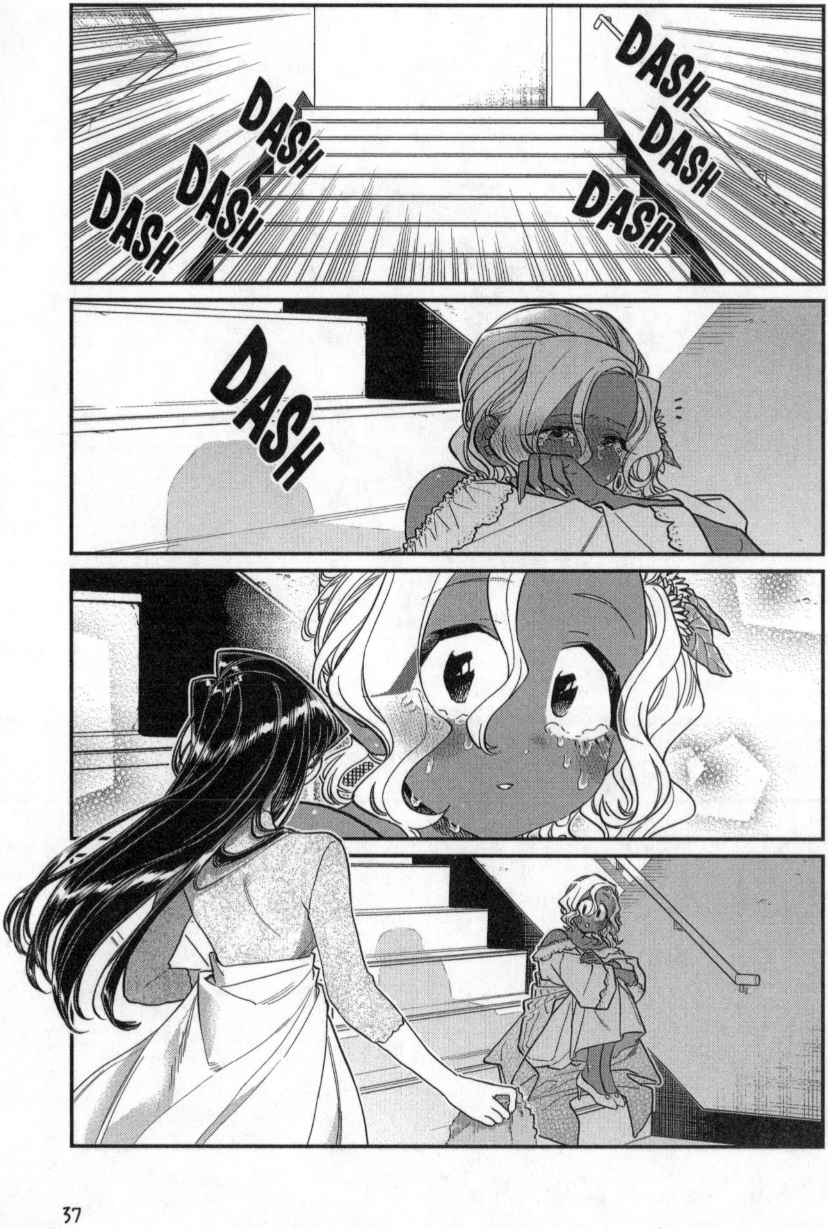
DASH
DASH
DASH
DASH
DASH
DASH
DASH

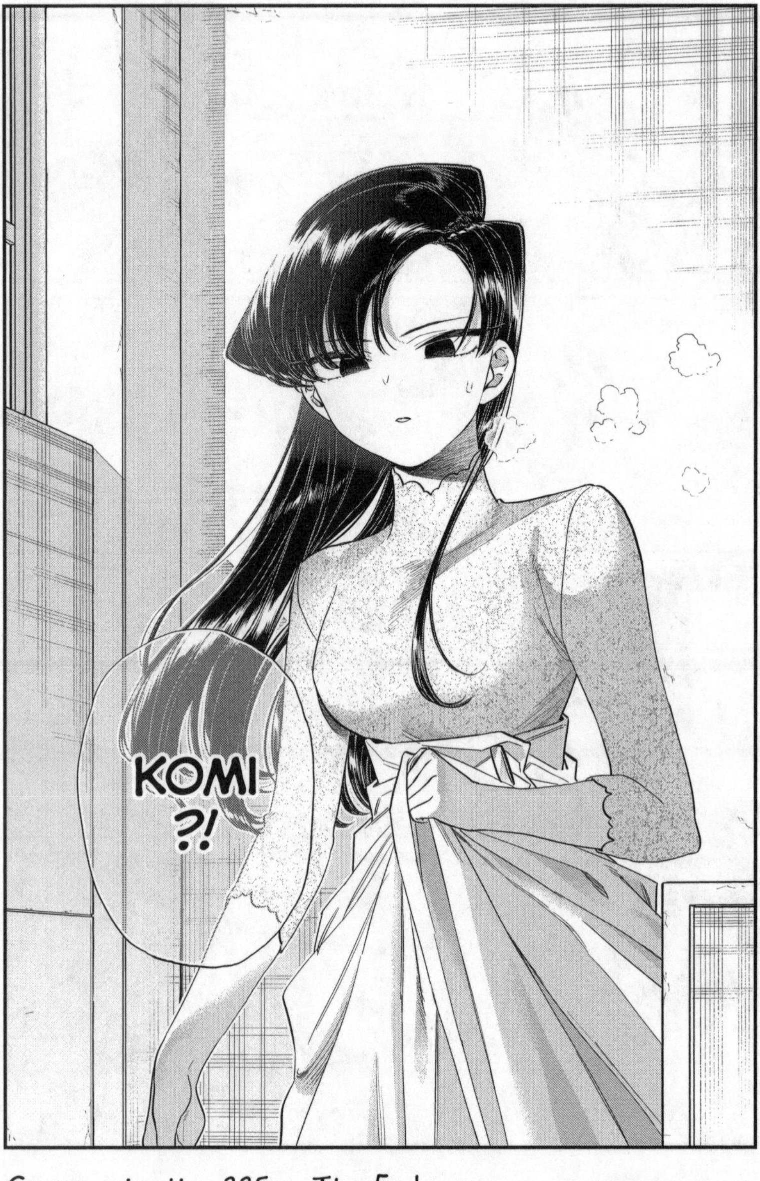
KOMI ?!

Communication 225 — The End

Komi Can't Communicate

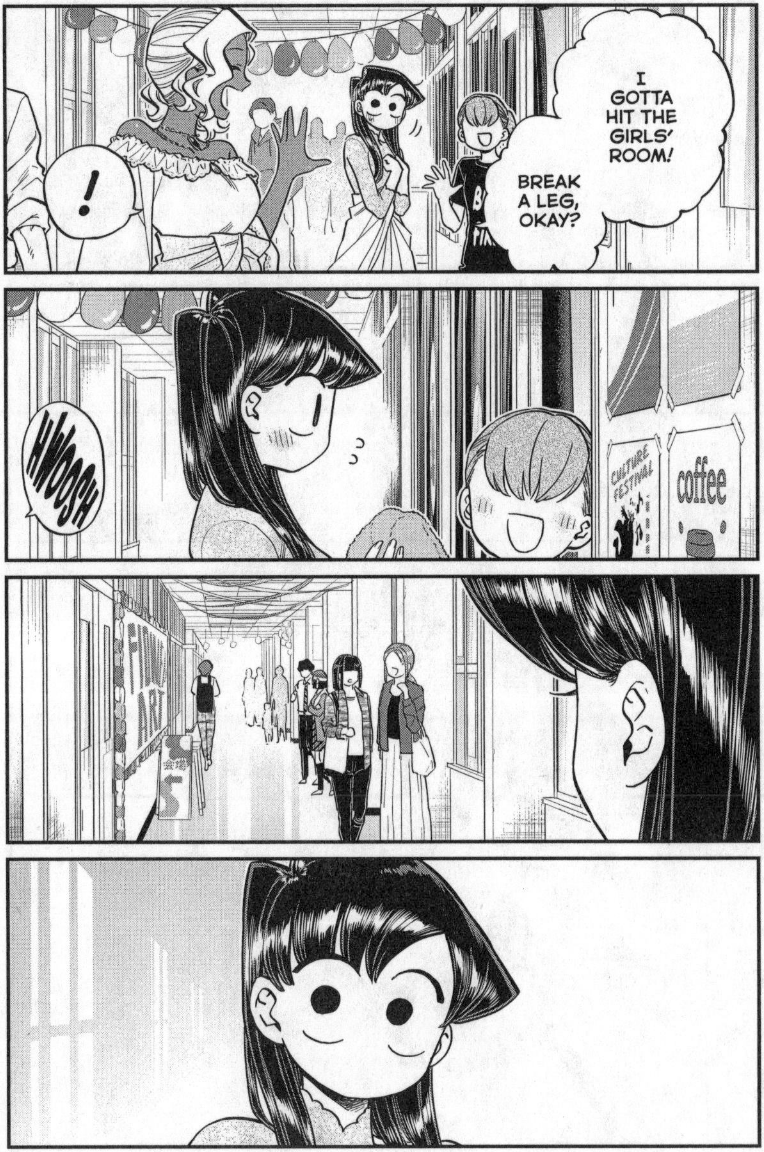

I GOTTA HIT THE GIRLS' ROOM!
BREAK A LEG, OKAY?
!
CULTURE FESTIVAL
coffee
WHOOSH

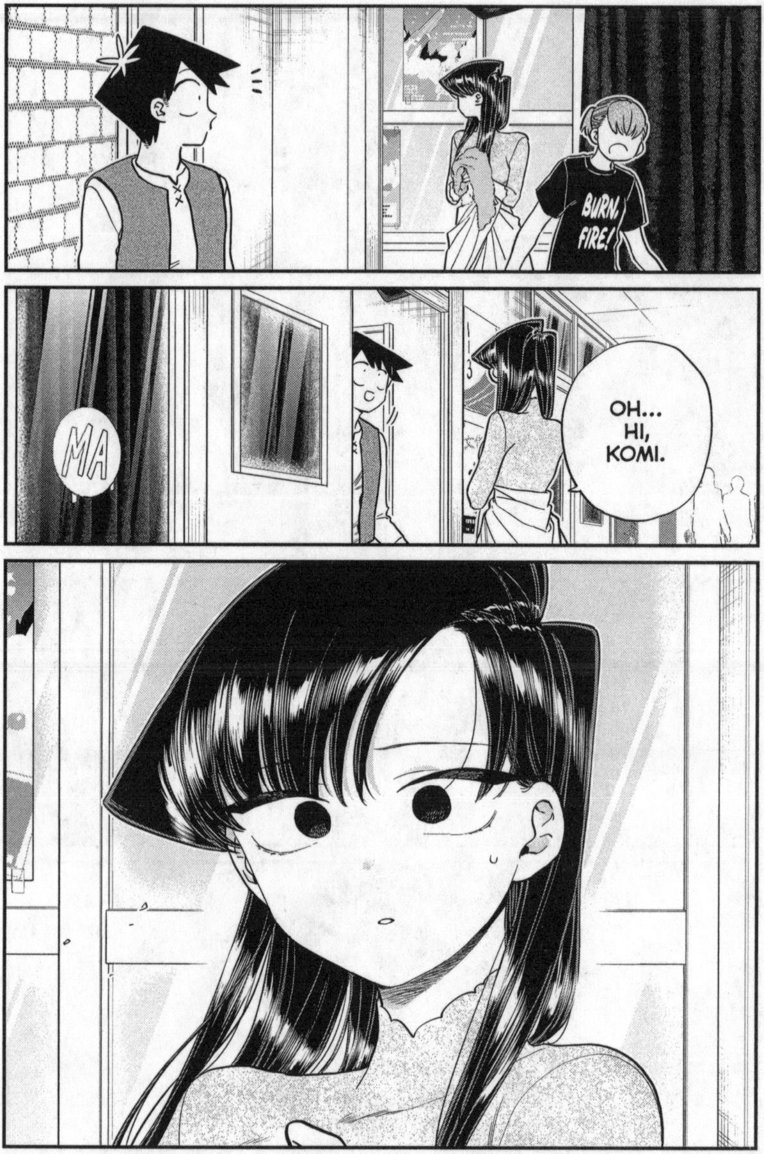
BURN, FIRE!
OH... HI, KOMI.
MA

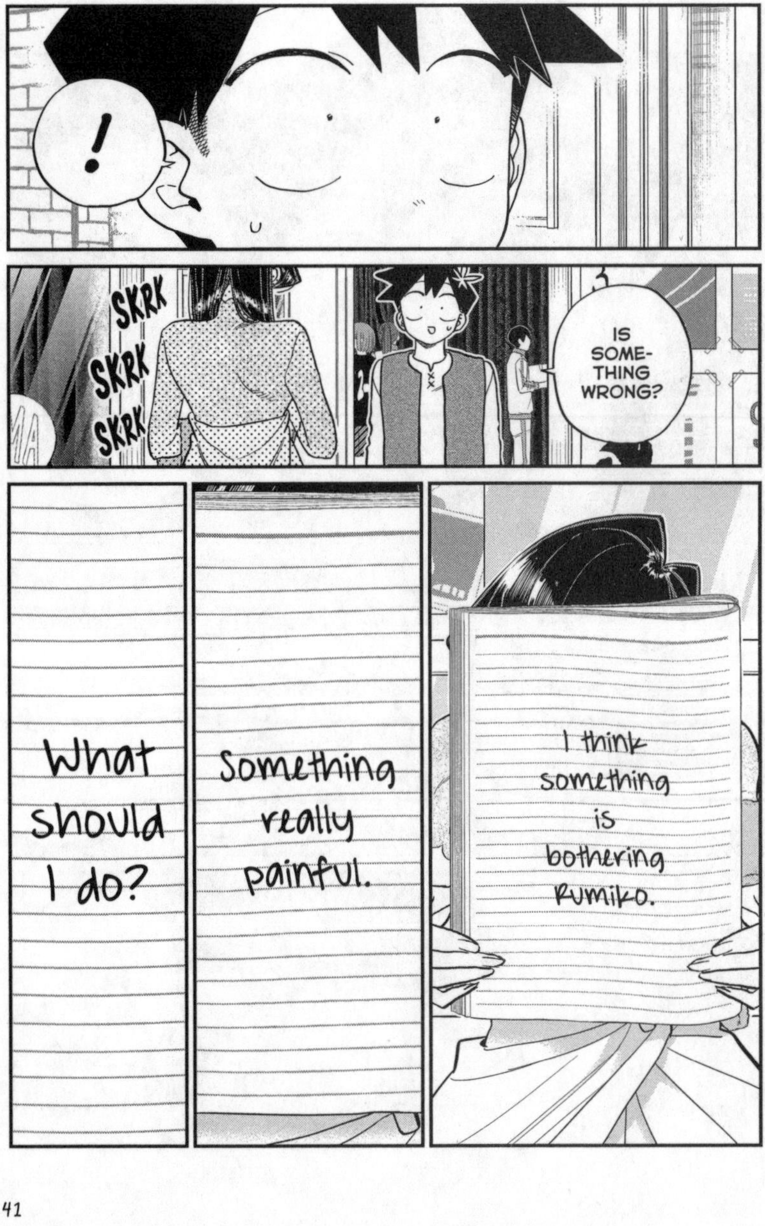
!
IS SOMETHING WRONG?
SKRK SKRK SKRK
I think something is bothering Rumiko.
Something really painful.
What should I do?

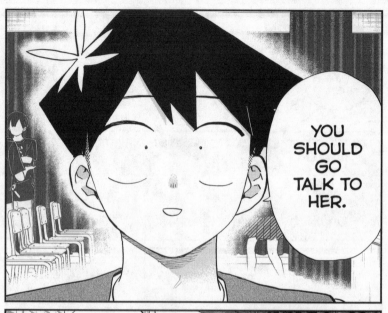

YOU SHOULD GO TALK TO HER.
I NOTICED IT TOO.
SHE'S ACTING UNUSUAL.
I'LL HANDLE THE PERFORMANCE SOMEHOW, SO IT'LL BE FINE...
...I HOPE.
...
...

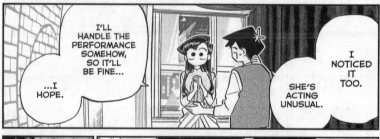

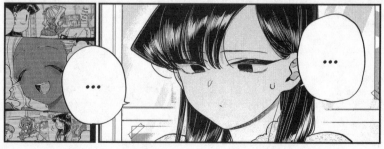

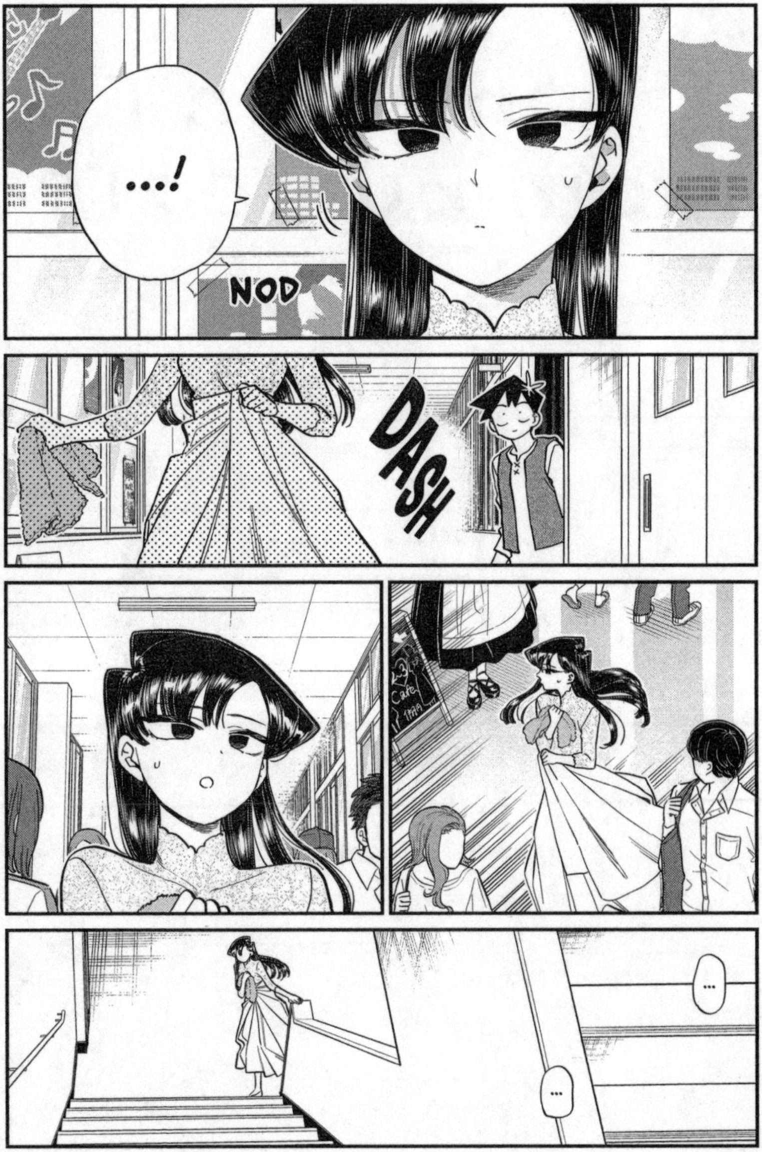
...!
NOD
DASH
...
...

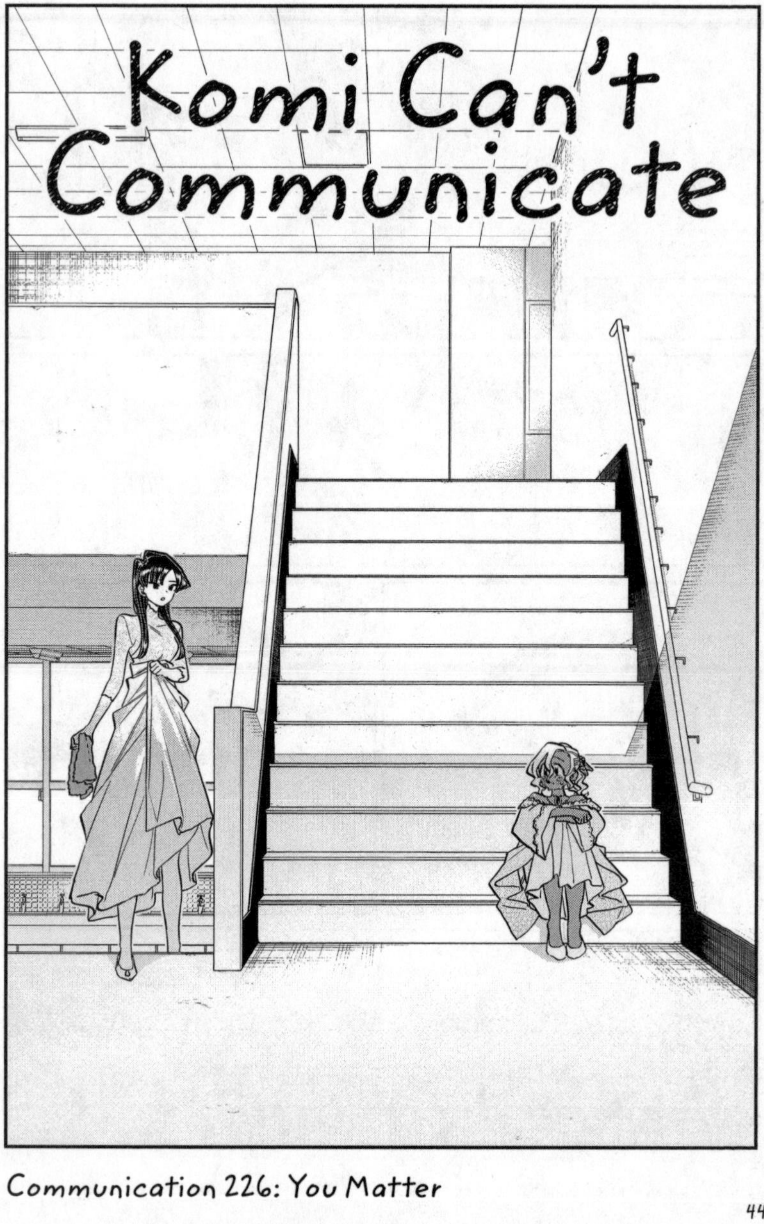
Komi Can't Communicate

Communication 226: You Matter

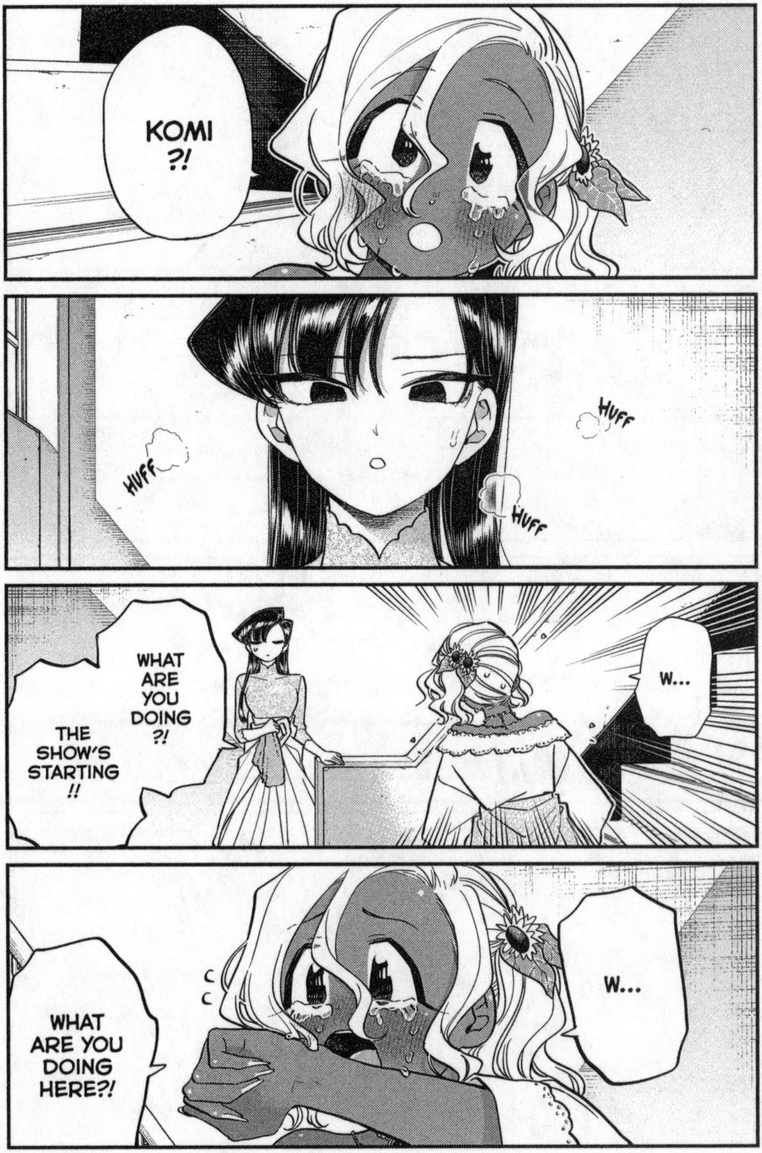
KOMI ?!
HUFF
HUFF
HUFF
W...
WHAT ARE YOU DOING ?!
THE SHOW'S STARTING !!
W...
WHAT ARE YOU DOING HERE?!

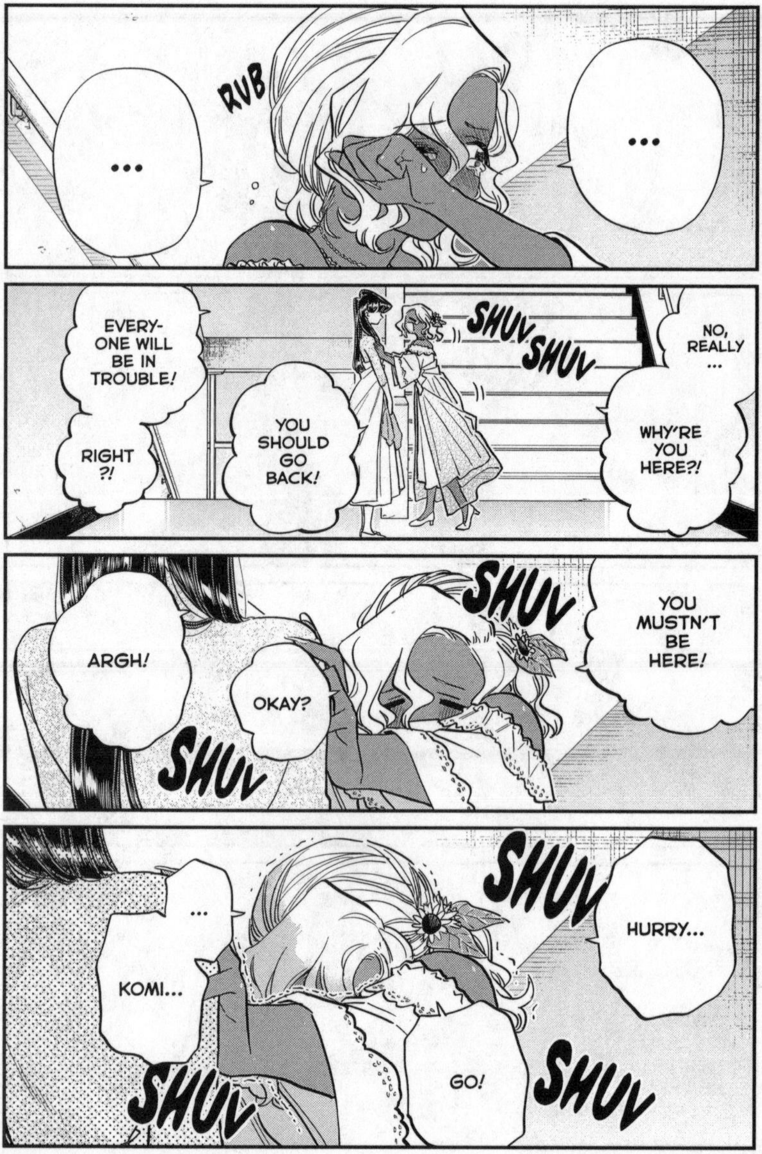
...
RUB
...
NO, REALLY ... WHY'RE YOU HERE?!
SHUV SHUV
YOU SHOULD GO BACK!
EVERY-ONE WILL BE IN TROUBLE! RIGHT?!
YOU MUSTN'T BE HERE!
SHUV
OKAY?
ARGH!
SHUV
SHUV
HURRY...
SHUV
GO!
... KOMI...
SHUV

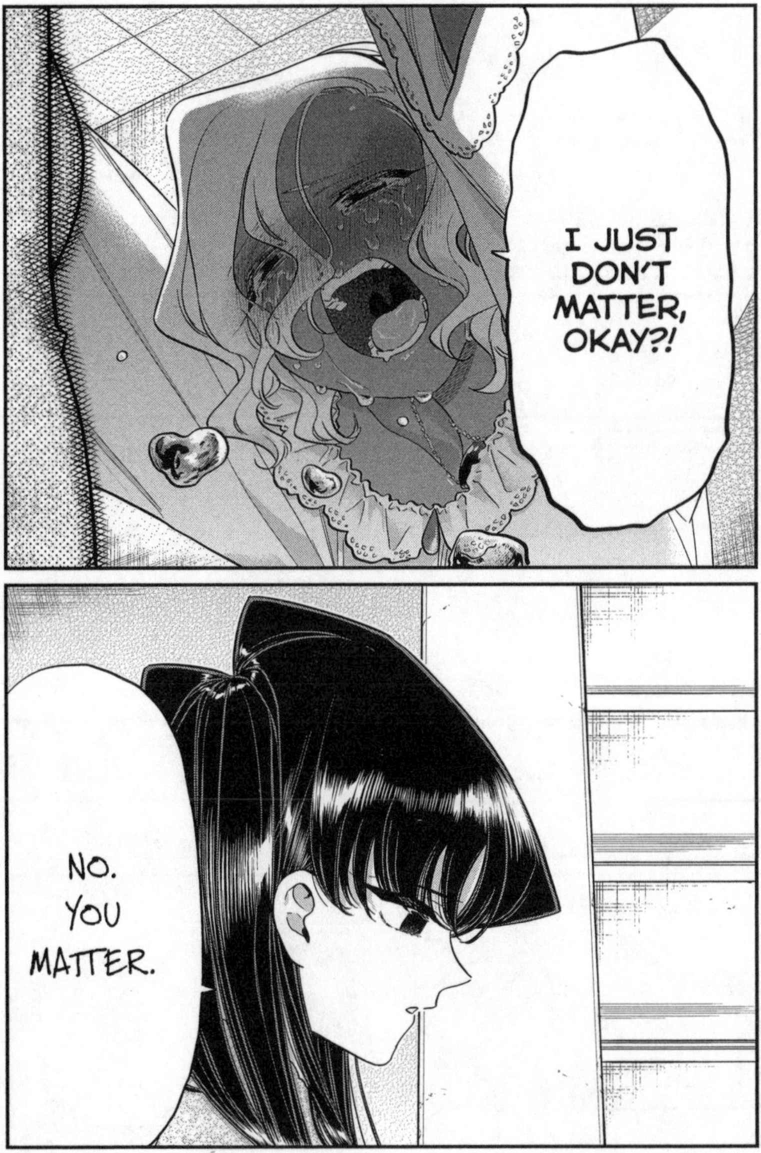
I JUST DON'T MATTER, OKAY?!
NO. YOU MATTER.

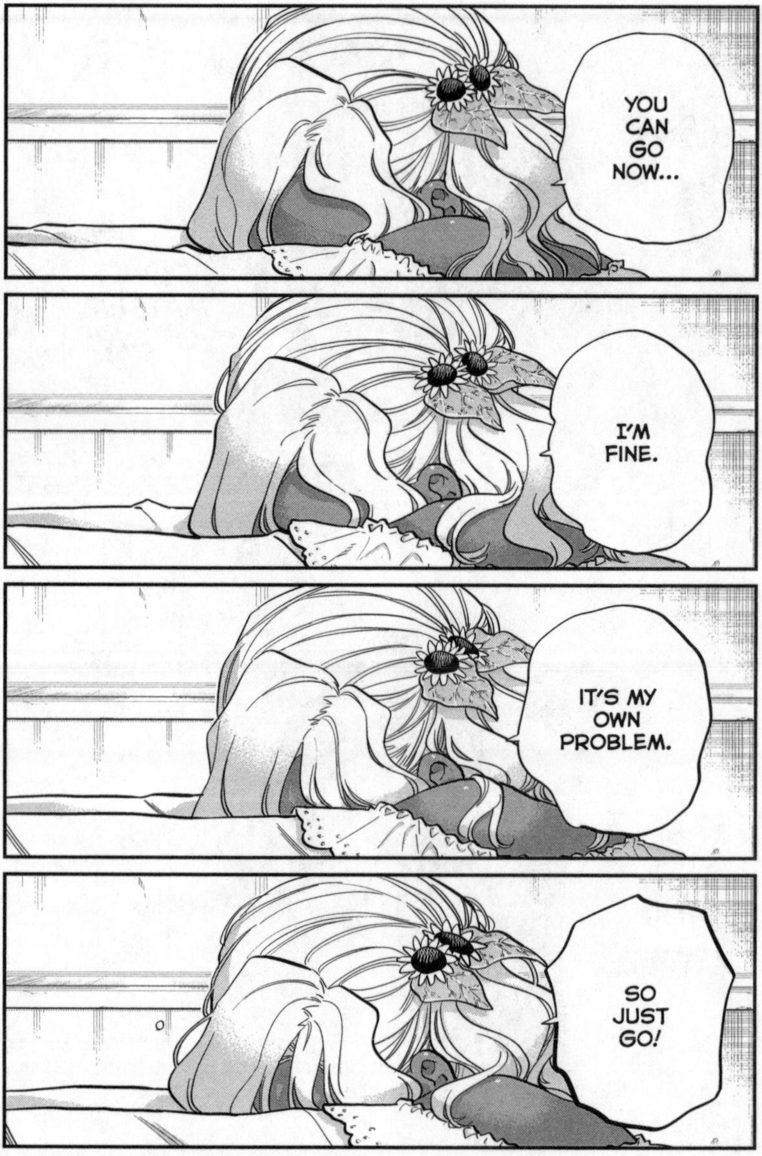
YOU CAN GO NOW...
I'M FINE.
IT'S MY OWN PROBLEM.
SO JUST GO!

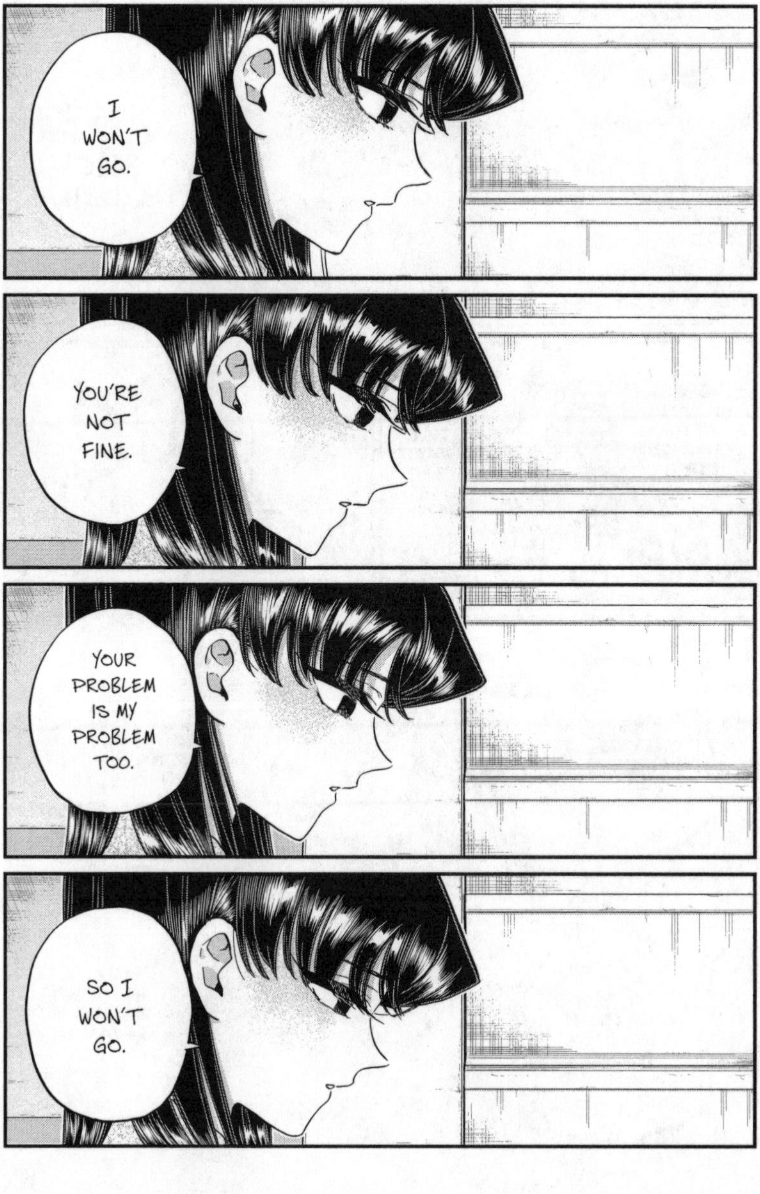
I WON'T GO.
YOU'RE NOT FINE.
YOUR PROBLEM IS MY PROBLEM TOO.
SO I WON'T GO.

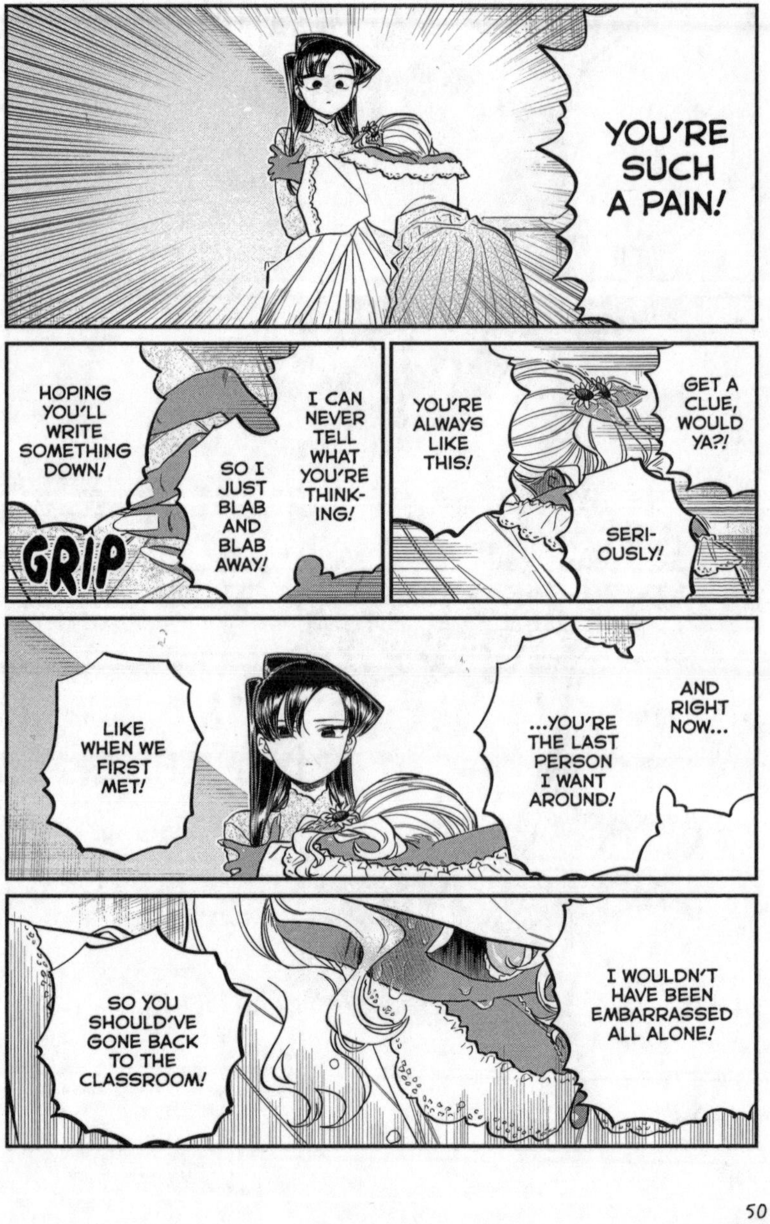
YOU'RE SUCH A PAIN!
GET A CLUE, WOULD YA?!
YOU'RE ALWAYS LIKE THIS!
SERI-OUSLY!
I CAN NEVER TELL WHAT YOU'RE THINKING!
SO I JUST BLAB AND BLAB AWAY!
HOPING YOU'LL WRITE SOMETHING DOWN!
GRIP
AND RIGHT NOW...
...YOU'RE THE LAST PERSON I WANT AROUND!
LIKE WHEN WE FIRST MET!
I WOULDN'T HAVE BEEN EMBARRASSED ALL ALONE!
SO YOU SHOULD'VE GONE BACK TO THE CLASSROOM!

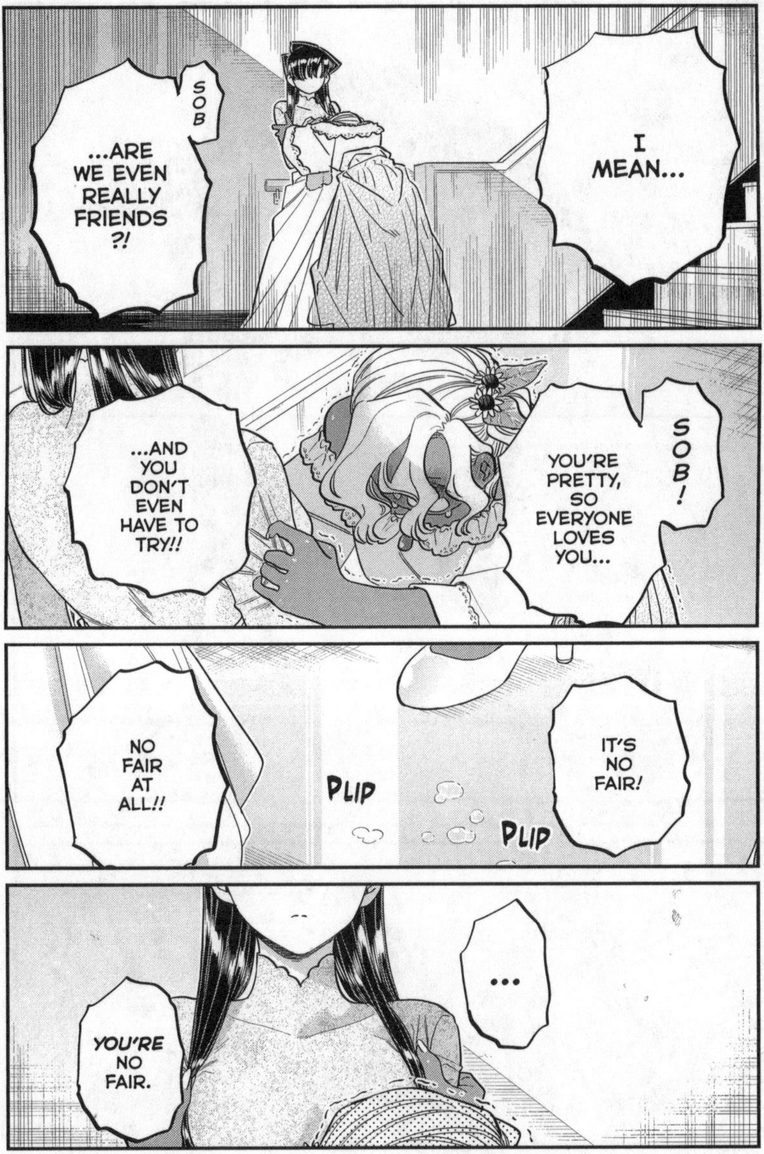
I MEAN...
SOB
...ARE WE EVEN REALLY FRIENDS ?!
SOB!
YOU'RE PRETTY, SO EVERYONE LOVES YOU...
...AND YOU DON'T EVEN HAVE TO TRY!!
IT'S NO FAIR!
PLIP
PLIP
NO FAIR AT ALL!!
...
YOU'RE NO FAIR.

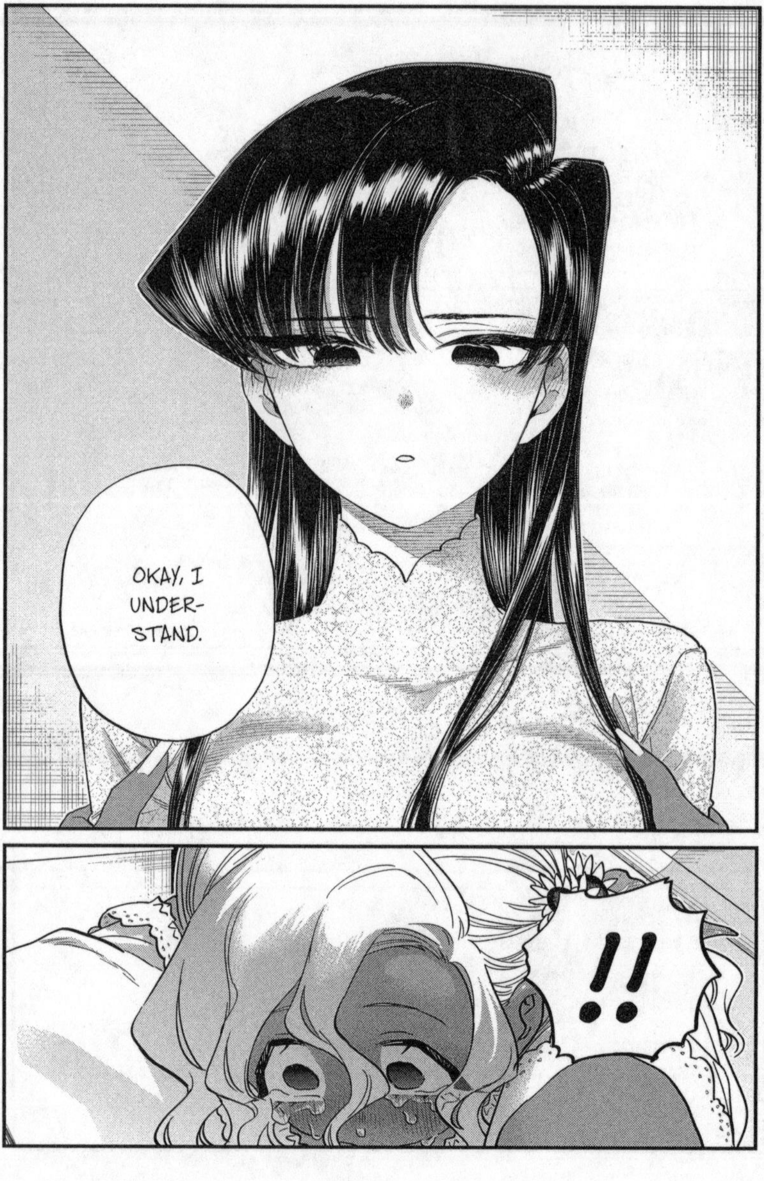
OKAY, I UNDER-STAND.
!!

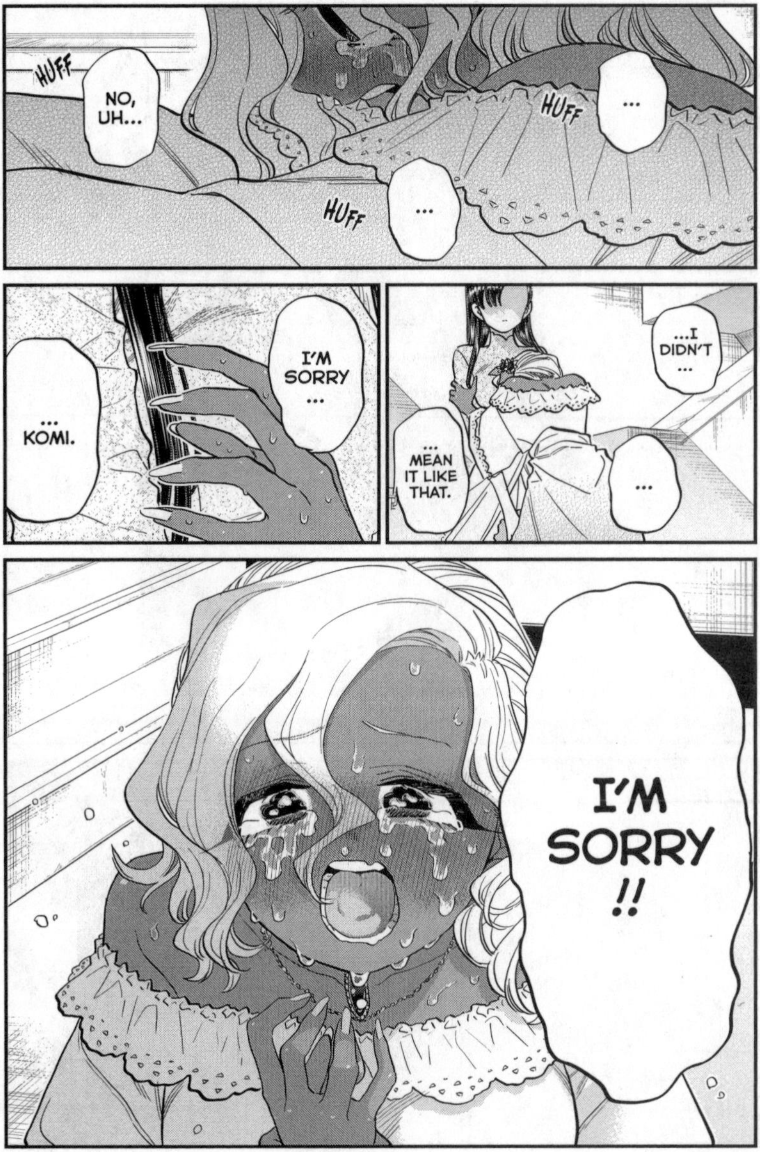
...
HUFF
...
HUFF
NO, UH...
HUFF
...I DIDN'T ...
... MEAN IT LIKE THAT.
...
I'M SORRY ...
... KOMI.
I'M SORRY !!

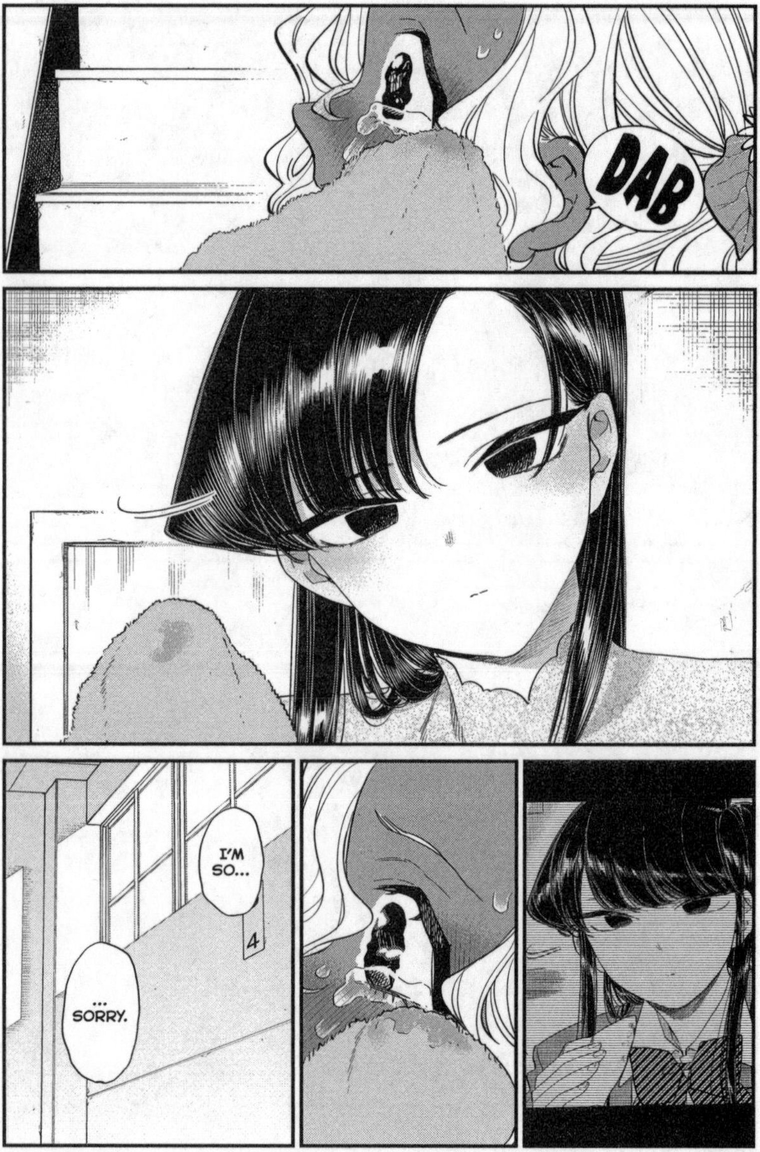
DAB
I'M SO...
... SORRY.

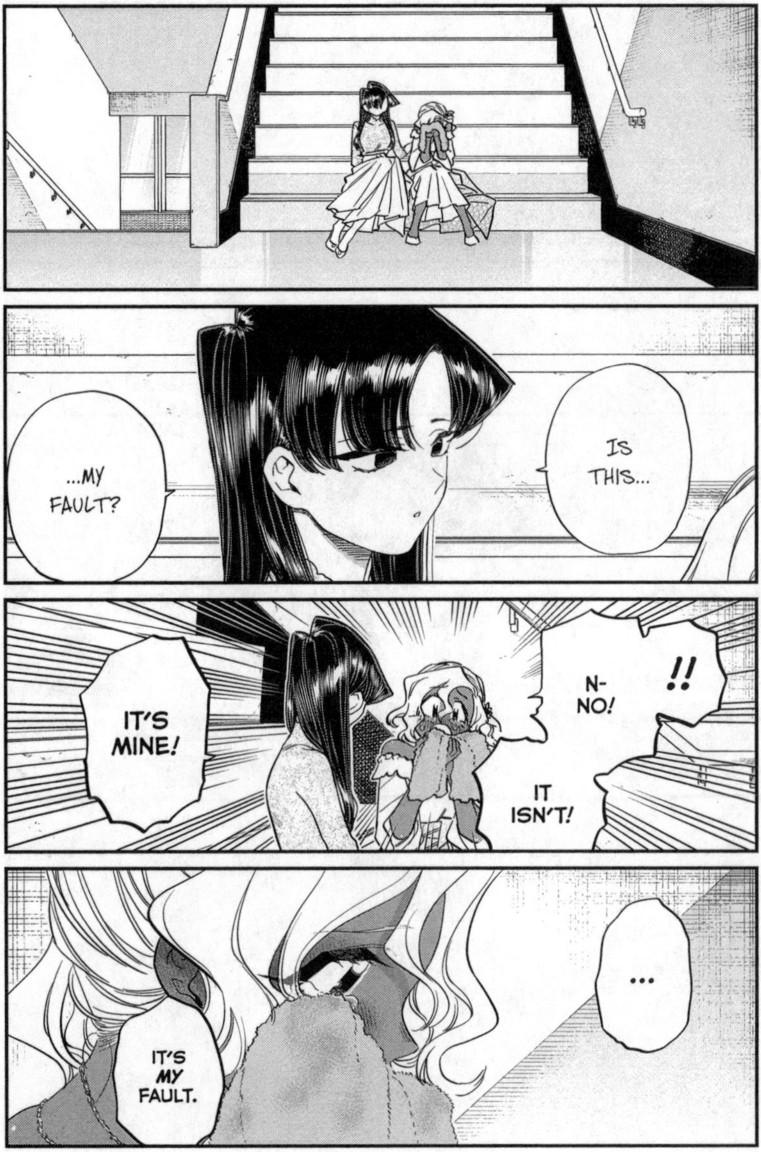
IS THIS...
...MY FAULT?
!!
N- NO!
IT ISN'T!
IT'S MINE!
...
IT'S MY FAULT.

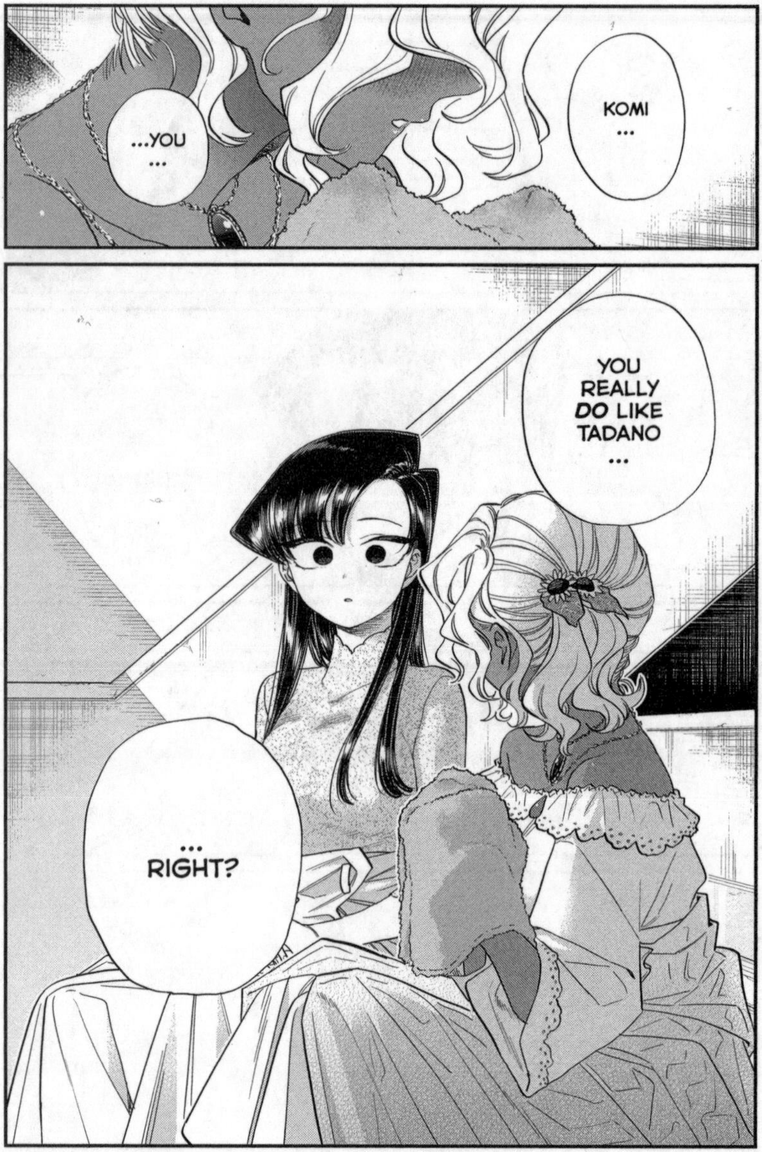
KOMI ...
...YOU ...
YOU REALLY *DO* LIKE TADANO ...
... RIGHT?

Communication 226 — The End

Hm? Where's Komi?
DO YOU HAVE A MINUTE, TAKARAZUKA?
WHAT DO YOU NEED?
MANBAGI ISN'T FEELING WELL, SO KOMI WENT TO CHECK ON HER.
INSTEAD OF DELAYING THE SHOW...
...MAYBE YOU COULD FILL IN FOR KOMI?
!
Why——?!
Whaaat?! Komi isn't here?!
Tadano! You must take responsibility for this!!
WILL KOMI BE BACK SOON?
MMPH MMPH
I DON'T KNOW.

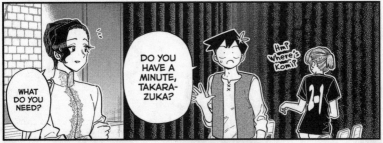

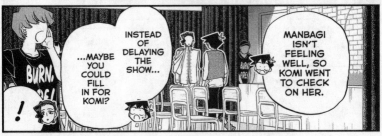

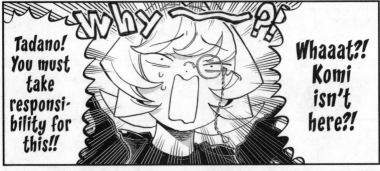

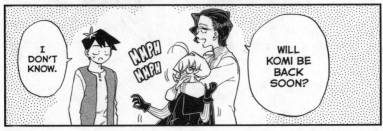

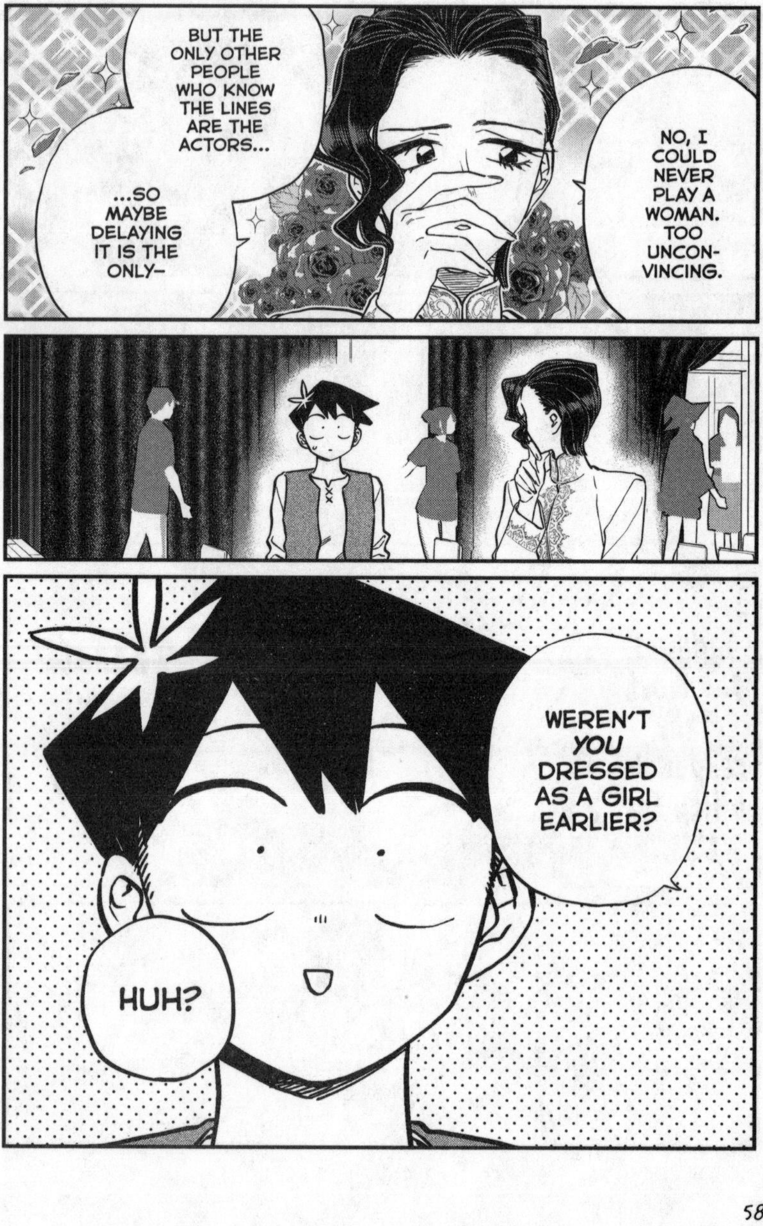
NO, I COULD NEVER PLAY A WOMAN. TOO UNCON-VINCING.
BUT THE ONLY OTHER PEOPLE WHO KNOW THE LINES ARE THE ACTORS...
...SO MAYBE DELAYING IT IS THE ONLY–
WEREN'T *YOU* DRESSED AS A GIRL EARLIER?
HUH?

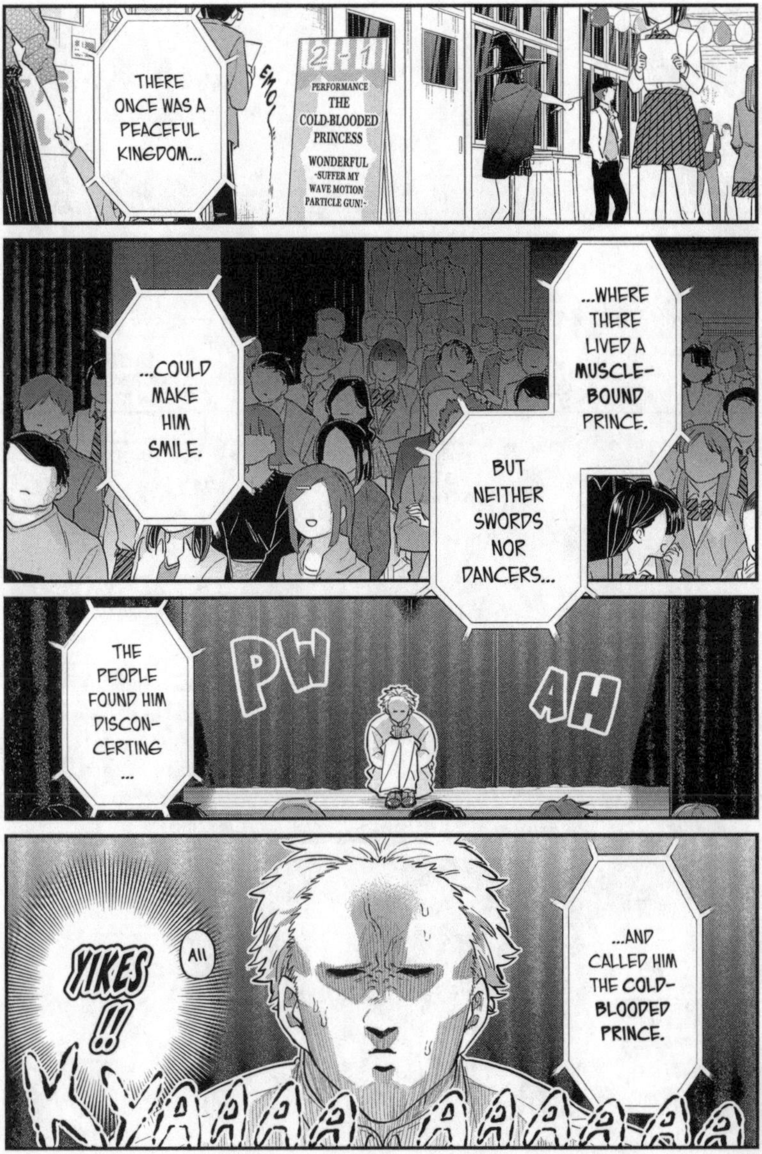
2-1
PERFORMANCE
THE COLD-BLOODED PRINCESS
WONDERFUL
-SUFFER MY WAVE MOTION PARTICLE GUN!-
EMO
THERE ONCE WAS A PEACEFUL KINGDOM...
...WHERE THERE LIVED A MUSCLE-BOUND PRINCE.
BUT NEITHER SWORDS NOR DANCERS...
...COULD MAKE HIM SMILE.
PWAH
THE PEOPLE FOUND HIM DISCONCERTING...
...AND CALLED HIM THE COLD-BLOODED PRINCE.
Ah
YIKES!!
KYAAAA AAAAAAA

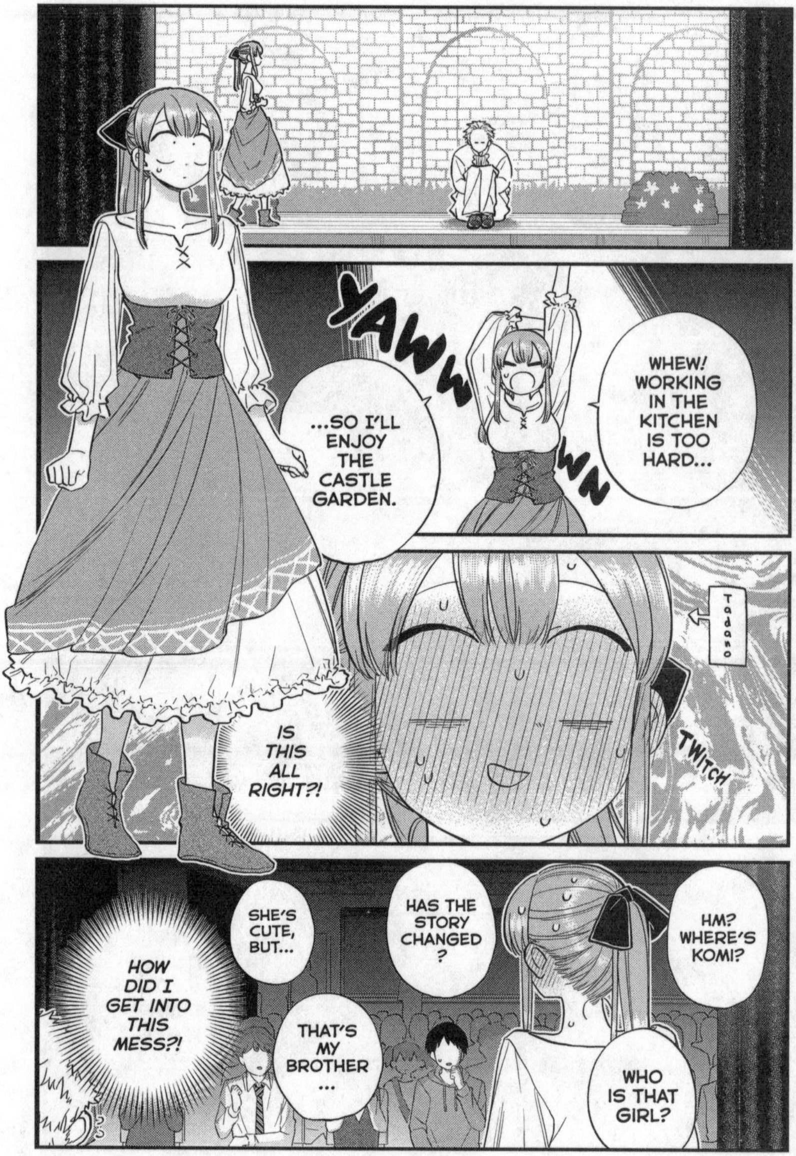
WHEW! WORKING IN THE KITCHEN IS TOO HARD...
YAWWW
WN
...SO I'LL ENJOY THE CASTLE GARDEN.
Tadano
TWITCH
IS THIS ALL RIGHT?!
HM? WHERE'S KOMI?
WHO IS THAT GIRL?
HAS THE STORY CHANGED?
SHE'S CUTE, BUT...
THAT'S MY BROTHER...
HOW DID I GET INTO THIS MESS?!

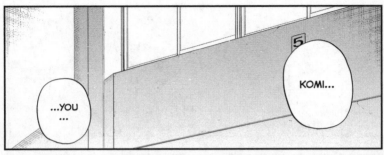

...YOU
...

KOMI...

YOU
REALLY
DO LIKE
TADANO
...

...RIGHT?

Komi Can't Communicate

Communication 227: No Surprise at All

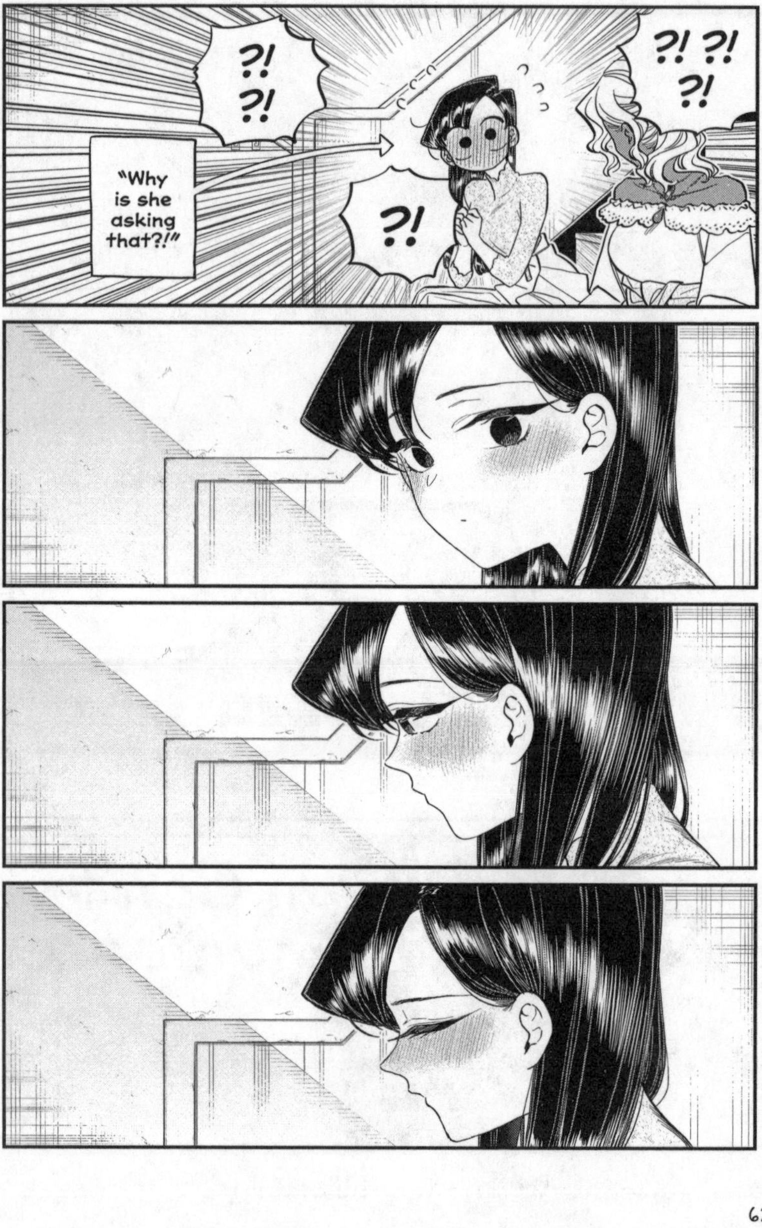
?! ?! ?!
?! ?!
?!
"Why is she asking that?!"

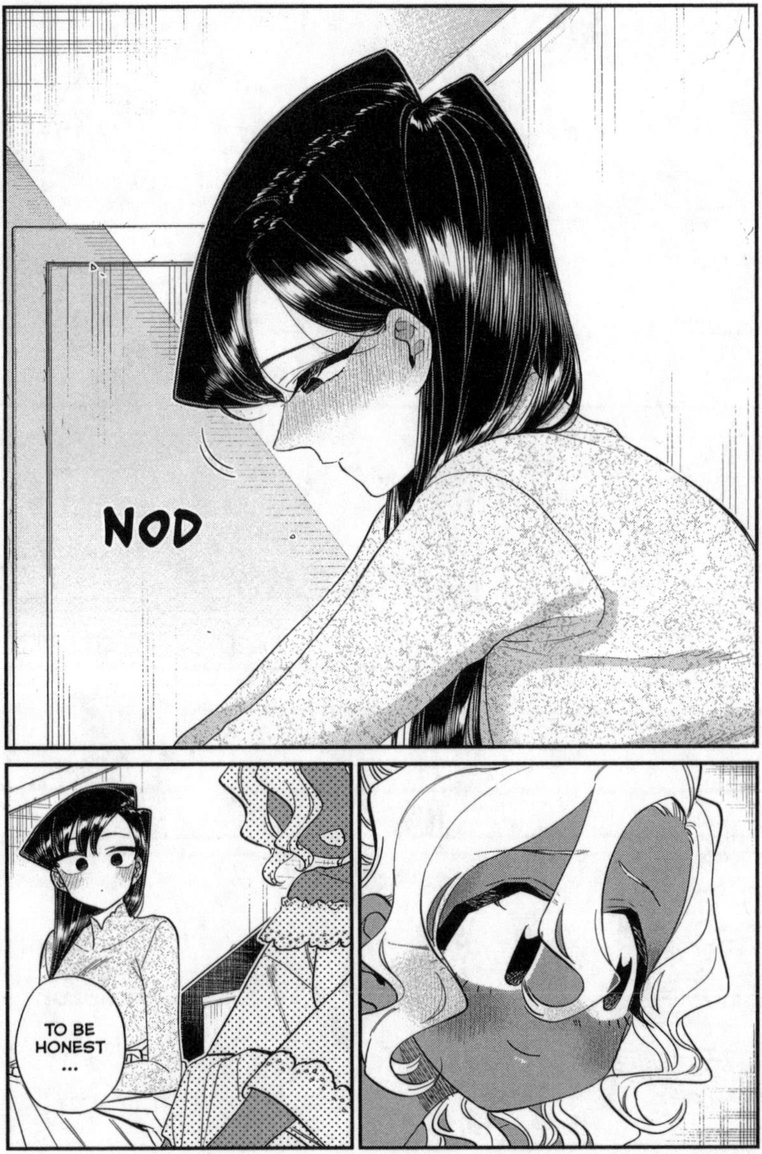
NOD
TO BE HONEST ...

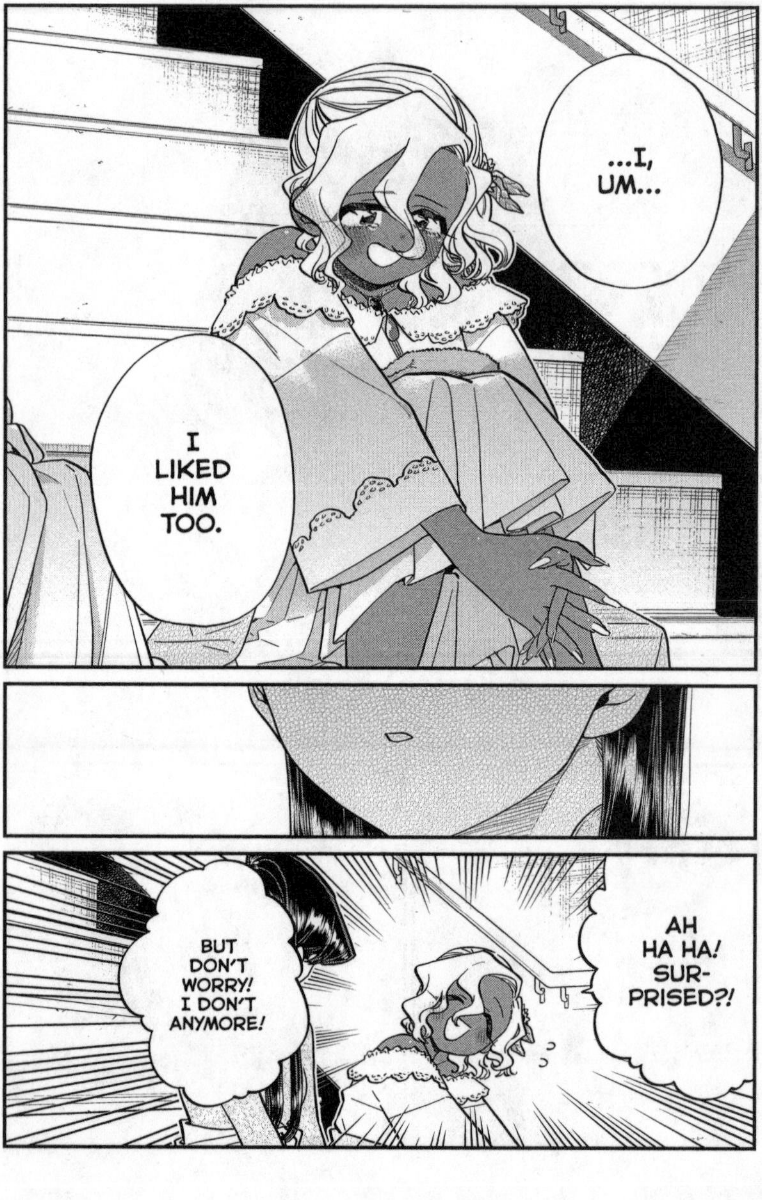
...I, UM...
I LIKED HIM TOO.
AH HA HA! SUR-PRISED?!
BUT DON'T WORRY! I DON'T ANYMORE!

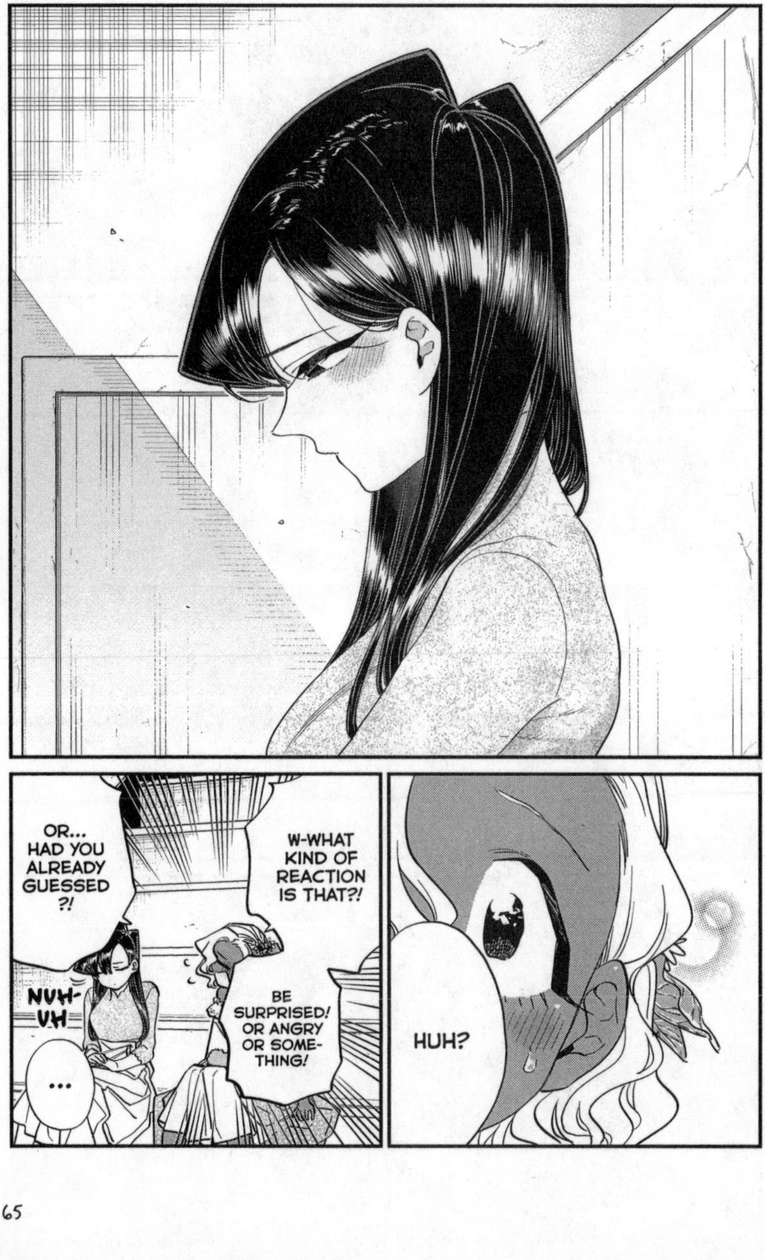
HUH?
W-WHAT KIND OF REACTION IS THAT?!
OR... HAD YOU ALREADY GUESSED ?!
BE SURPRISED! OR ANGRY OR SOME-THING!
NUH-UH
...

ACTUALLY, IT'S NO SURPRISE AT ALL.
?!
BECAUSE TADANO IS COOL.
?!
NO, IT'S A TOTAL SHOCKER!!
?!
HE ISN'T CONVEN-TIONALLY COOL AT ALL!
FWIP
FWIP
FWIP
FWIP
?!

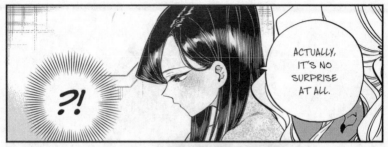

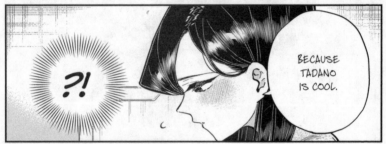

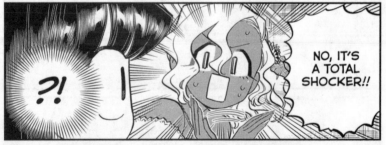

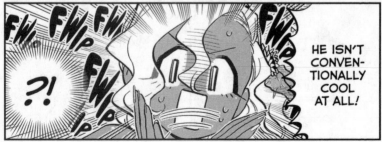

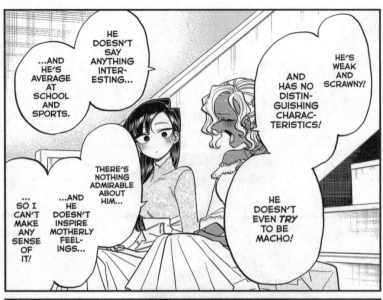

HE'S WEAK AND SCRAWNY!
AND HAS NO DISTINGUISHING CHARACTERISTICS!
HE DOESN'T EVEN *TRY* TO BE MACHO!
HE DOESN'T SAY ANYTHING INTERESTING...
...AND HE'S AVERAGE AT SCHOOL AND SPORTS.
THERE'S NOTHING ADMIRABLE ABOUT HIM...
...AND HE DOESN'T INSPIRE MOTHERLY FEELINGS...
...SO I CAN'T MAKE ANY SENSE OF IT!
I KNOW.

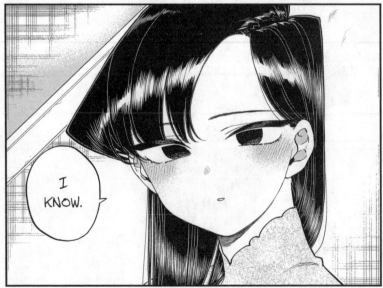

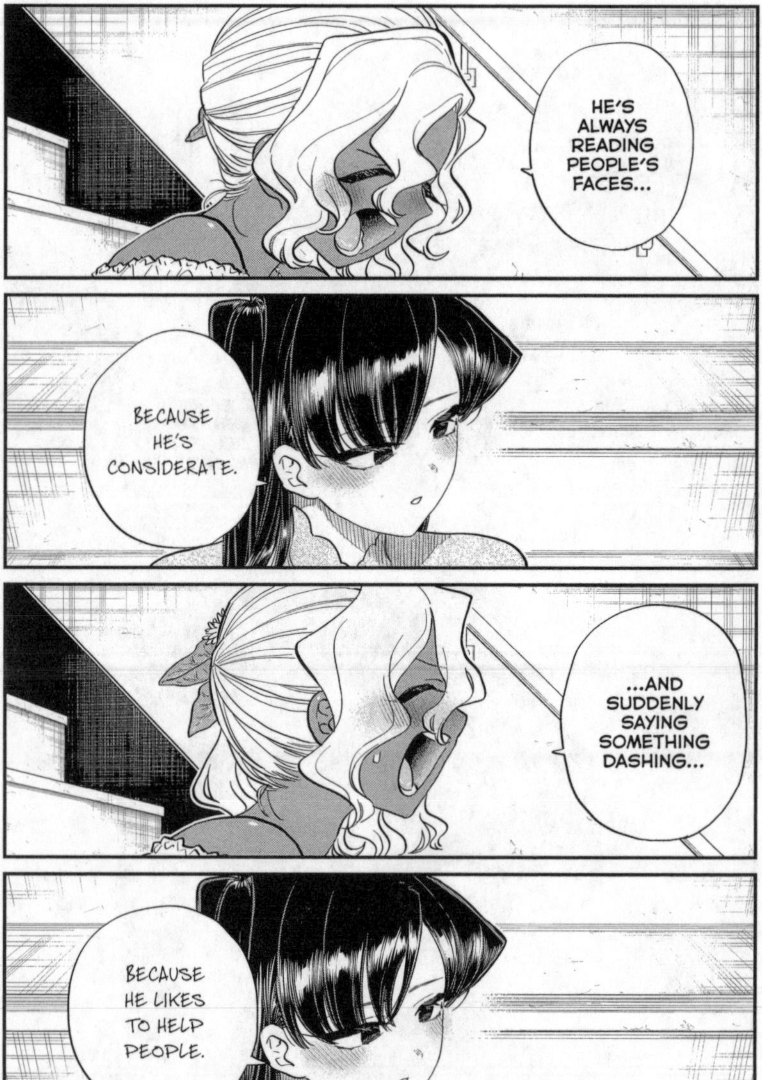
HE'S ALWAYS READING PEOPLE'S FACES...
BECAUSE HE'S CONSIDERATE.
...AND SUDDENLY SAYING SOMETHING DASHING...
BECAUSE HE LIKES TO HELP PEOPLE.

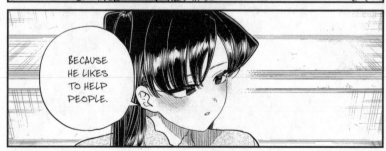

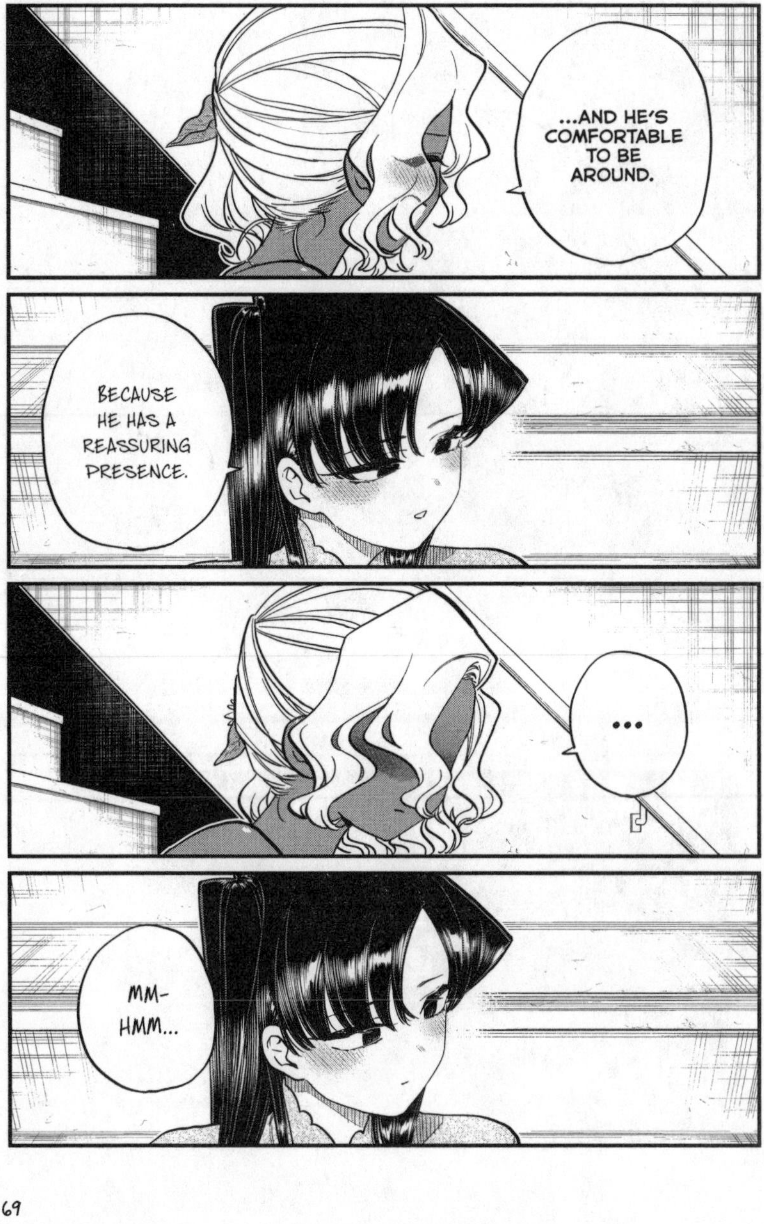
...AND HE'S COMFORTABLE TO BE AROUND.
BECAUSE HE HAS A REASSURING PRESENCE.
...
MM-HMM...

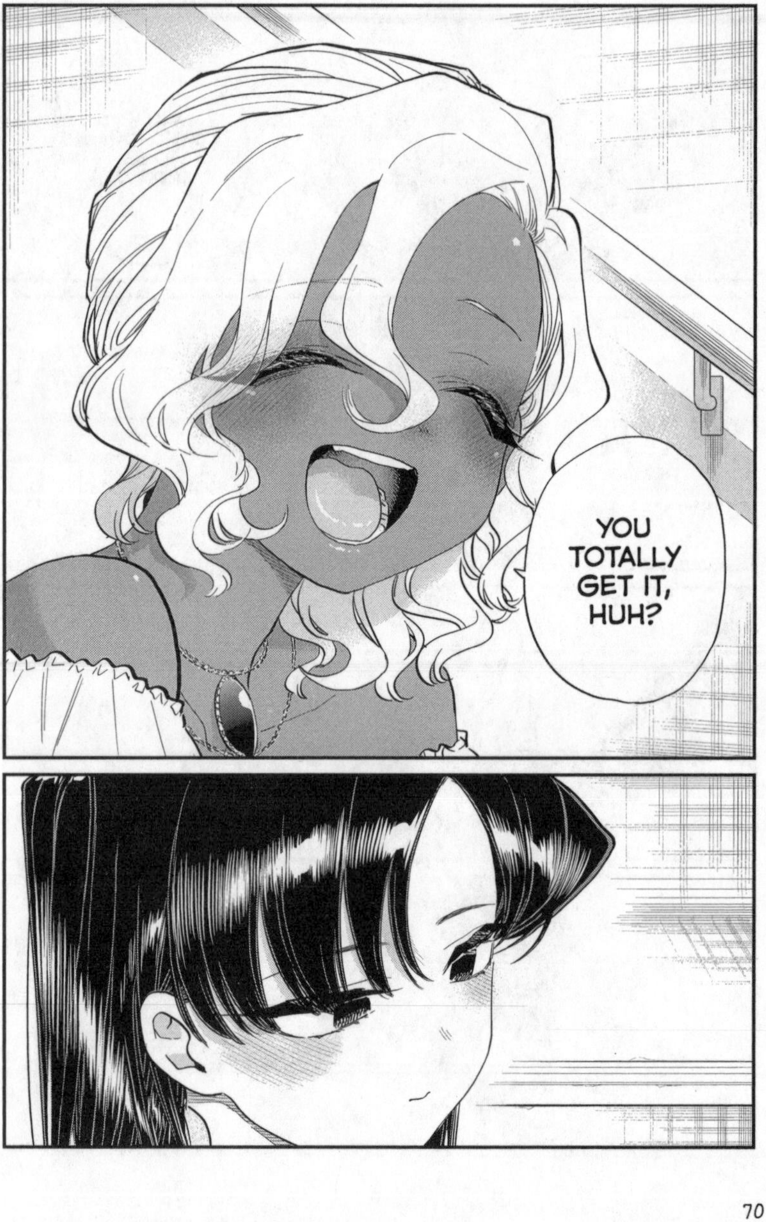
YOU TOTALLY GET IT, HUH?

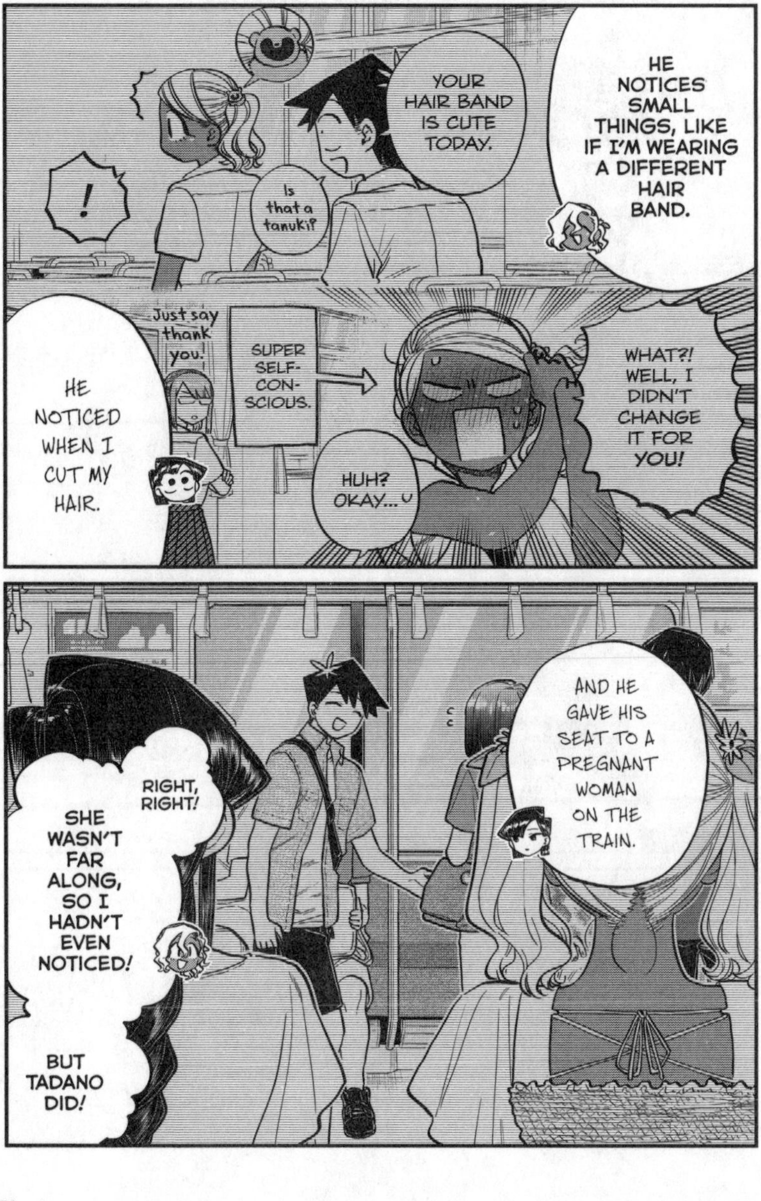
HE NOTICES SMALL THINGS, LIKE IF I'M WEARING A DIFFERENT HAIR BAND.
YOUR HAIR BAND IS CUTE TODAY.
Is that a tanuki?
!
WHAT?! WELL, I DIDN'T CHANGE IT FOR YOU!
HUH? OKAY...
SUPER SELF-CONSCIOUS.
Just say thank you.
HE NOTICED WHEN I CUT MY HAIR.
AND HE GAVE HIS SEAT TO A PREGNANT WOMAN ON THE TRAIN.
RIGHT, RIGHT!
SHE WASN'T FAR ALONG, SO I HADN'T EVEN NOTICED!
BUT TADANO DID!

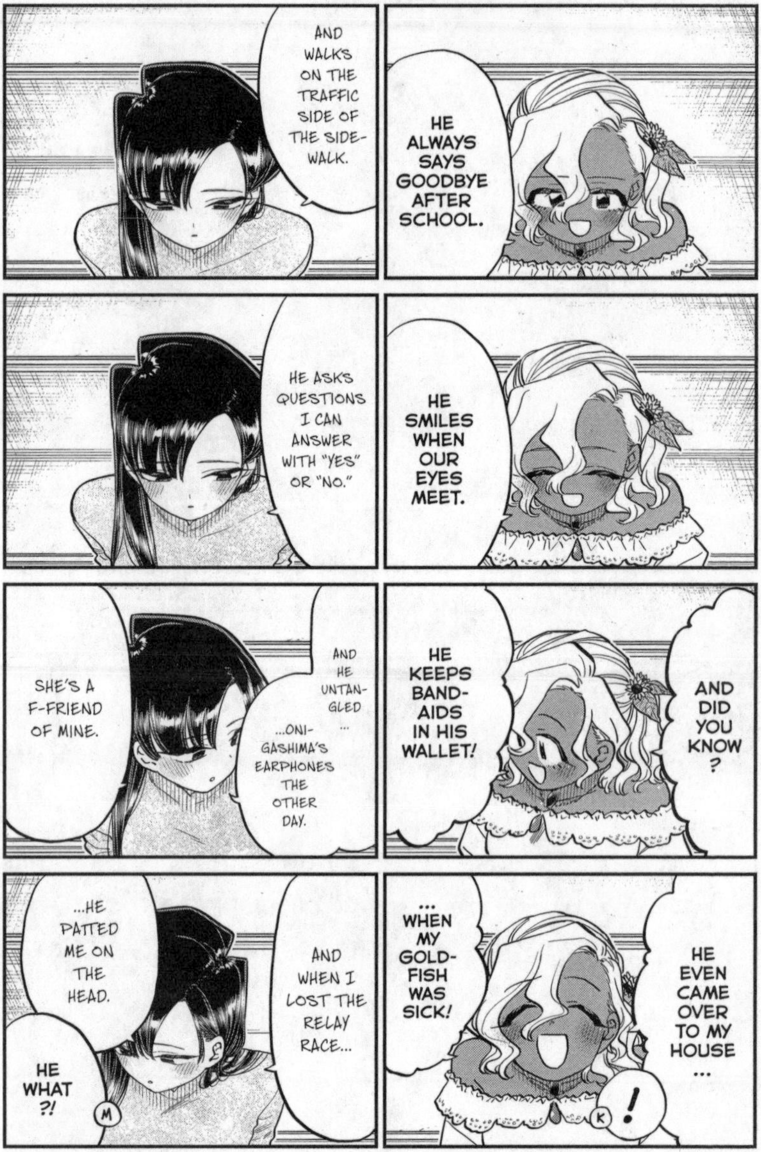
HE ALWAYS SAYS GOODBYE AFTER SCHOOL.
AND WALKS ON THE TRAFFIC SIDE OF THE SIDE-WALK.
HE SMILES WHEN OUR EYES MEET.
HE ASKS QUESTIONS I CAN ANSWER WITH "YES" OR "NO."
HE KEEPS BAND-AIDS IN HIS WALLET!
AND DID YOU KNOW ?
AND HE UNTANGLED ...
...ONI-GASHIMA'S EARPHONES THE OTHER DAY.
SHE'S A F-FRIEND OF MINE.
HE EVEN CAME OVER TO MY HOUSE ...
... WHEN MY GOLD-FISH WAS SICK!
K
!
AND WHEN I LOST THE RELAY RACE...
...HE PATTED ME ON THE HEAD.
HE WHAT ?!
M

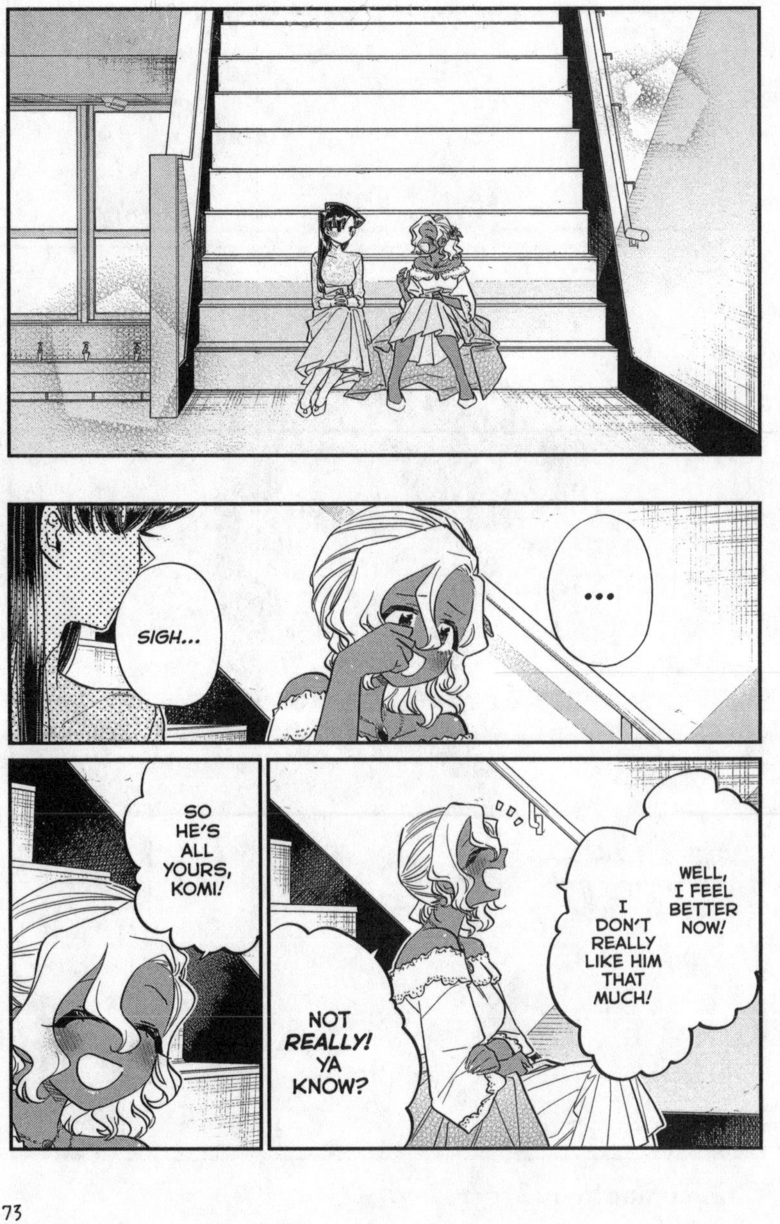
...
SIGH...
WELL, I FEEL BETTER NOW!
I DON'T REALLY LIKE HIM THAT MUCH!
NOT *REALLY!* YA KNOW?
SO HE'S ALL YOURS, KOMI!

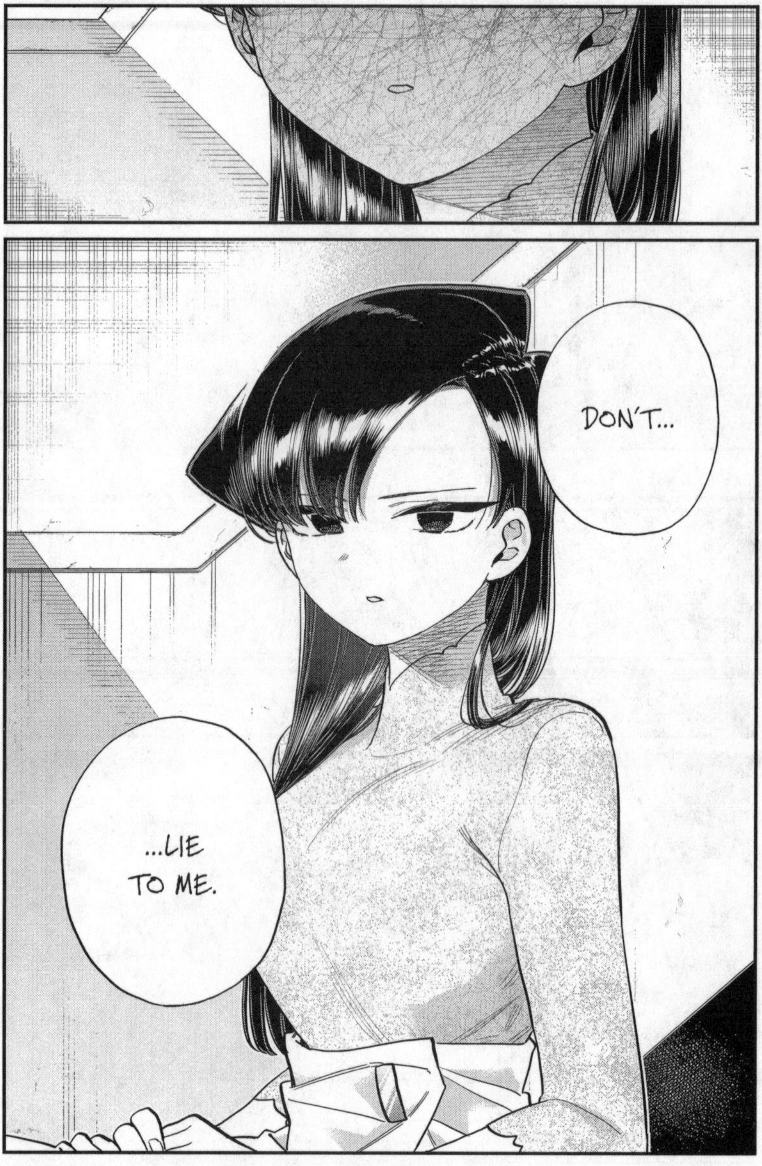
DON'T...
...LIE TO ME.

Communication 227 — The End

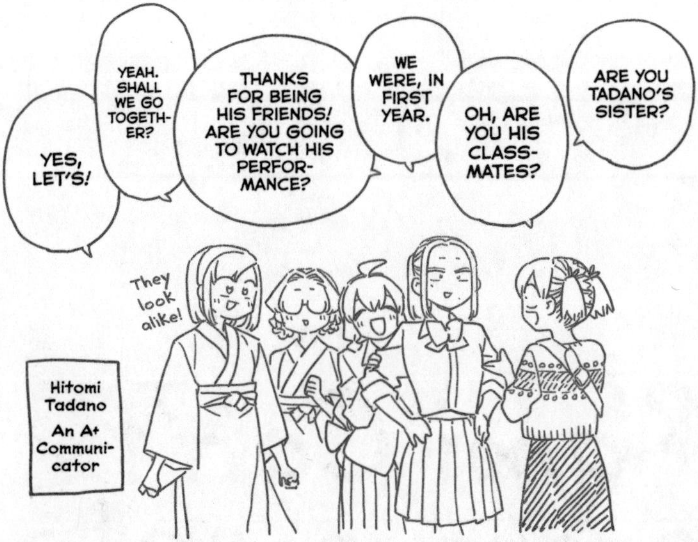
ARE YOU TADANO'S SISTER?
OH, ARE YOU HIS CLASSMATES?
WE WERE, IN FIRST YEAR.
THANKS FOR BEING HIS FRIENDS! ARE YOU GOING TO WATCH HIS PERFORMANCE?
YEAH. SHALL WE GO TOGETHER?
YES, LET'S!
They look alike!
Hitomi Tadano
An A+ Communicator

Komi Can't
Communicate

Komi Can't Communicate

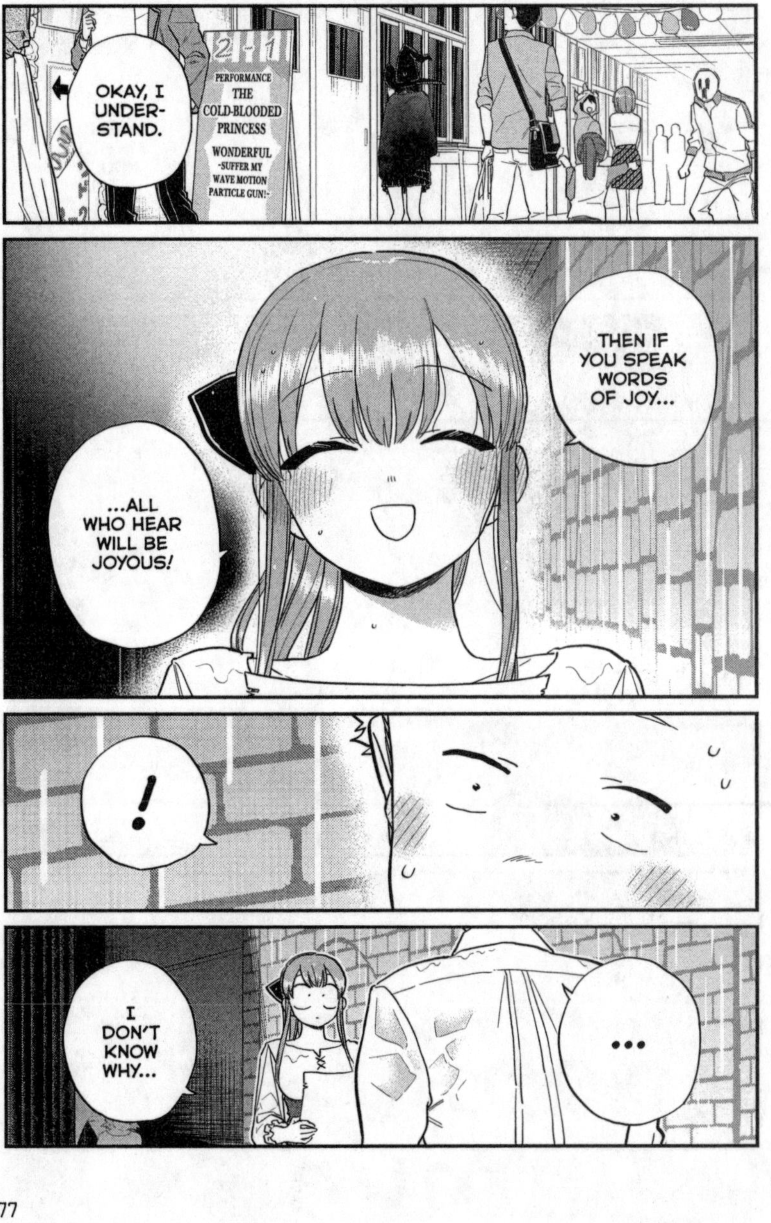
2-1
PERFORMANCE
THE COLD-BLOODED PRINCESS
WONDERFUL -SUFFER MY WAVE MOTION PARTICLE GUN!-
OKAY, I UNDERSTAND.
THEN IF YOU SPEAK WORDS OF JOY...
...ALL WHO HEAR WILL BE JOYOUS!
!
...
I DON'T KNOW WHY...

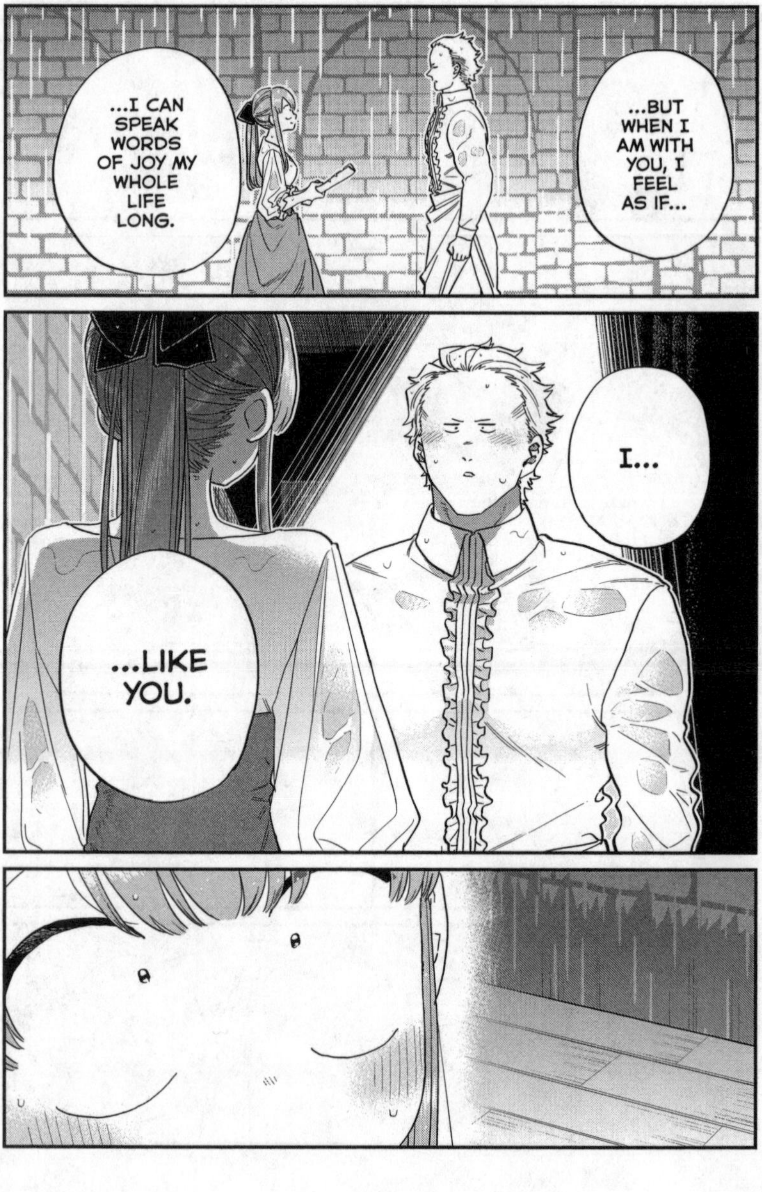
...BUT WHEN I AM WITH YOU, I FEEL AS IF...
...I CAN SPEAK WORDS OF JOY MY WHOLE LIFE LONG.
I...
...LIKE YOU.

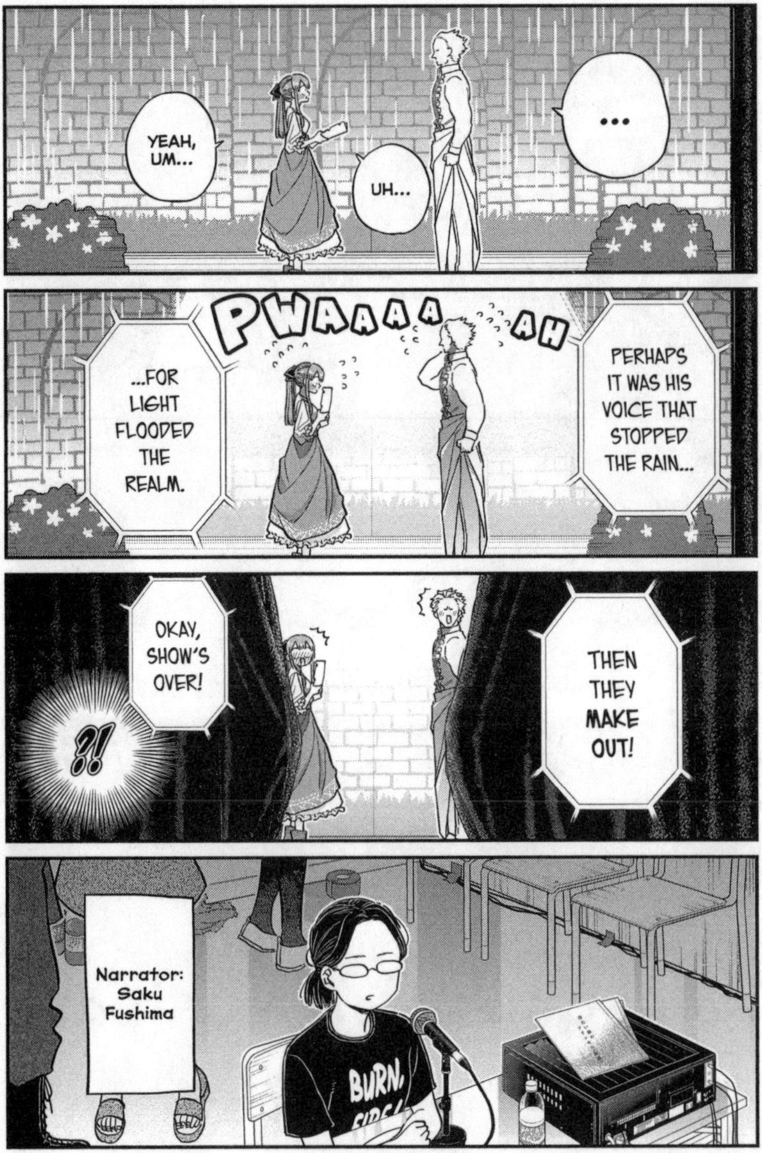
...
UH...
YEAH, UM...
PERHAPS IT WAS HIS VOICE THAT STOPPED THE RAIN...
PWAAAAAH
...FOR LIGHT FLOODED THE REALM.
THEN THEY MAKE OUT!
OKAY, SHOW'S OVER!
?!
Narrator: Saku Fushima
BURN,

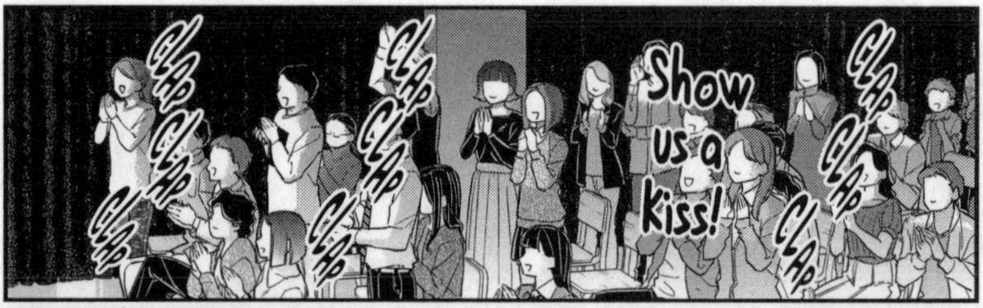
CLAP CLAP
CLAP
Show us a kiss!
CLAP CLAP CLAP
CLAP CLAP CLAP

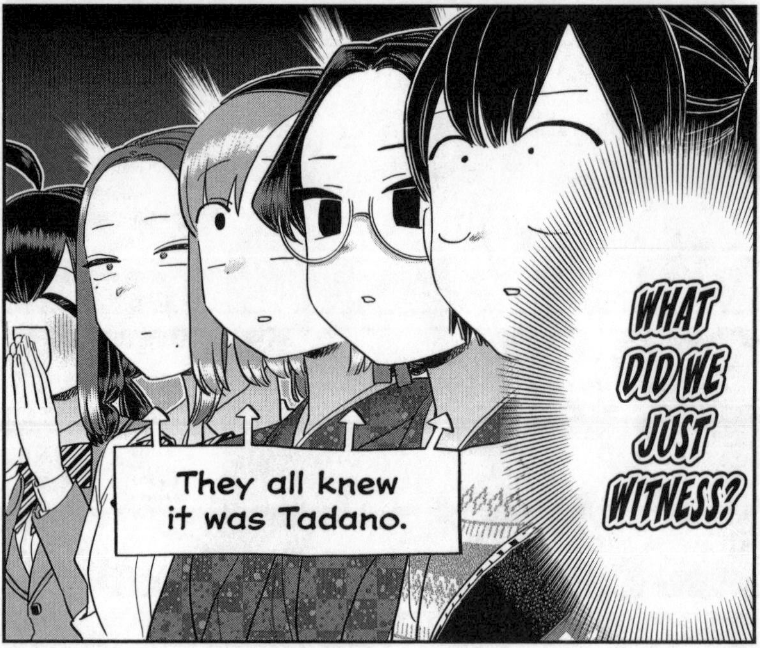
WHAT DID WE JUST WITNESS?
They all knew it was Tadano.

Komi Can't Communicate

Communication 228: Out of the Question

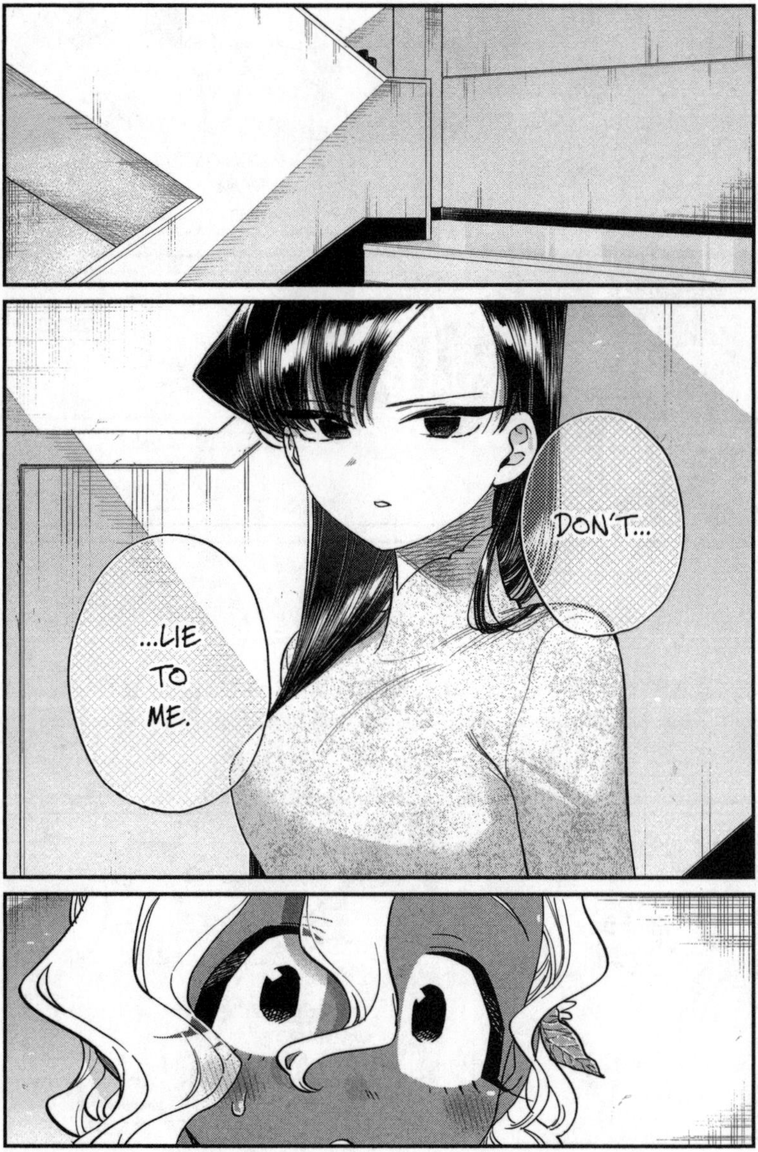
DON'T...
...LIE TO ME.

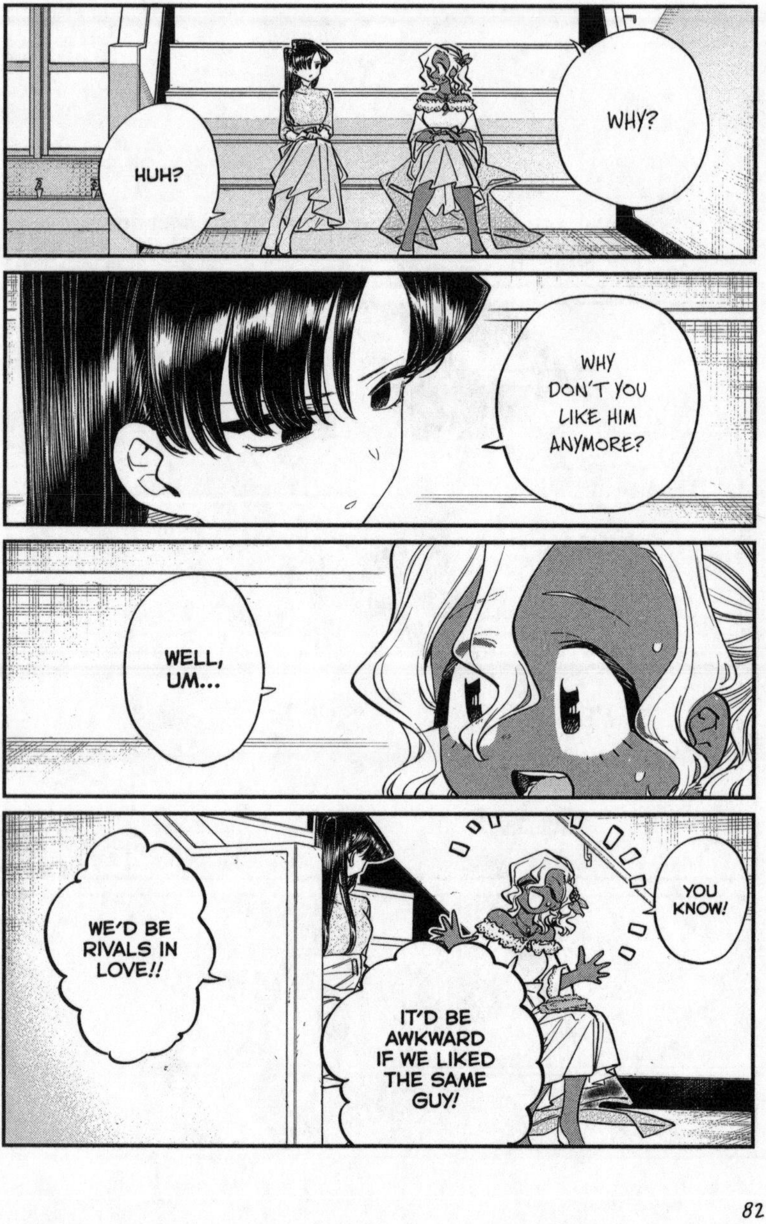
WHY?
HUH?
WHY DON'T YOU LIKE HIM ANYMORE?
WELL, UM...
YOU KNOW!
IT'D BE AWKWARD IF WE LIKED THE SAME GUY!
WE'D BE RIVALS IN LOVE!!

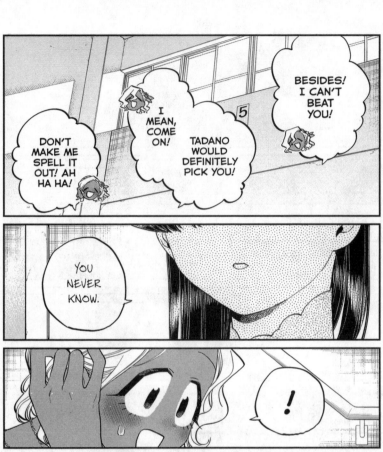

BESIDES! I CAN'T BEAT YOU!
I MEAN, COME ON!
TADANO WOULD DEFINITELY PICK YOU!
DON'T MAKE ME SPELL IT OUT! AH HA HA!
YOU NEVER KNOW.
!
IF TWO PEOPLE LIKE THE SAME PERSON...
...WHY DOES ONE HAVE TO GIVE UP?

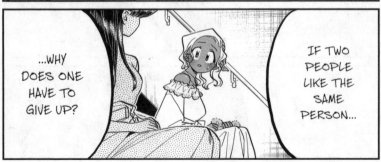

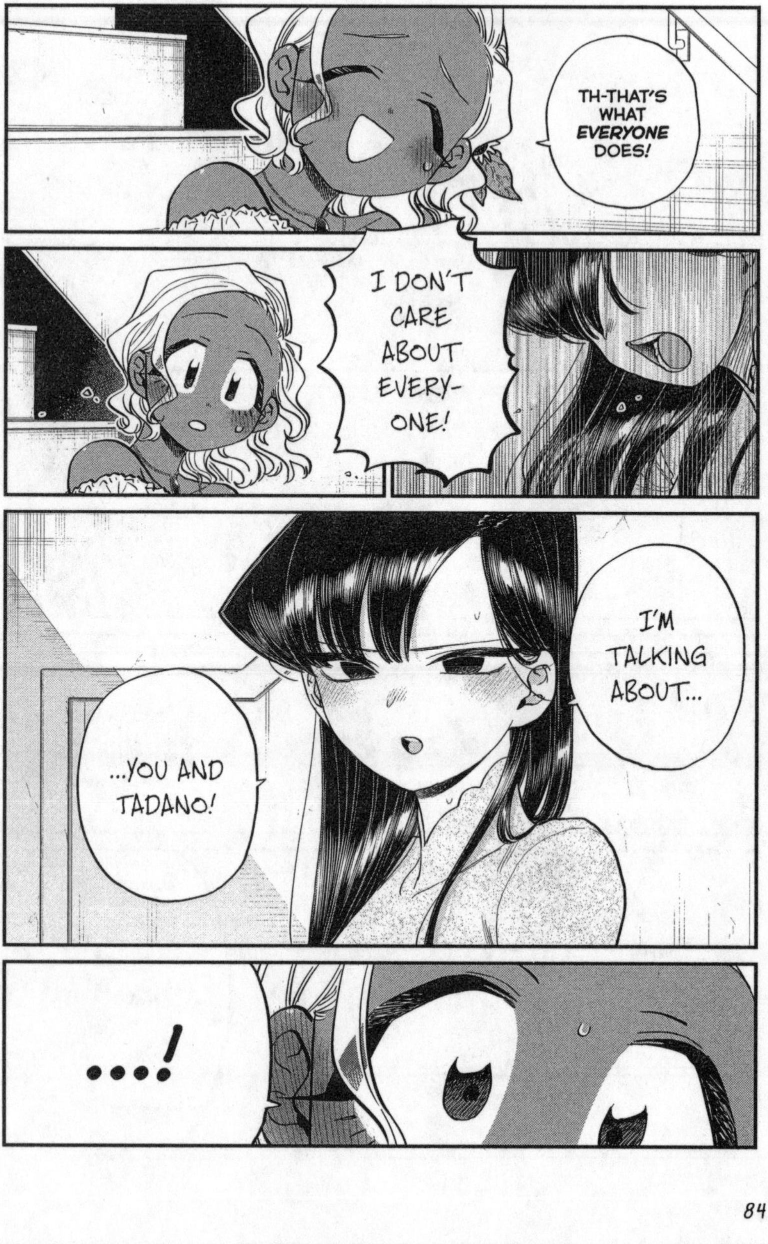
TH-THAT'S WHAT EVERYONE DOES!
I DON'T CARE ABOUT EVERY-ONE!
I'M TALKING ABOUT...
...YOU AND TADANO!
...!

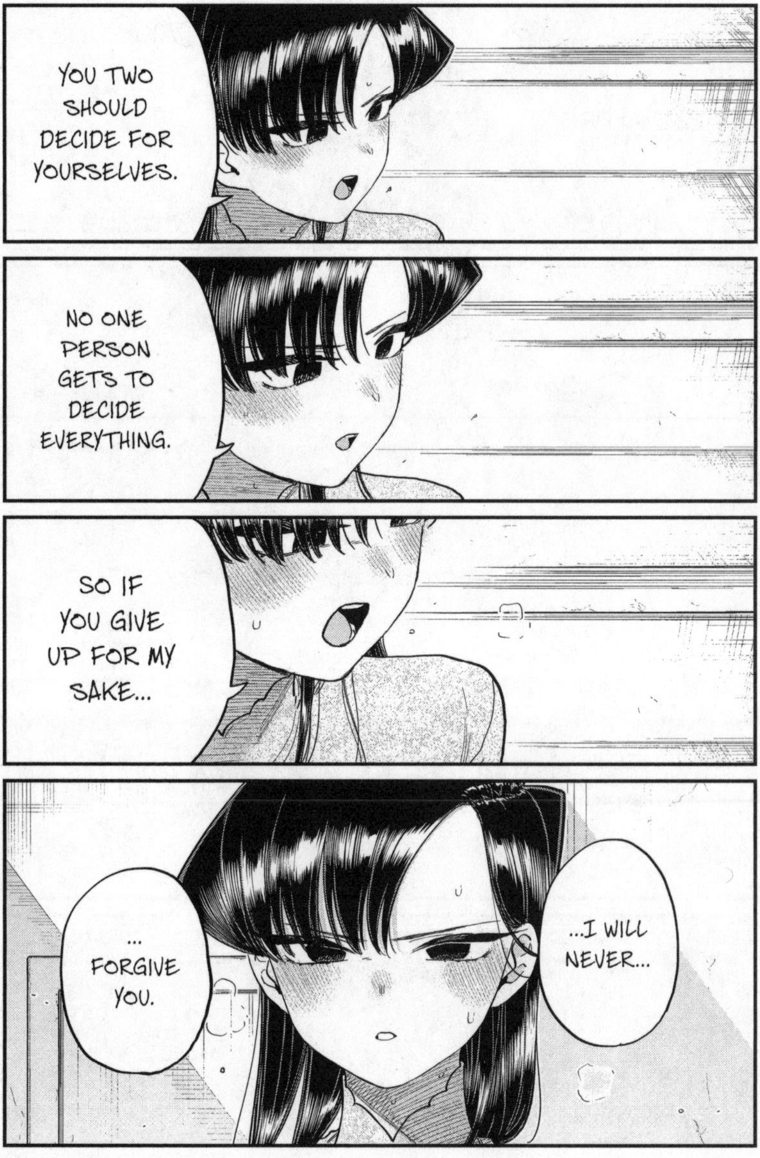
YOU TWO SHOULD DECIDE FOR YOURSELVES.
NO ONE PERSON GETS TO DECIDE EVERYTHING.
SO IF YOU GIVE UP FOR MY SAKE...
...I WILL NEVER...
... FORGIVE YOU.

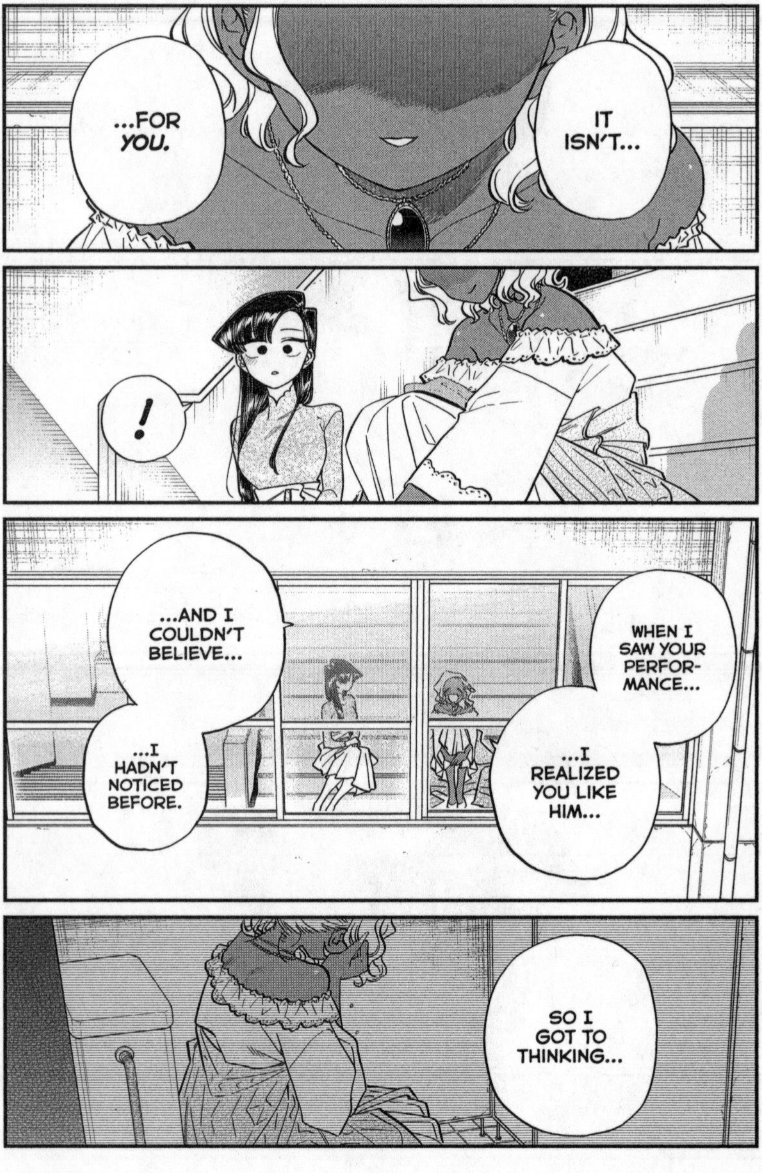
IT ISN'T...
...FOR YOU.
!
WHEN I SAW YOUR PERFOR-MANCE...
...I REALIZED YOU LIKE HIM...
...AND I COULDN'T BELIEVE...
...I HADN'T NOTICED BEFORE.
SO I GOT TO THINKING...

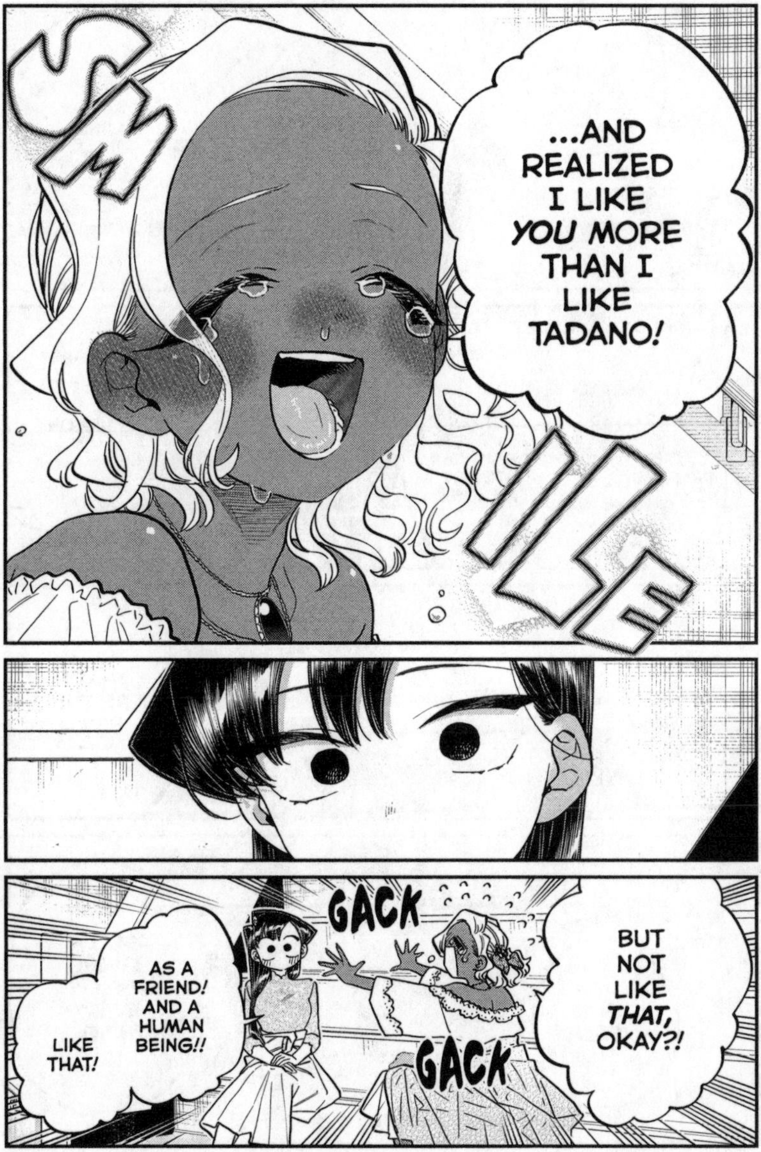
SMILE
...AND REALIZED I LIKE *YOU* MORE THAN I LIKE TADANO!
BUT NOT LIKE *THAT*, OKAY?!
GACK
GACK
AS A FRIEND! AND A HUMAN BEING!!
LIKE THAT!

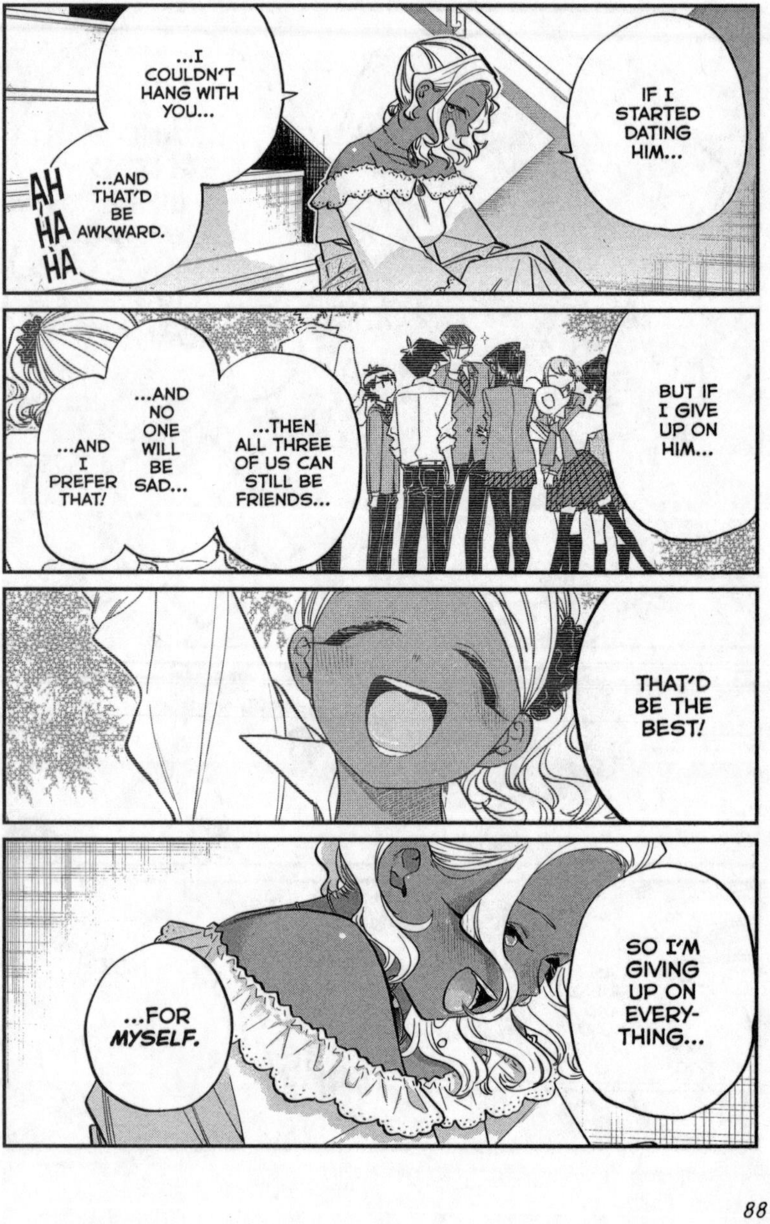
IF I STARTED DATING HIM...
...I COULDN'T HANG WITH YOU...
...AND THAT'D BE AWKWARD.
AH HA HA HA
BUT IF I GIVE UP ON HIM...
...THEN ALL THREE OF US CAN STILL BE FRIENDS...
...AND NO ONE WILL BE SAD...
...AND I PREFER THAT!
THAT'D BE THE BEST!
SO I'M GIVING UP ON EVERY-THING...
...FOR *MYSELF.*

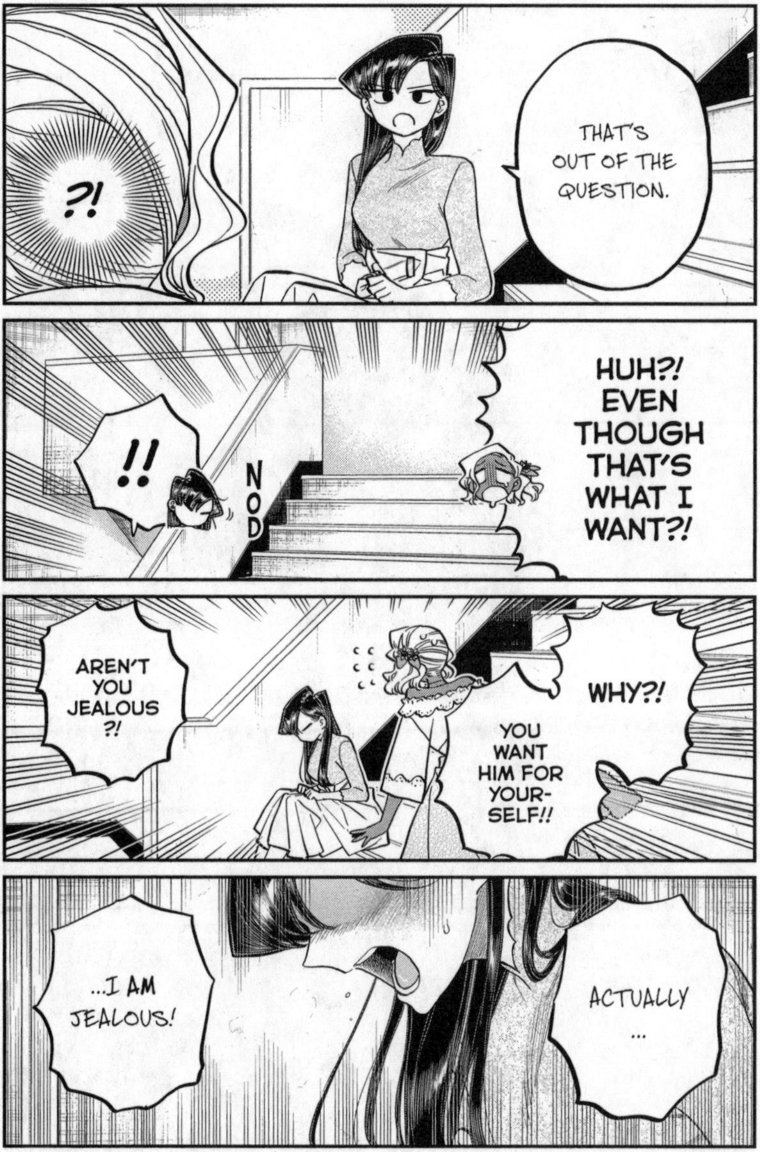
THAT'S OUT OF THE QUESTION.
?!
HUH?! EVEN THOUGH THAT'S WHAT I WANT?!
NOD
!!
WHY?!
YOU WANT HIM FOR YOUR-SELF!!
AREN'T YOU JEALOUS ?!
ACTUALLY ...
...I AM JEALOUS!

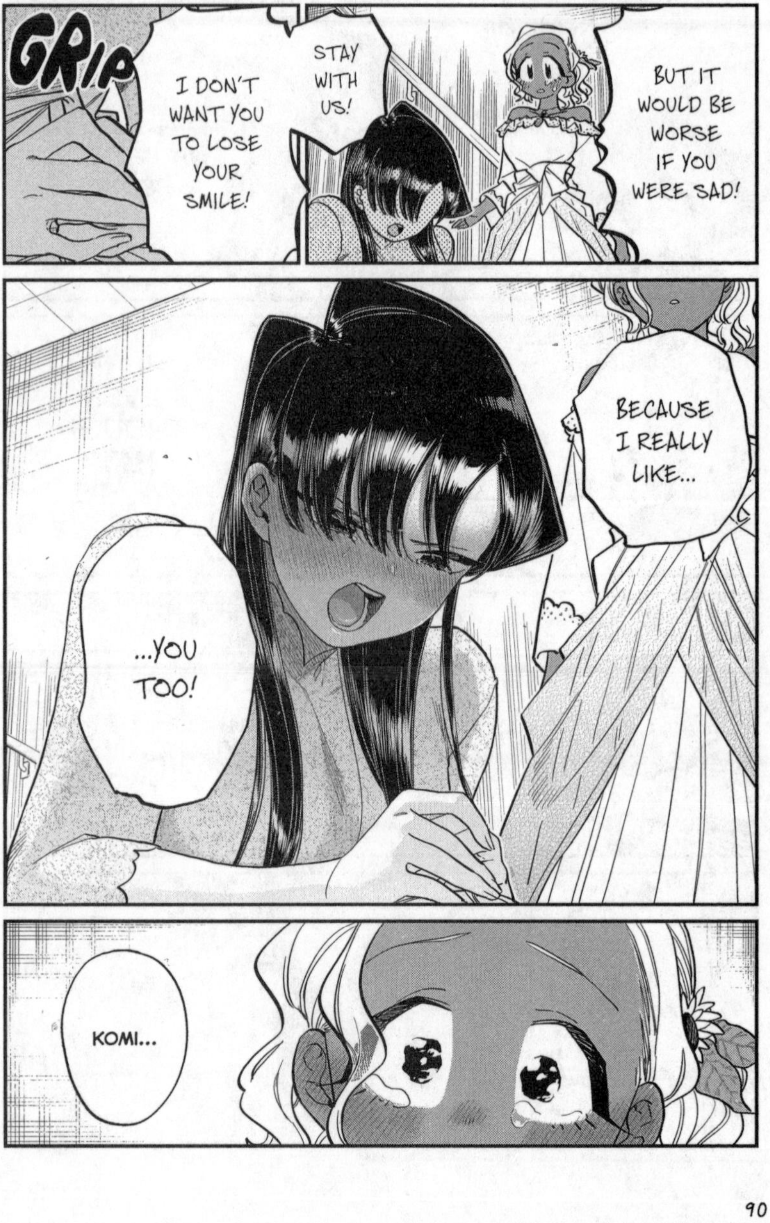
BUT IT WOULD BE WORSE IF YOU WERE SAD!
STAY WITH US!
I DON'T WANT YOU TO LOSE YOUR SMILE!
GRIP
BECAUSE I REALLY LIKE...
...YOU TOO!
KOMI...

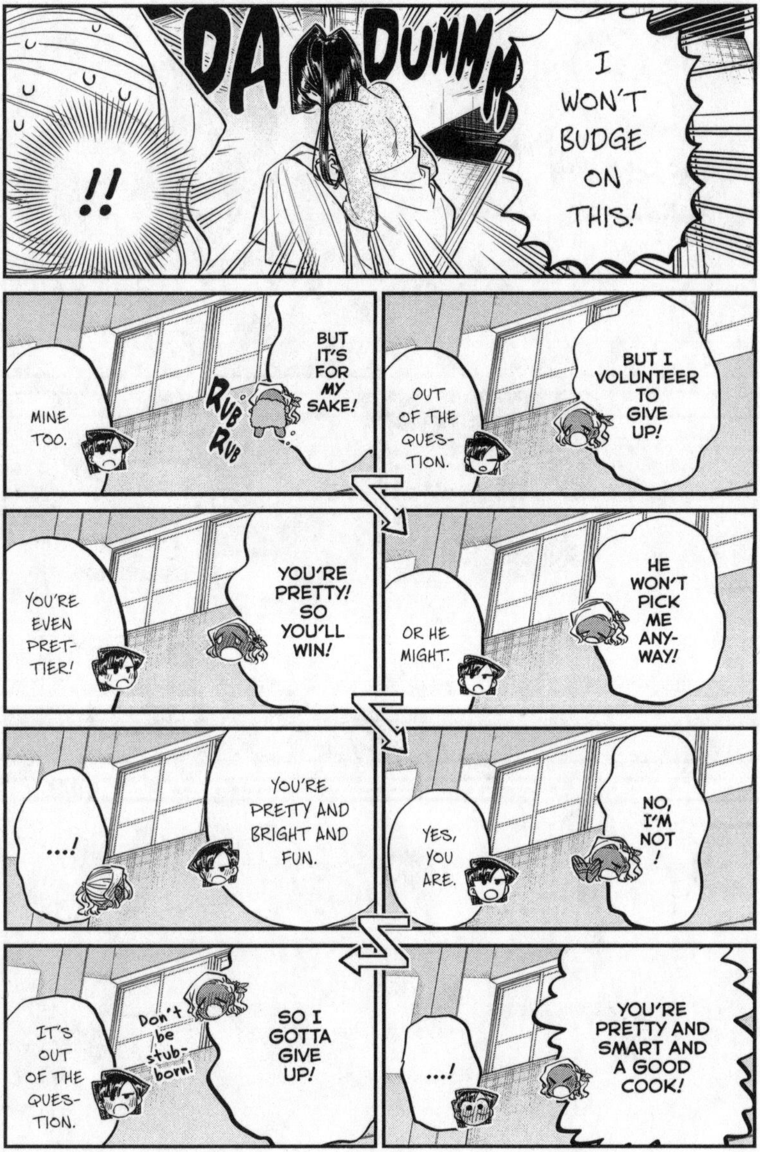
DA DUMMM
I WON'T BUDGE ON THIS!
!!
BUT I VOLUNTEER TO GIVE UP!
OUT OF THE QUESTION.
BUT IT'S FOR MY SAKE!
RUB RUB
MINE TOO.
HE WON'T PICK ME ANYWAY!
OR HE MIGHT.
YOU'RE PRETTY! SO YOU'LL WIN!
YOU'RE EVEN PRETTIER!
NO, I'M NOT!
YES, YOU ARE.
YOU'RE PRETTY AND BRIGHT AND FUN.
...!
YOU'RE PRETTY AND SMART AND A GOOD COOK!
...!
SO I GOTTA GIVE UP!
Don't be stubborn!
IT'S OUT OF THE QUESTION.

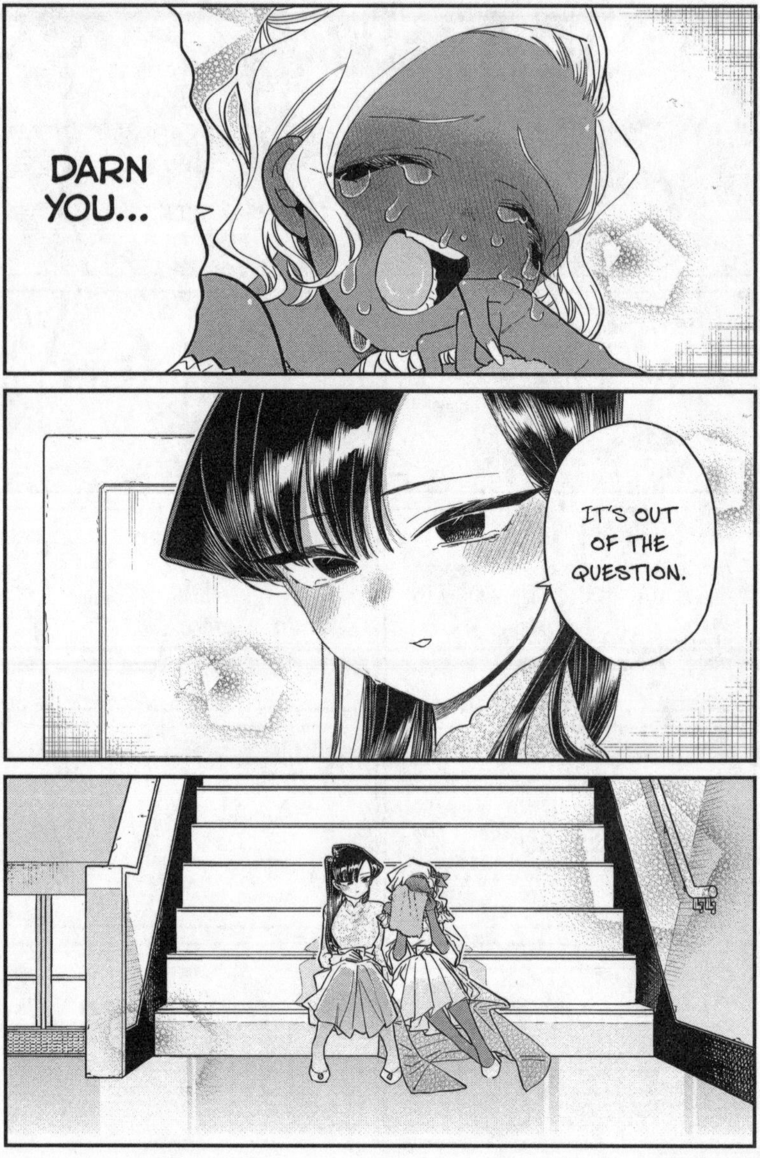
DARN YOU...
IT'S OUT OF THE QUESTION.

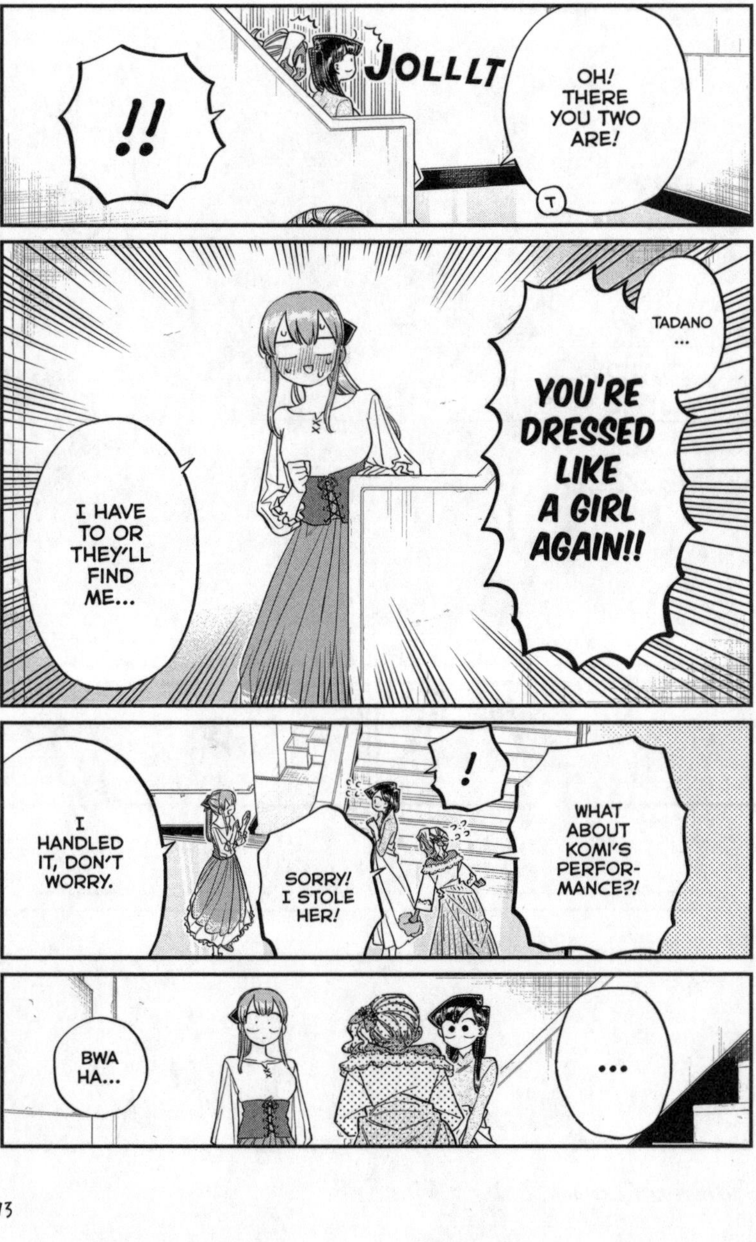
OH! THERE YOU TWO ARE!
T
JOLLLT
!!
TADANO ...
YOU'RE DRESSED LIKE A GIRL AGAIN!!
I HAVE TO OR THEY'LL FIND ME...
!
WHAT ABOUT KOMI'S PERFORMANCE?!
SORRY! I STOLE HER!
I HANDLED IT, DON'T WORRY.
...
BWA HA...

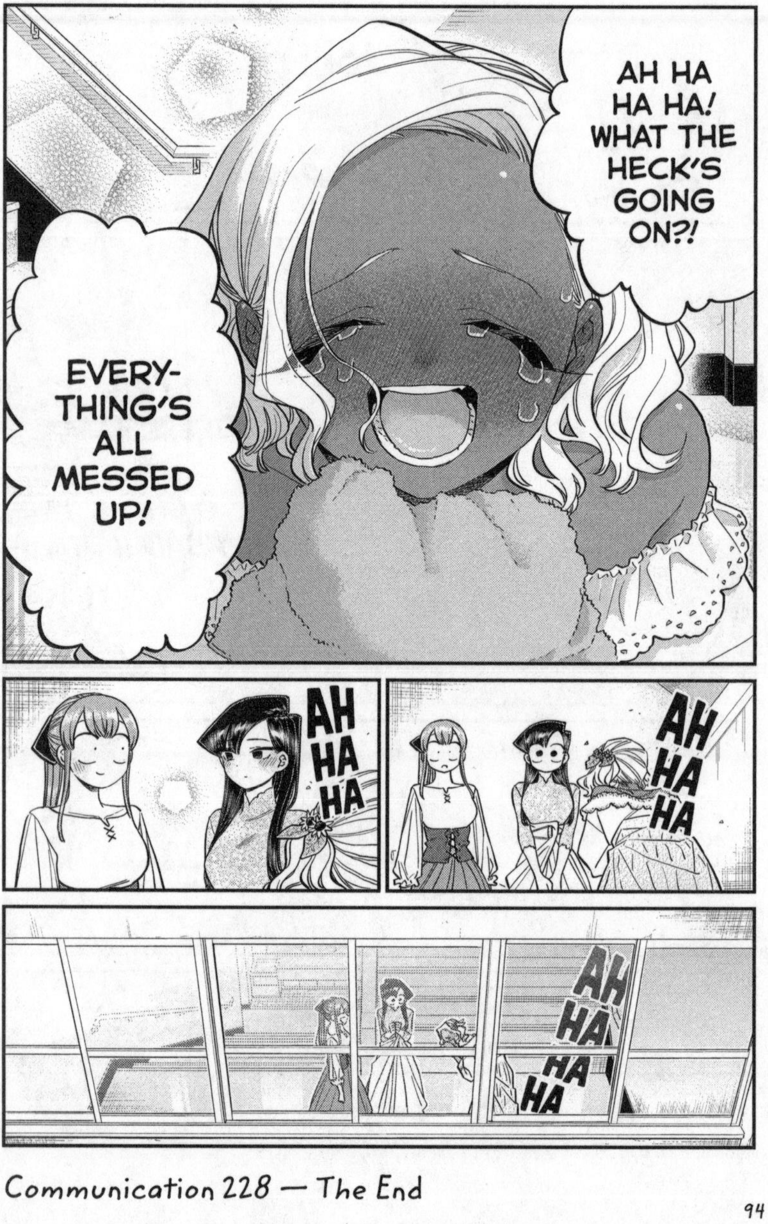
AH HA HA HA! WHAT THE HECK'S GOING ON?!
EVERY-THING'S ALL MESSED UP!
AH HA HA HA
AH HA HA
AH HA HA HA HA

Communication 228 — The End

Komi Can't Communicate

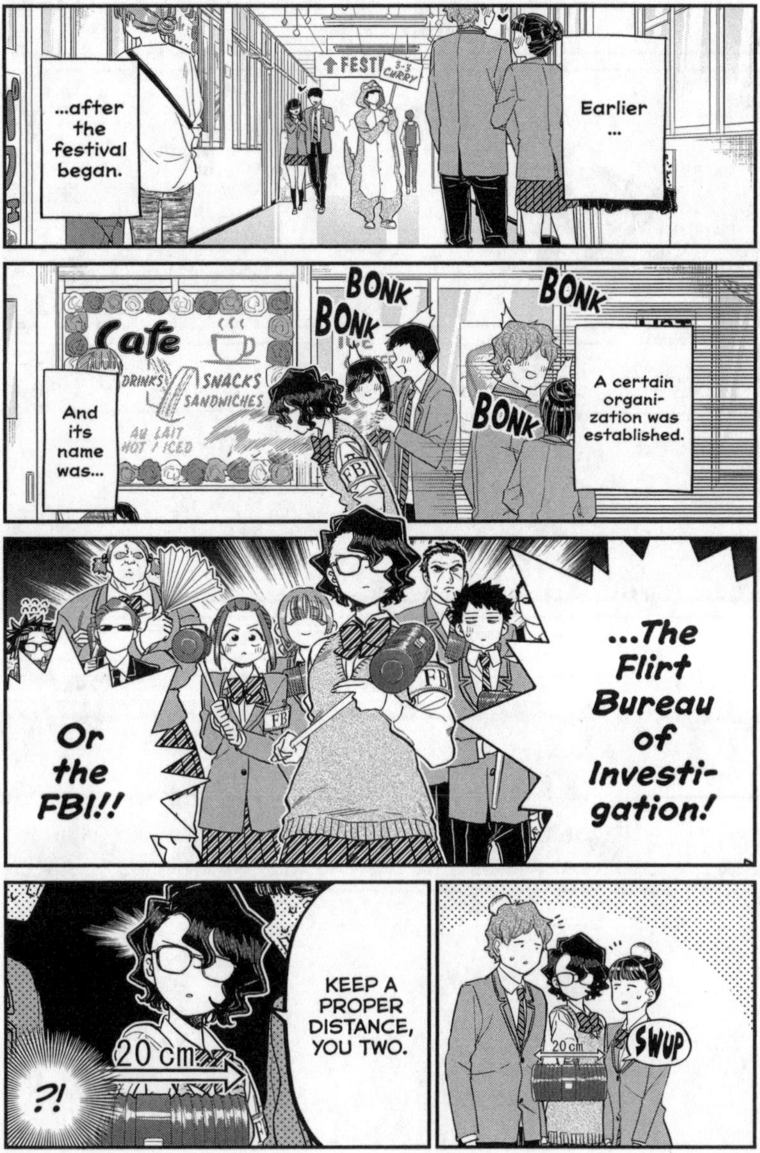
Earlier ...
FESTI
3-3 CURRY
...after the festival began.
A certain organization was established.
BONK
BONK
BONK
BONK
Cafe
DRINKS
SNACKS
SANDWICHES
AU LAIT
HOT / ICED
FBI
And its name was...
...The Flirt Bureau of Investigation!
Or the FBI!!
SWUP
20 cm
KEEP A PROPER DISTANCE, YOU TWO.
20 cm
?!

Communication 229: The FBI

FBI Case Files
LIVE
BONK
BONK
BONK
FBI
BONK
?!
THWAK

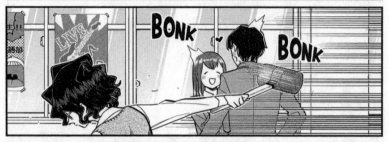

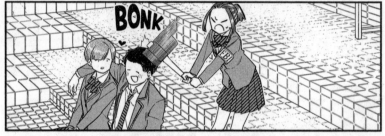

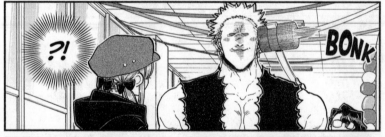

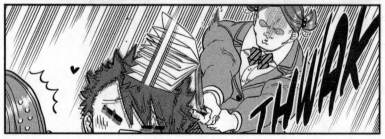

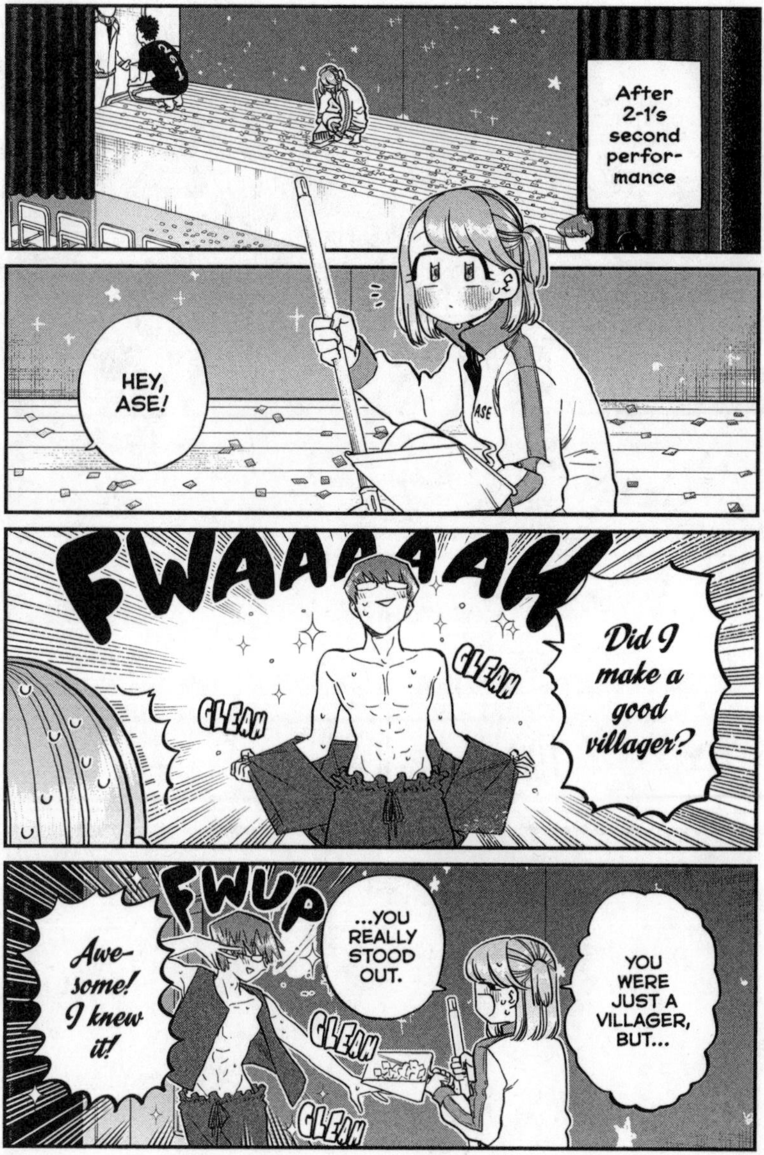
After 2-1's second performance
HEY, ASE!
FWAAAAAH
Did I make a good villager?
CLEAN
CLEAN
YOU WERE JUST A VILLAGER, BUT...
...YOU REALLY STOOD OUT.
FWUP
Awe-some! I knew it!
CLEAN
CLEAN

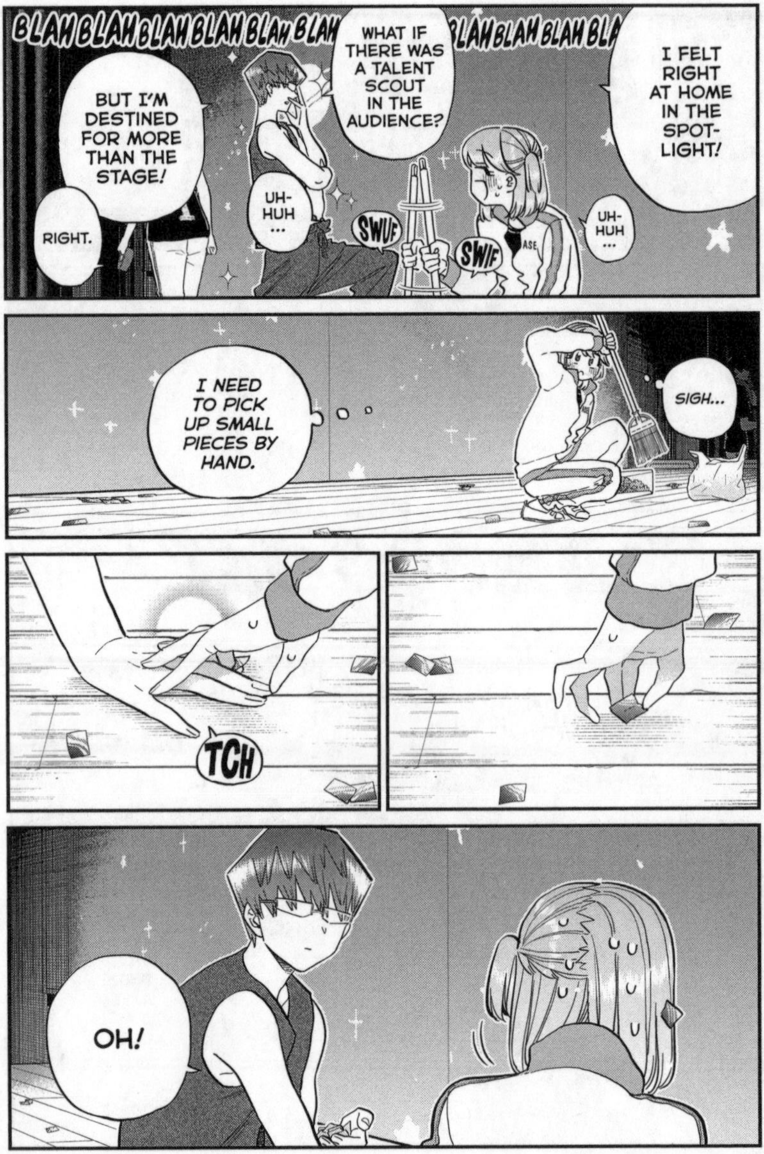

I FELT RIGHT AT HOME IN THE SPOT-LIGHT!
BLAH BLAH BLAH BLA
UH-HUH...
SWIF
WHAT IF THERE WAS A TALENT SCOUT IN THE AUDIENCE?
BLAH BLAH BLAH BLAH BLAH BLAH
SWUF
UH-HUH...
BUT I'M DESTINED FOR MORE THAN THE STAGE!
RIGHT.
SIGH...
I NEED TO PICK UP SMALL PIECES BY HAND.
TCH
OH!

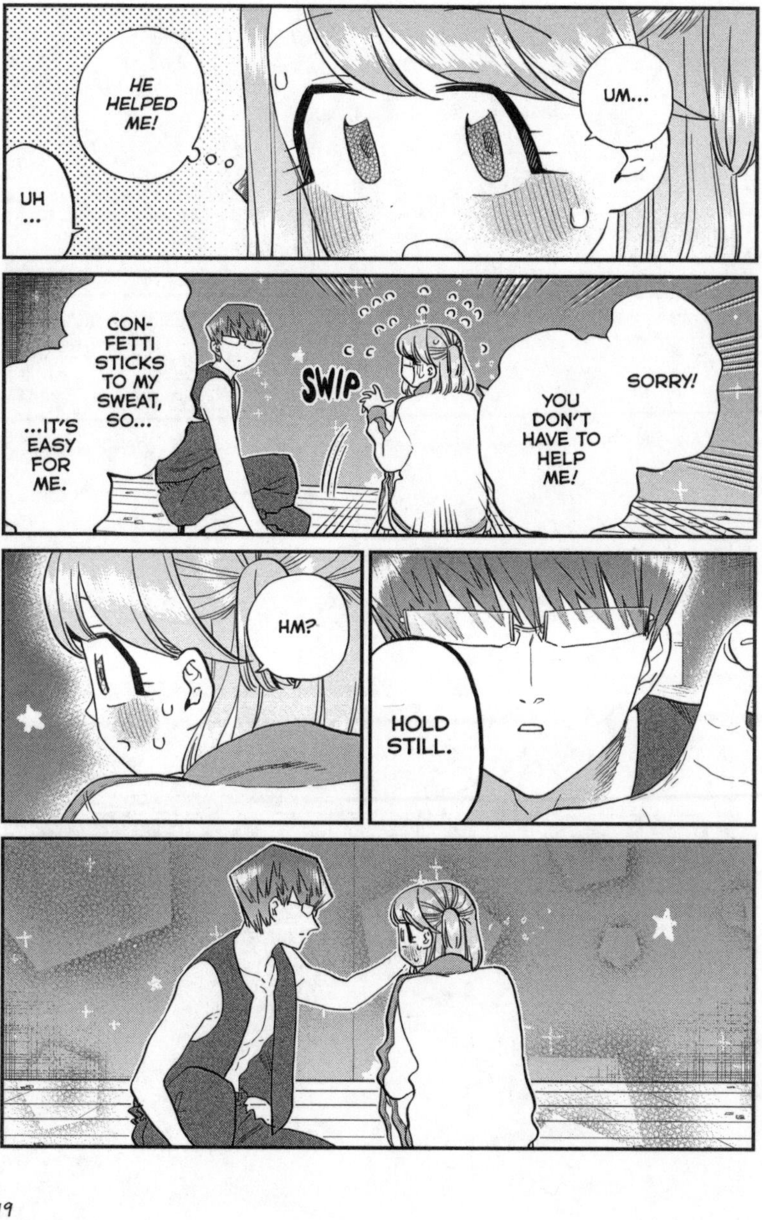
UM...
HE HELPED ME!
UH ...
SORRY!
YOU DON'T HAVE TO HELP ME!
SWIP
CON-FETTI STICKS TO MY SWEAT, SO...
...IT'S EASY FOR ME.
HOLD STILL.
HM?

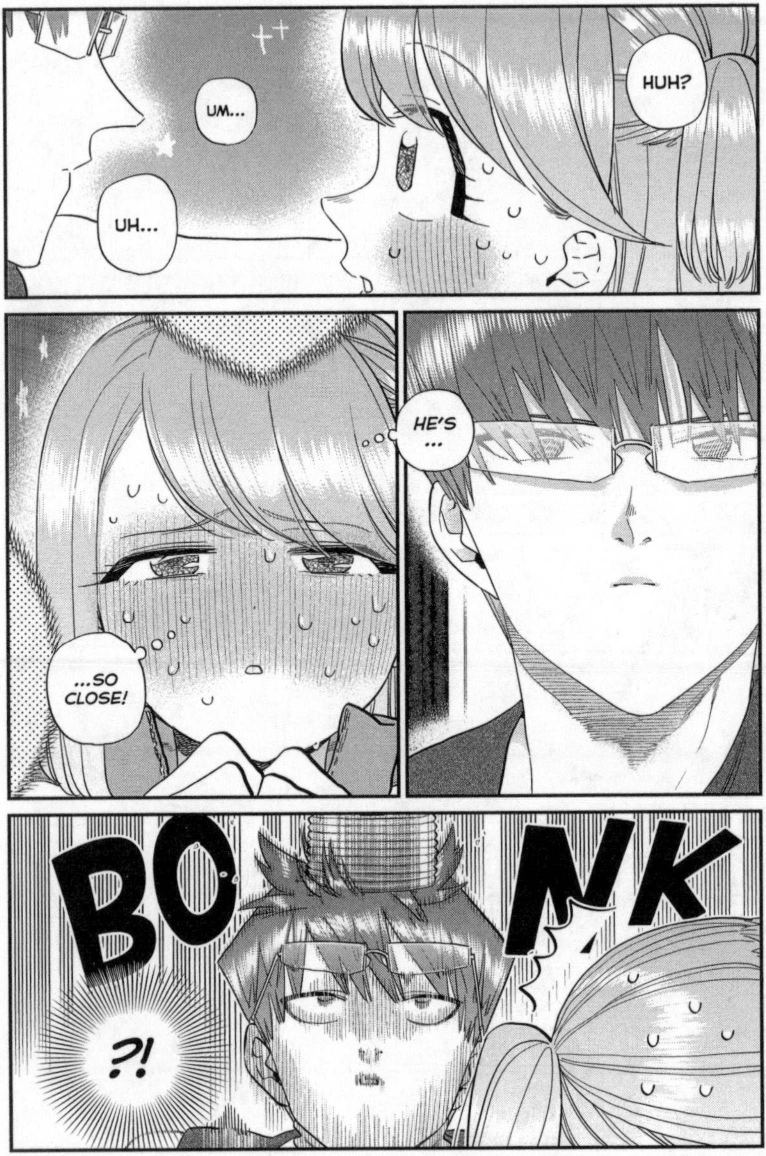
HUH?
UM...
UH...
HE'S ...
...SO CLOSE!
BONK
?!

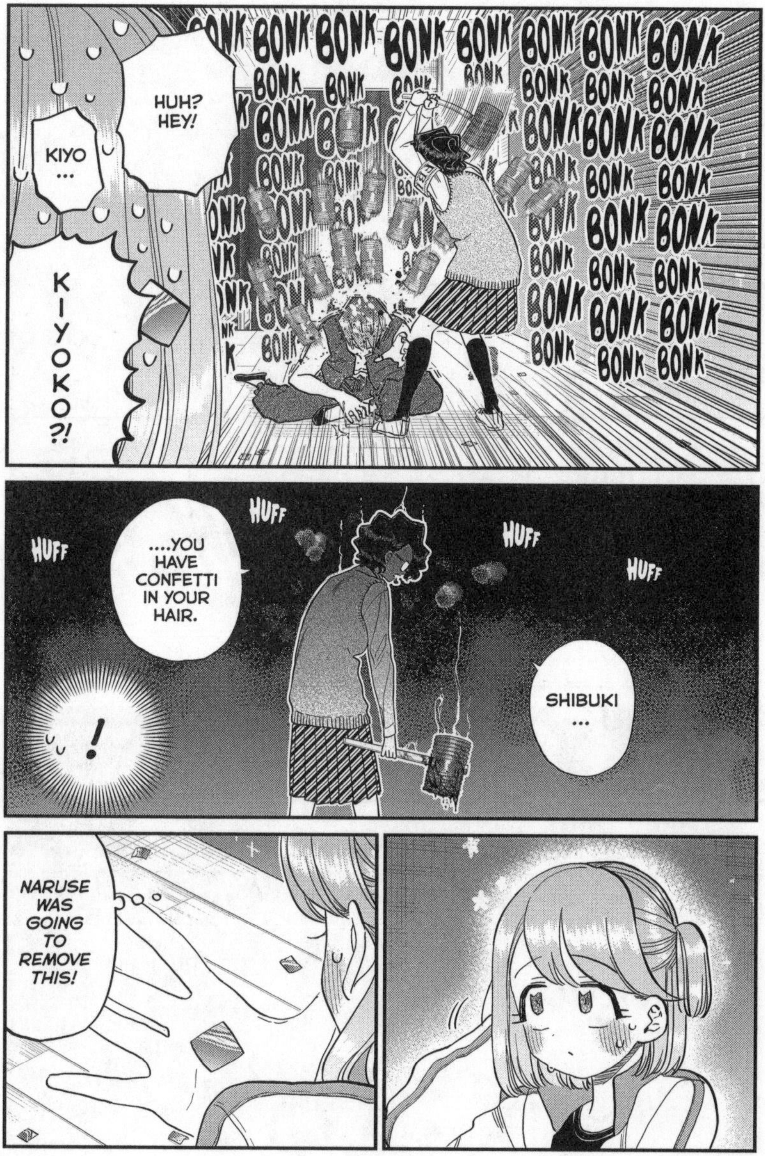
BONK BONK BONK BONK BONK BONK BONK BONK
HUH? HEY!
KIYO ...
KIYOKO?!
HUFF HUFF HUFF HUFF
....YOU HAVE CONFETTI IN YOUR HAIR.
SHIBUKI ...
!
NARUSE WAS GOING TO REMOVE THIS!

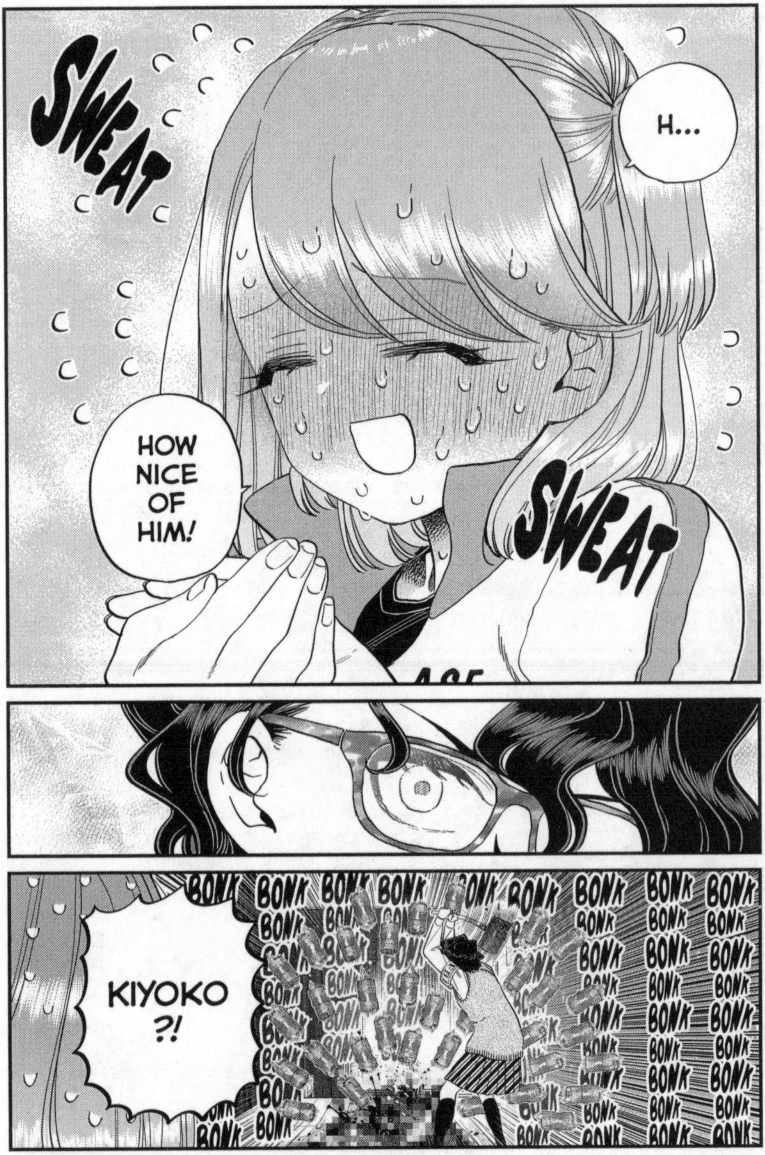
H...
SWEAT
HOW NICE OF HIM!
SWEAT
BONK BONK BONK BONK
KIYOKO ?!

Communication 229 — The End

Komi Can't Communicate

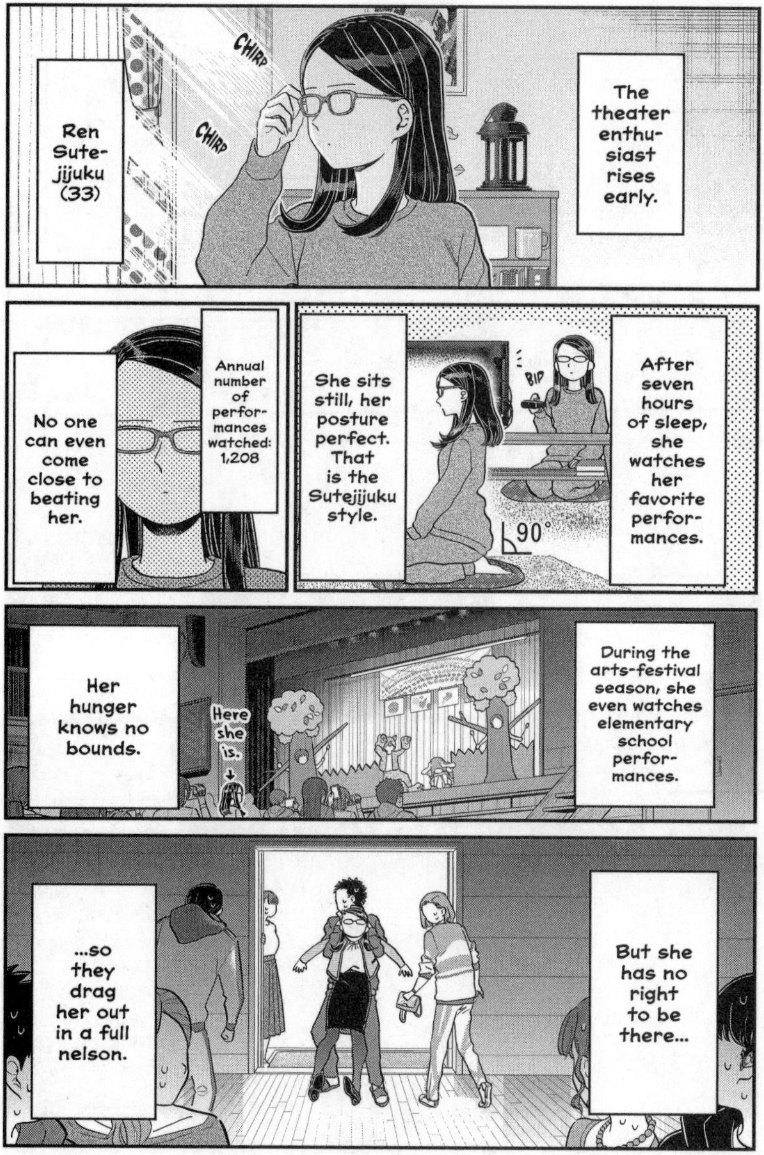
The theater enthusiast rises early.
CHIRP
CHIRP
Ren Sutejijuku (33)
After seven hours of sleep, she watches her favorite performances.
BIP
90°
She sits still, her posture perfect. That is the Sutejijuku style.
Annual number of performances watched: 1,208
No one can even come close to beating her.
During the arts-festival season, she even watches elementary school performances.
Here she is.
Her hunger knows no bounds.
But she has no right to be there...
...so they drag her out in a full nelson.

Communication 230: Performance

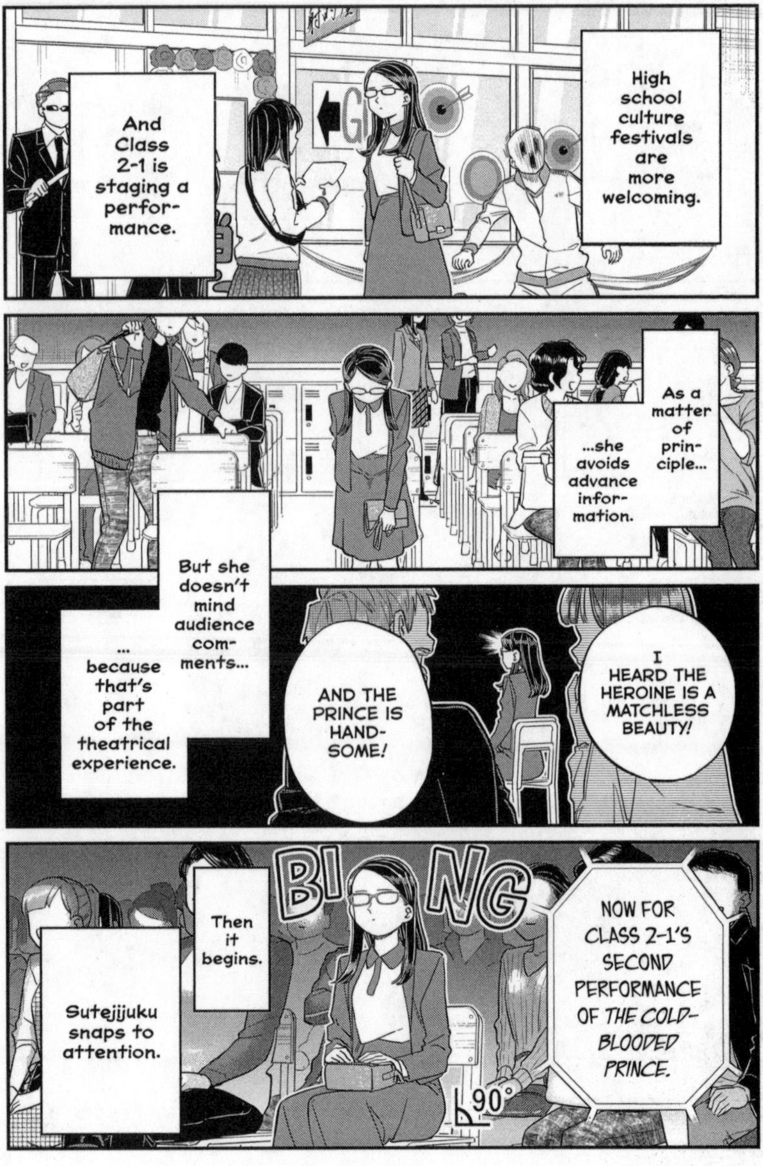
High school culture festivals are more welcoming.
And Class 2-1 is staging a performance.
As a matter of principle...
...she avoids advance information.
I HEARD THE HEROINE IS A MATCHLESS BEAUTY!
AND THE PRINCE IS HANDSOME!
But she doesn't mind audience comments...
... because that's part of the theatrical experience.
BING
NOW FOR CLASS 2-1'S SECOND PERFORMANCE OF THE COLD-BLOODED PRINCE.
Then it begins.
90°
Sutejijuku snaps to attention.

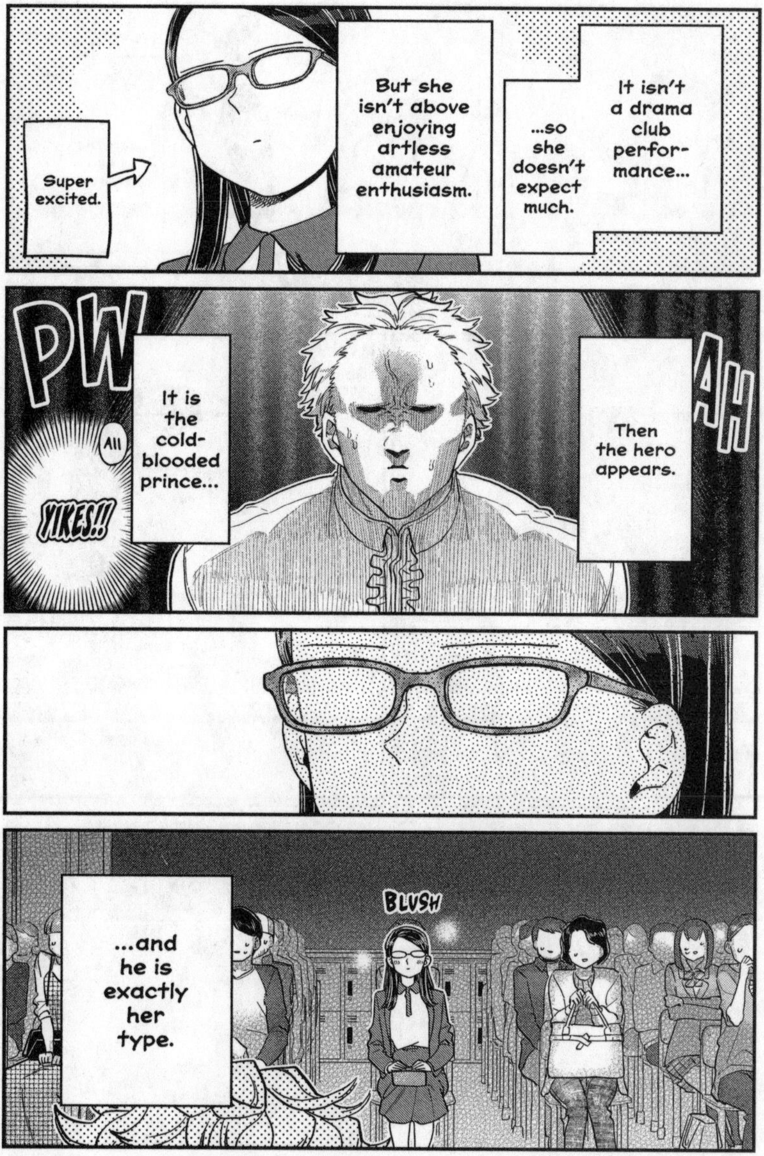
It isn't a drama club performance...
...so she doesn't expect much.
But she isn't above enjoying artless amateur enthusiasm.
Super excited.
Then the hero appears.
AH
It is the cold-blooded prince...
PW
All
YIKES!!
BLUSH
...and he is exactly her type.

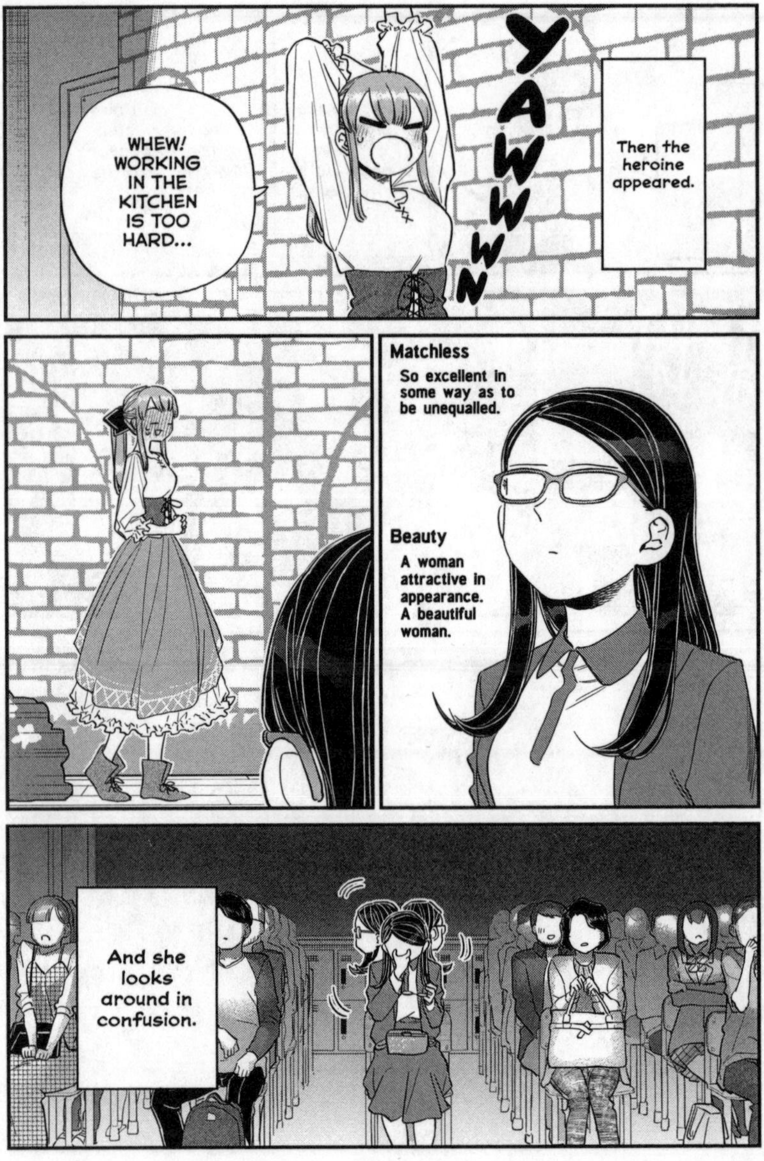
Then the heroine appeared.
YAWWWN
WHEW! WORKING IN THE KITCHEN IS TOO HARD...
Matchless
So excellent in some way as to be unequalled.
Beauty
A woman attractive in appearance. A beautiful woman.
And she looks around in confusion.

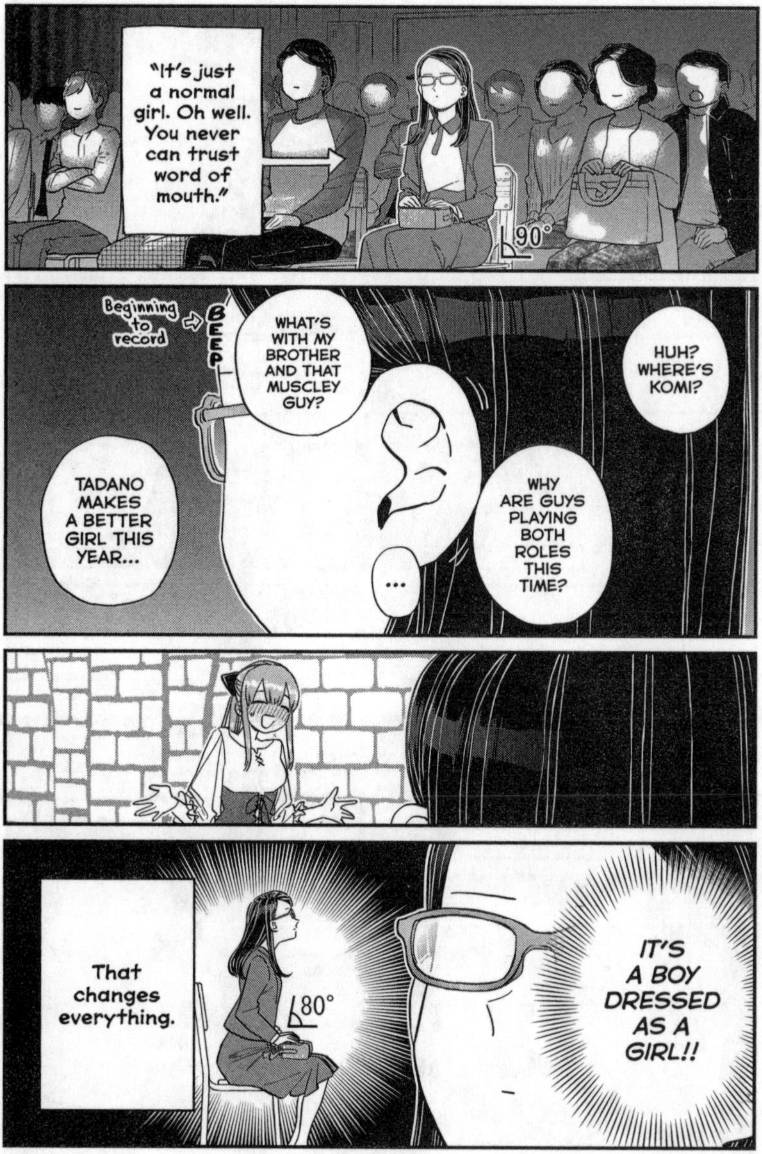

"It's just a normal girl. Oh well. You never can trust word of mouth."
90°
HUH? WHERE'S KOMI?
WHAT'S WITH MY BROTHER AND THAT MUSCLEY GUY?
BEEP
Beginning to record
WHY ARE GUYS PLAYING BOTH ROLES THIS TIME?
...
TADANO MAKES A BETTER GIRL THIS YEAR...
IT'S A BOY DRESSED AS A GIRL!!
80°
That changes everything.

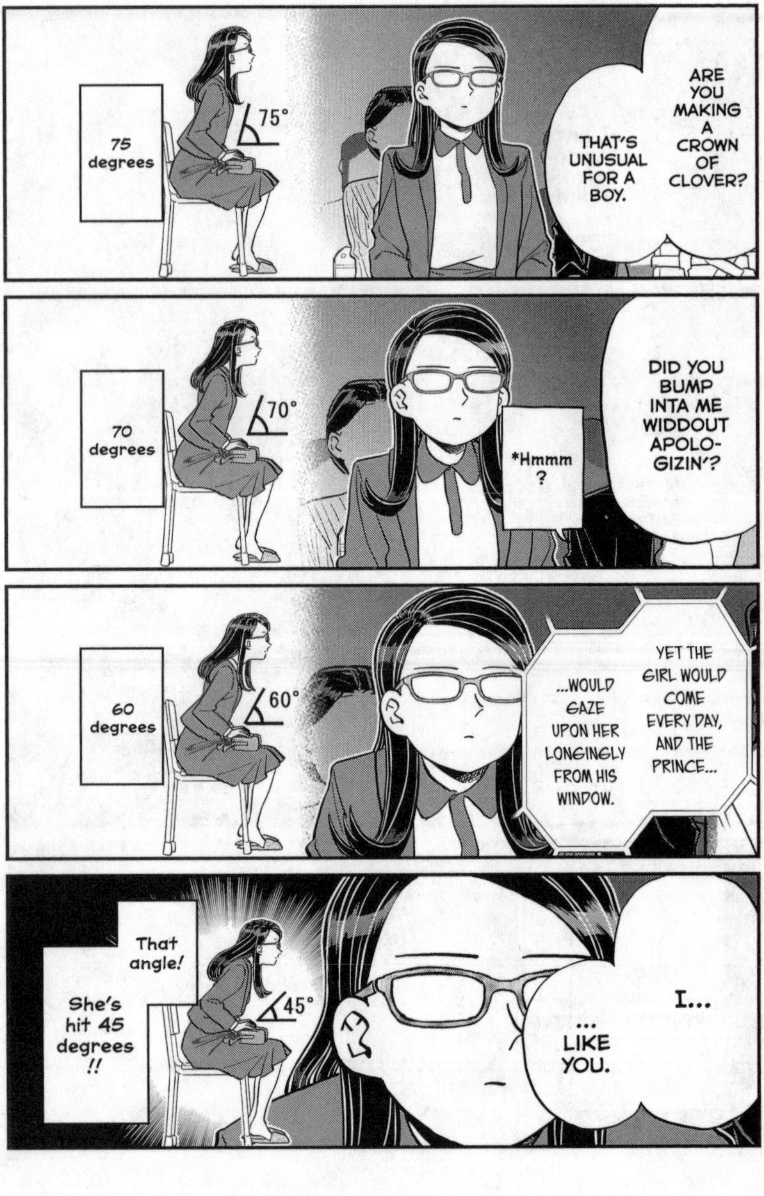
ARE YOU MAKING A CROWN OF CLOVER?
THAT'S UNUSUAL FOR A BOY.
75°
75 degrees
DID YOU BUMP INTA ME WIDDOUT APOLO-GIZIN'?
*Hmmm ?
70°
70 degrees
YET THE GIRL WOULD COME EVERY DAY, AND THE PRINCE...
...WOULD GAZE UPON HER LONGINGLY FROM HIS WINDOW.
60°
60 degrees
I...
... LIKE YOU.
45°
That angle!
She's hit 45 degrees !!

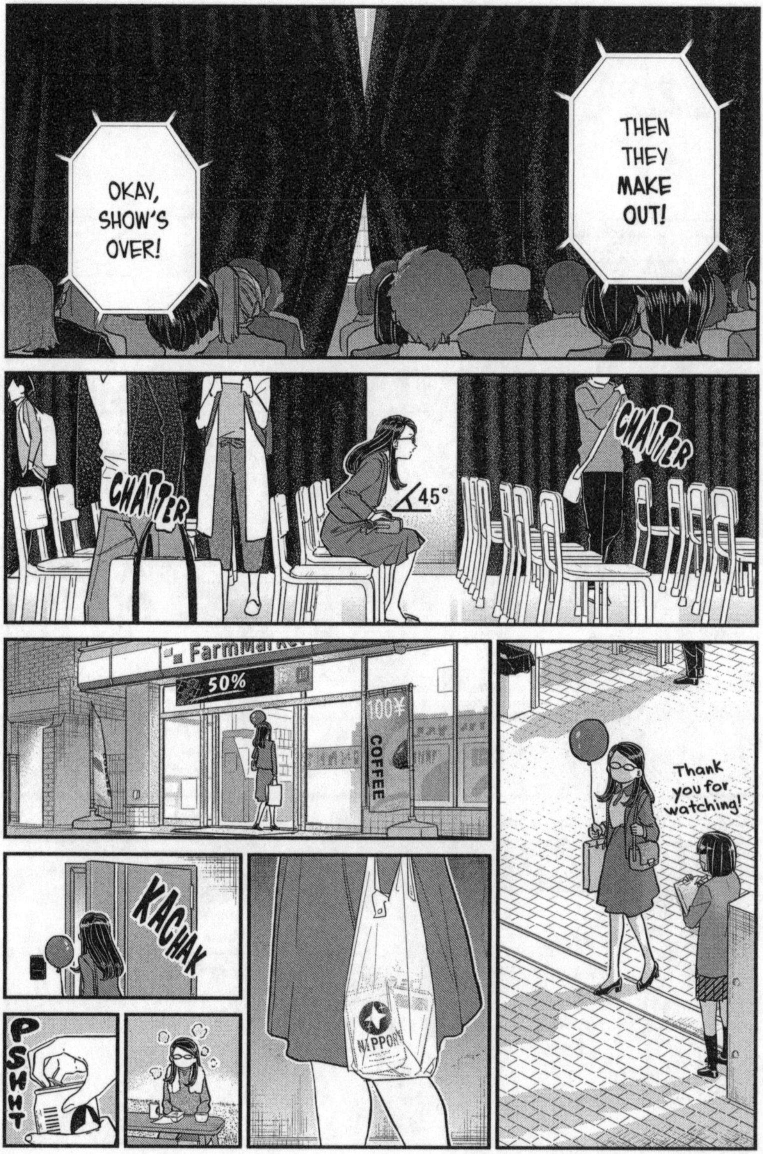
THEN THEY MAKE OUT!
OKAY, SHOW'S OVER!
CHATTER
45°
CHATTER
Thank you for watching!
50%
100¥
COFFEE
KACHAK
PSHHT

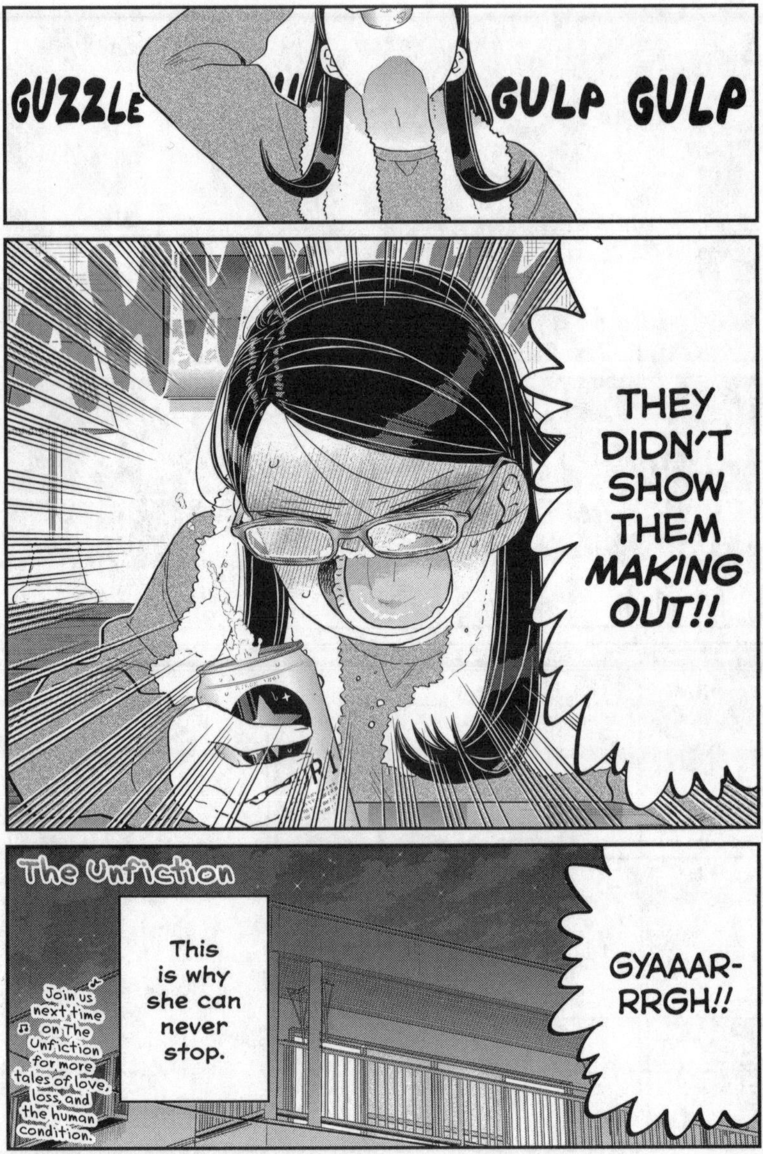
GULP GULP
GUZZLE
THEY DIDN'T SHOW THEM *MAKING* OUT!!
GYAAAR-RRGH!!
The Unfiction
This is why she can never stop.
Join us next time on The Unfiction for more tales of love, loss, and the human condition.

Communication 230 — The End

Sutejijjuku's Favorite Snacks, Ranked!!

👑 **1.** Roasted stingray fin

2. Blue cheese

3. Omelet with fermented soybeans

SIZZ

FLIK FLIK

Komi Can't
Communicate

Komi Can't Communicate

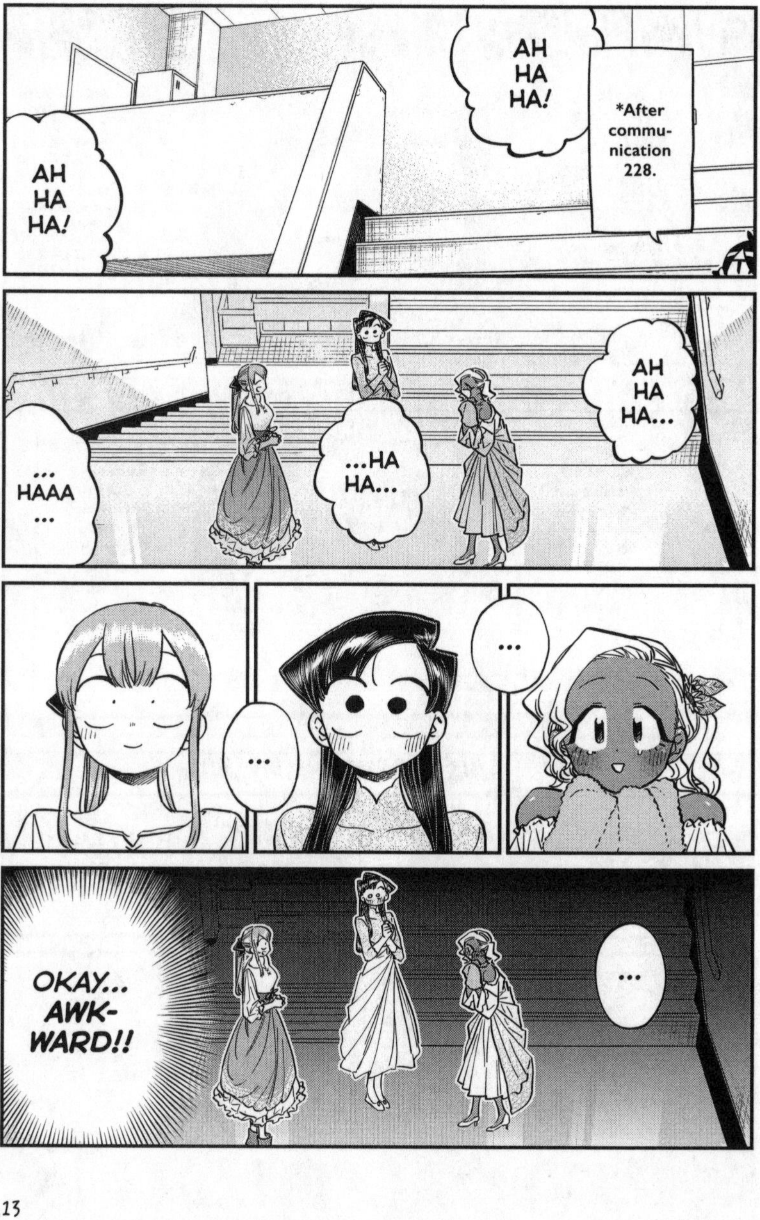
AH HA HA!
*After communication 228.
AH HA HA!
AH HA HA...
...HA HA...
... HAAA ...
...
...
...
OKAY... AWK-WARD!!

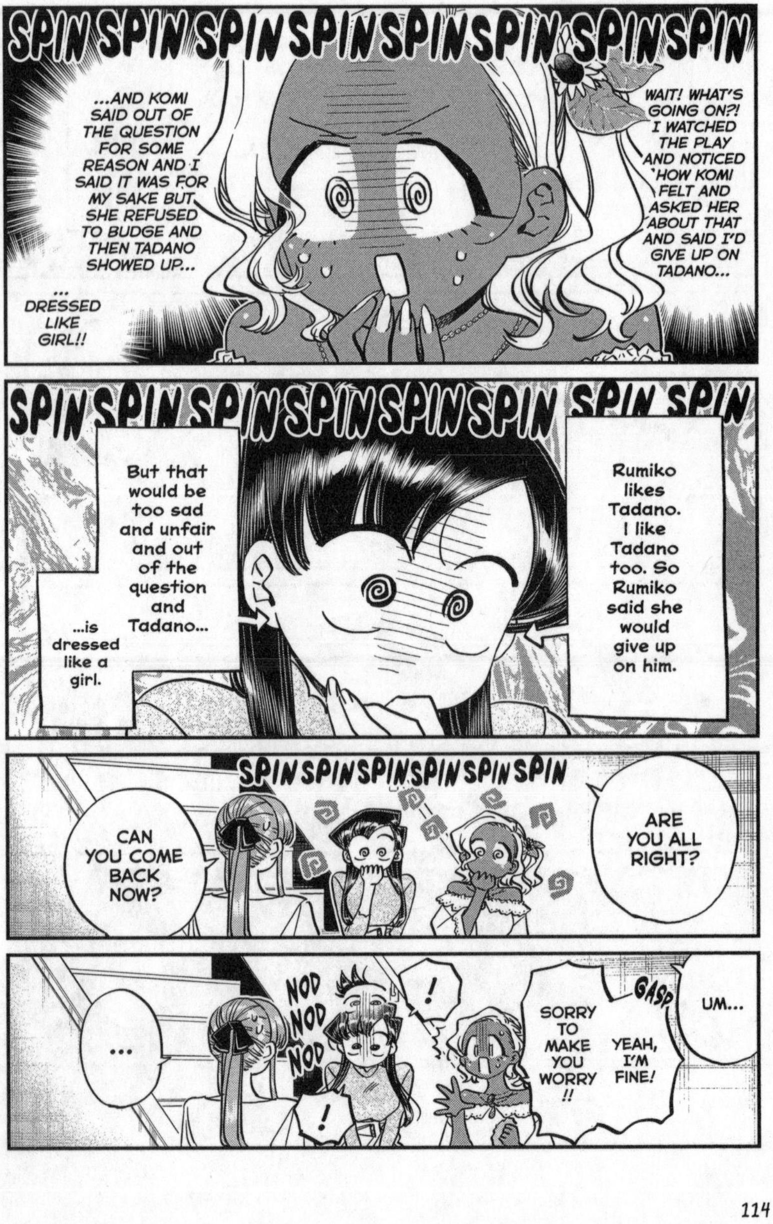
SPIN SPIN SPIN SPIN SPIN SPIN SPIN SPIN
WAIT! WHAT'S GOING ON?! I WATCHED THE PLAY AND NOTICED HOW KOMI FELT AND ASKED HER ABOUT THAT AND SAID I'D GIVE UP ON TADANO...
...AND KOMI SAID OUT OF THE QUESTION FOR SOME REASON AND I SAID IT WAS FOR MY SAKE BUT SHE REFUSED TO BUDGE AND THEN TADANO SHOWED UP...
...DRESSED LIKE GIRL!!
SPIN SPIN SPIN SPIN SPIN SPIN SPIN SPIN
Rumiko likes Tadano. I like Tadano too. So Rumiko said she would give up on him.
But that would be too sad and unfair and out of the question and Tadano...
...is dressed like a girl.
SPIN SPIN SPIN SPIN SPIN SPIN
ARE YOU ALL RIGHT?
CAN YOU COME BACK NOW?
UM...
GASP
YEAH, I'M FINE!
SORRY TO MAKE YOU WORRY!!
!
NOD NOD NOD
!
...

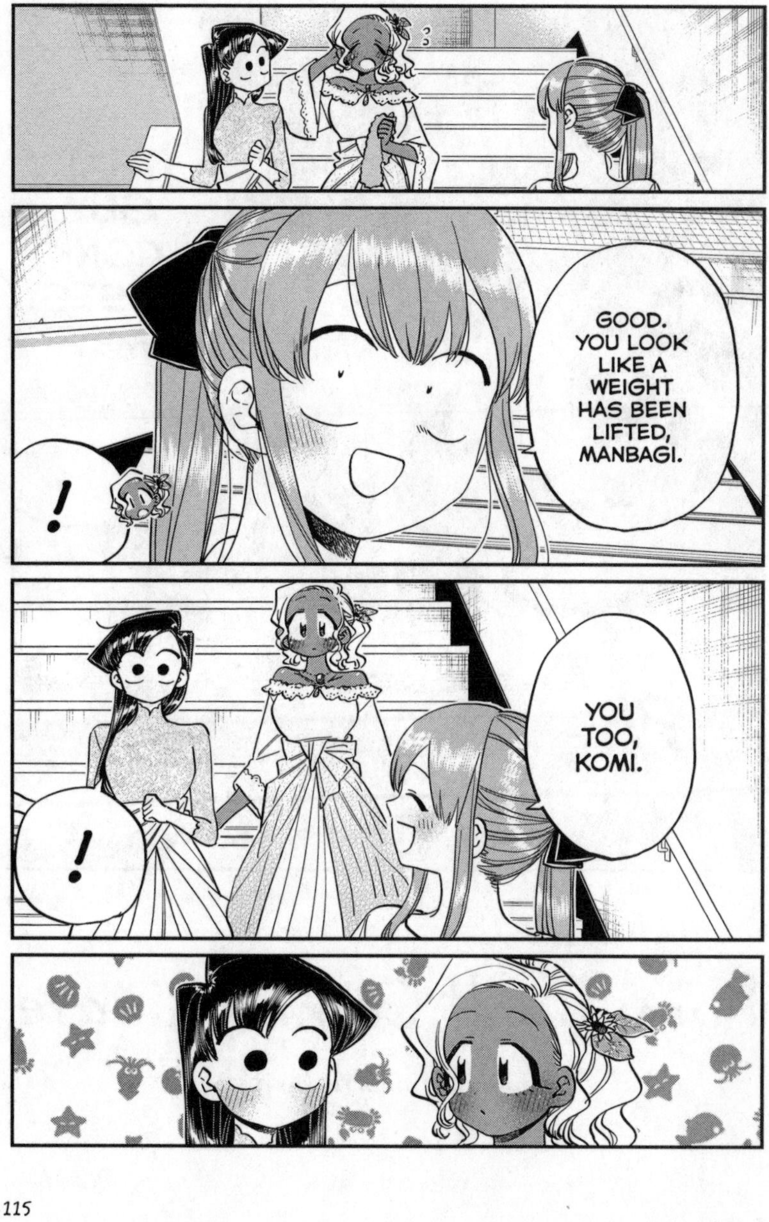
GOOD. YOU LOOK LIKE A WEIGHT HAS BEEN LIFTED, MANBAGI.
!
YOU TOO, KOMI.
!

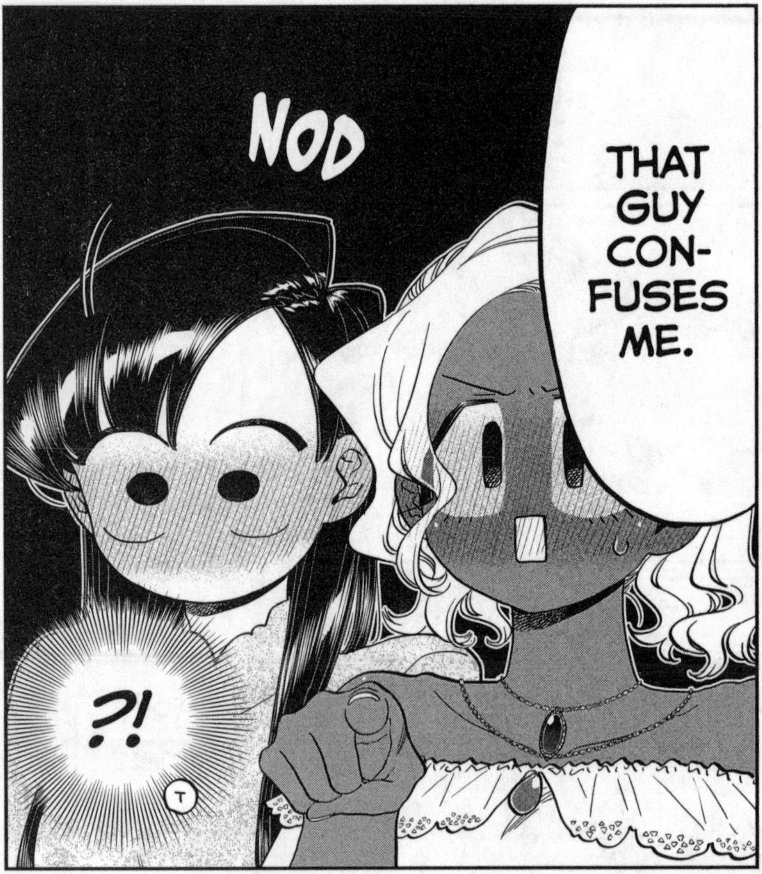
THAT GUY CON-FUSES ME.
NOD
?!
T

Komi Can't Communicate

Communication 231: Invitation

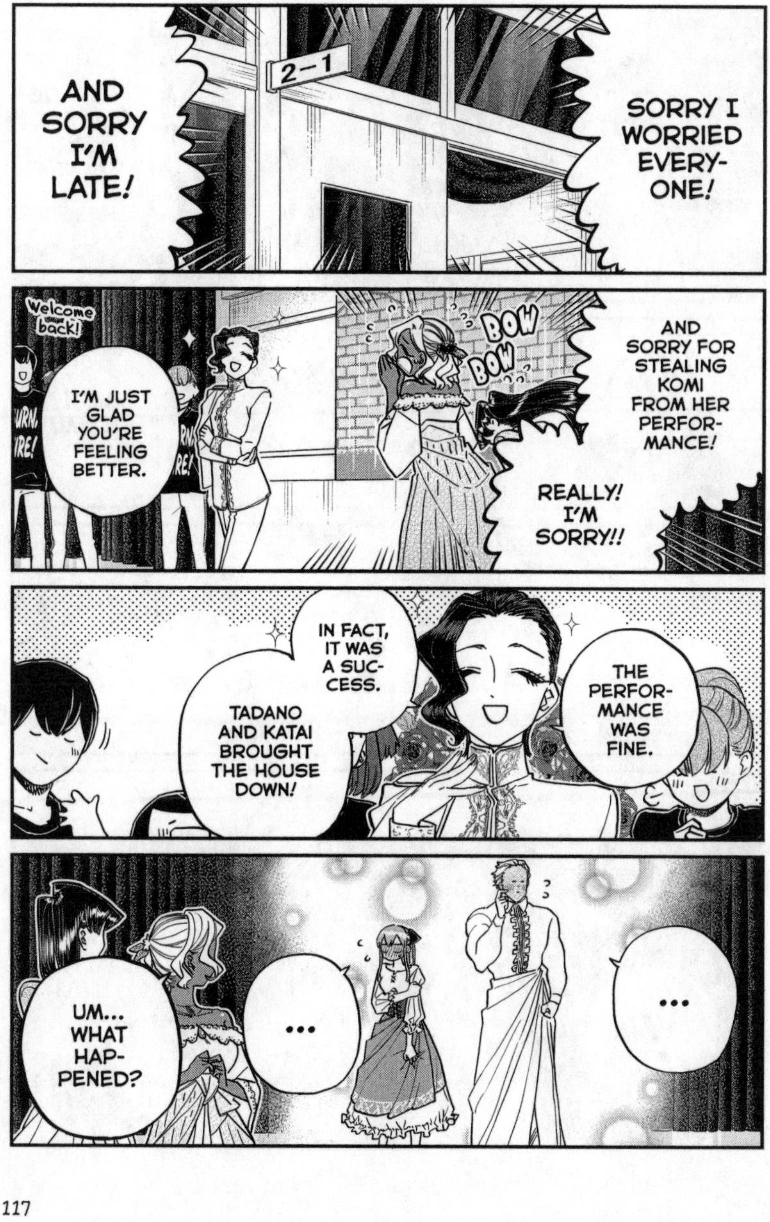
2-1
SORRY I WORRIED EVERY-ONE!
AND SORRY I'M LATE!
AND SORRY FOR STEALING KOMI FROM HER PERFOR-MANCE!
BOW BOW
REALLY! I'M SORRY!!
I'M JUST GLAD YOU'RE FEELING BETTER.
Welcome back!
THE PERFOR-MANCE WAS FINE.
IN FACT, IT WAS A SUC-CESS.
TADANO AND KATAI BROUGHT THE HOUSE DOWN!
...
...
UM... WHAT HAP-PENED?

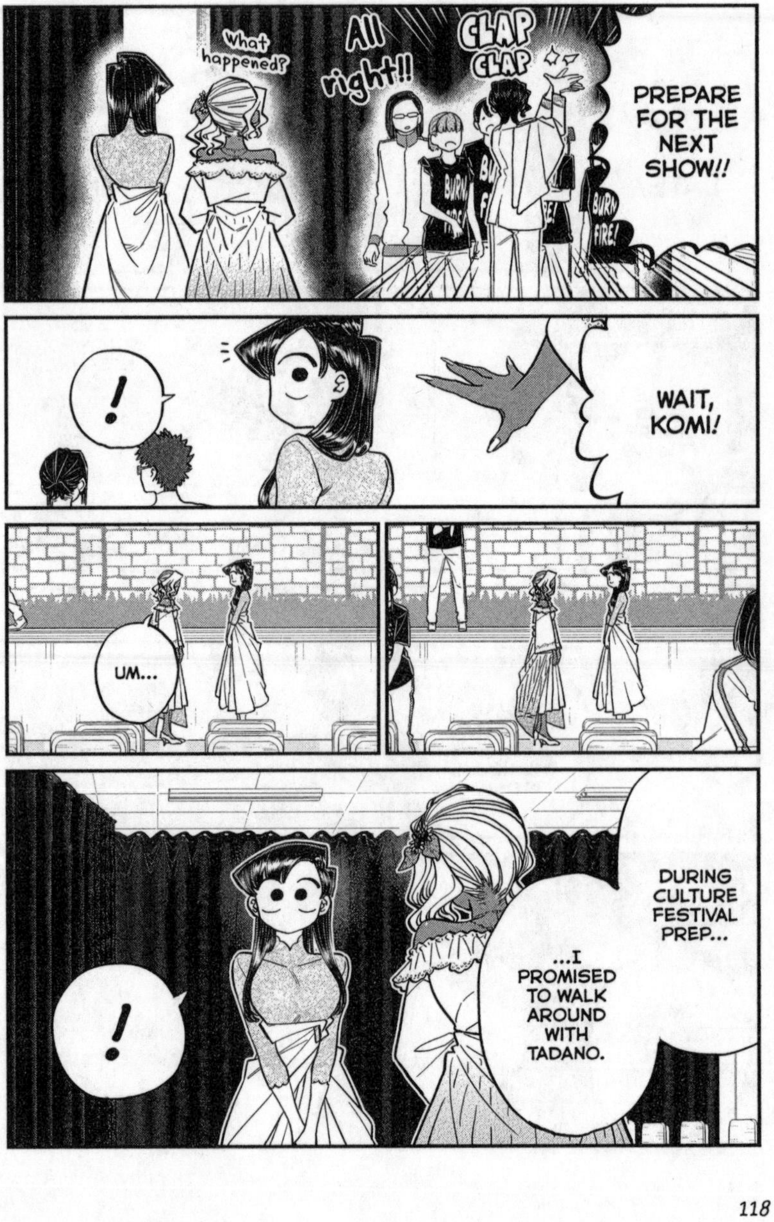
PREPARE FOR THE NEXT SHOW!!
CLAP CLAP
All right!!
What happened?
WAIT, KOMI!
!
UM...
DURING CULTURE FESTIVAL PREP...
...I PROMISED TO WALK AROUND WITH TADANO.
!

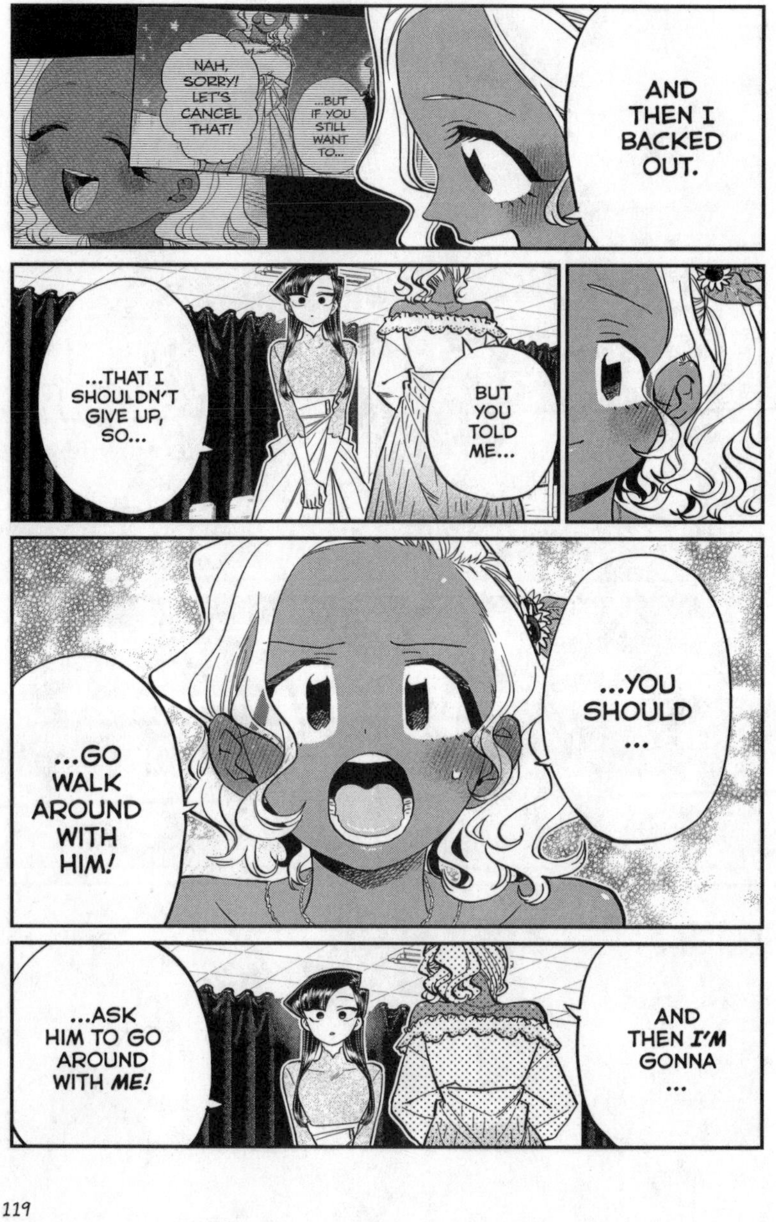
AND THEN I BACKED OUT.
...BUT IF YOU STILL WANT TO...
NAH, SORRY! LET'S CANCEL THAT!
BUT YOU TOLD ME...
...THAT I SHOULDN'T GIVE UP, SO...
...YOU SHOULD ...
...GO WALK AROUND WITH HIM!
AND THEN *I'M* GONNA ...
...ASK HIM TO GO AROUND WITH *ME!*

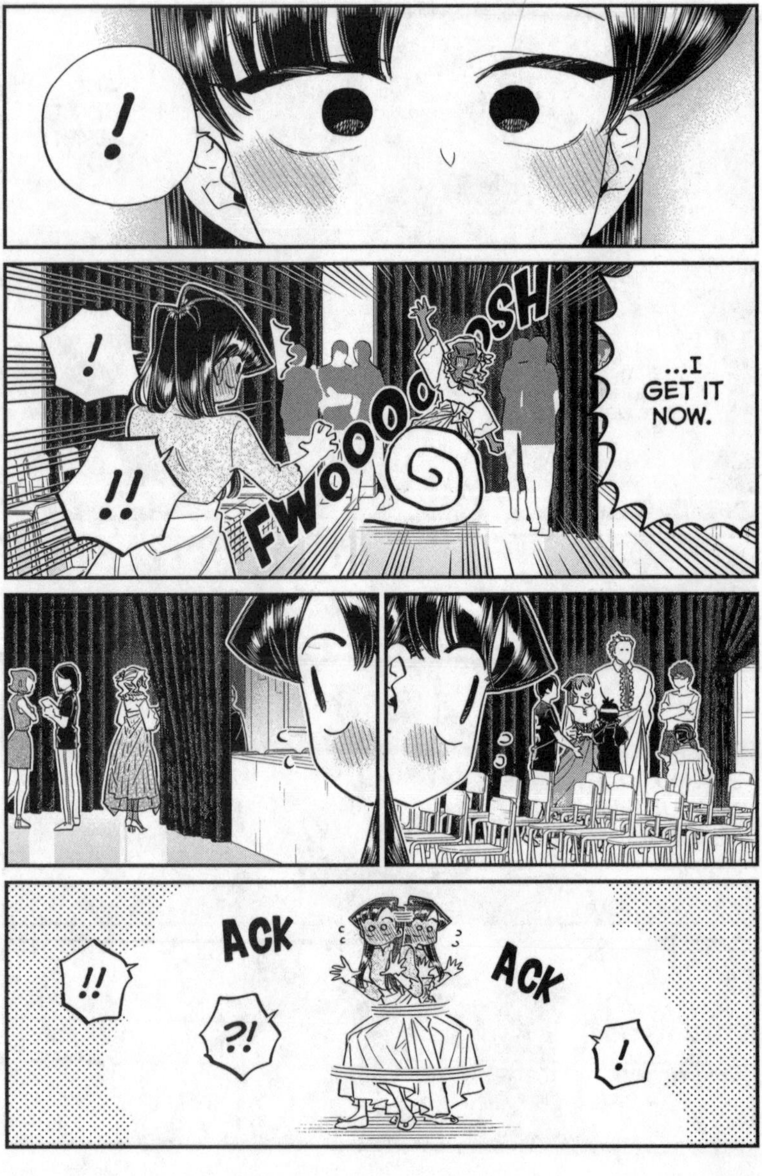
!
...I GET IT NOW.
FWOOOOOOSH
!
!!
!
ACK
ACK
?!
!!

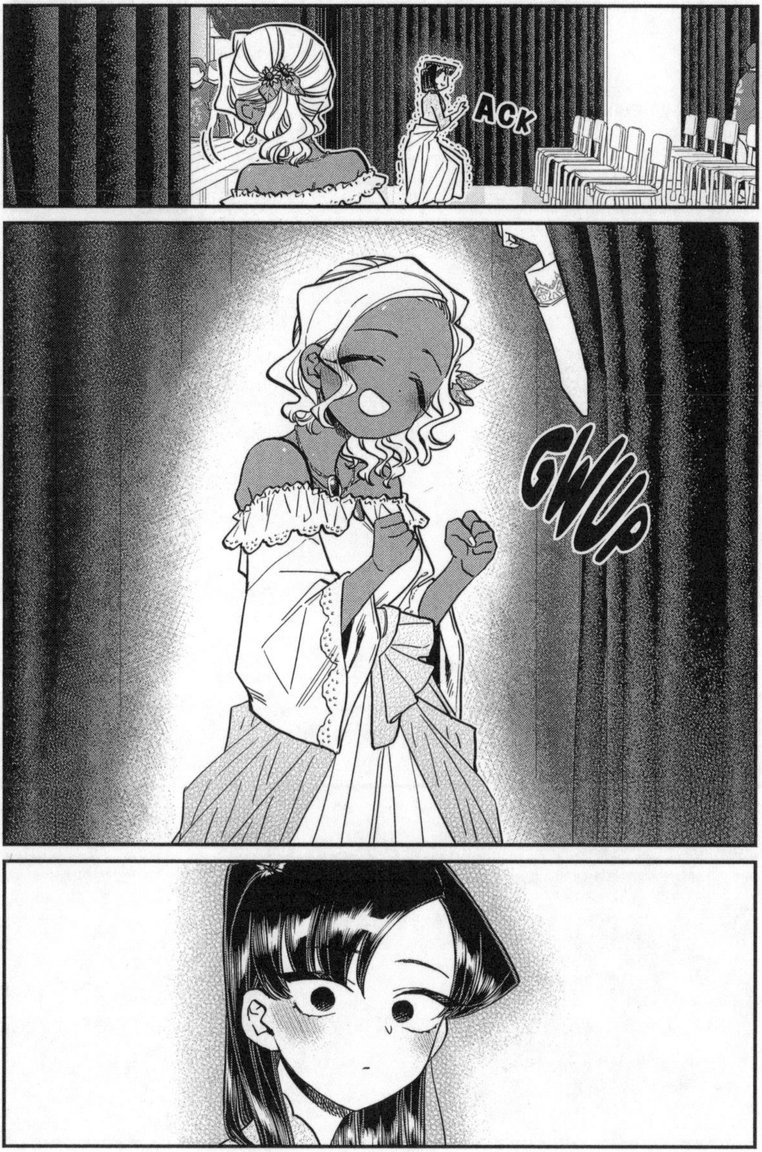
ACK
GWUP

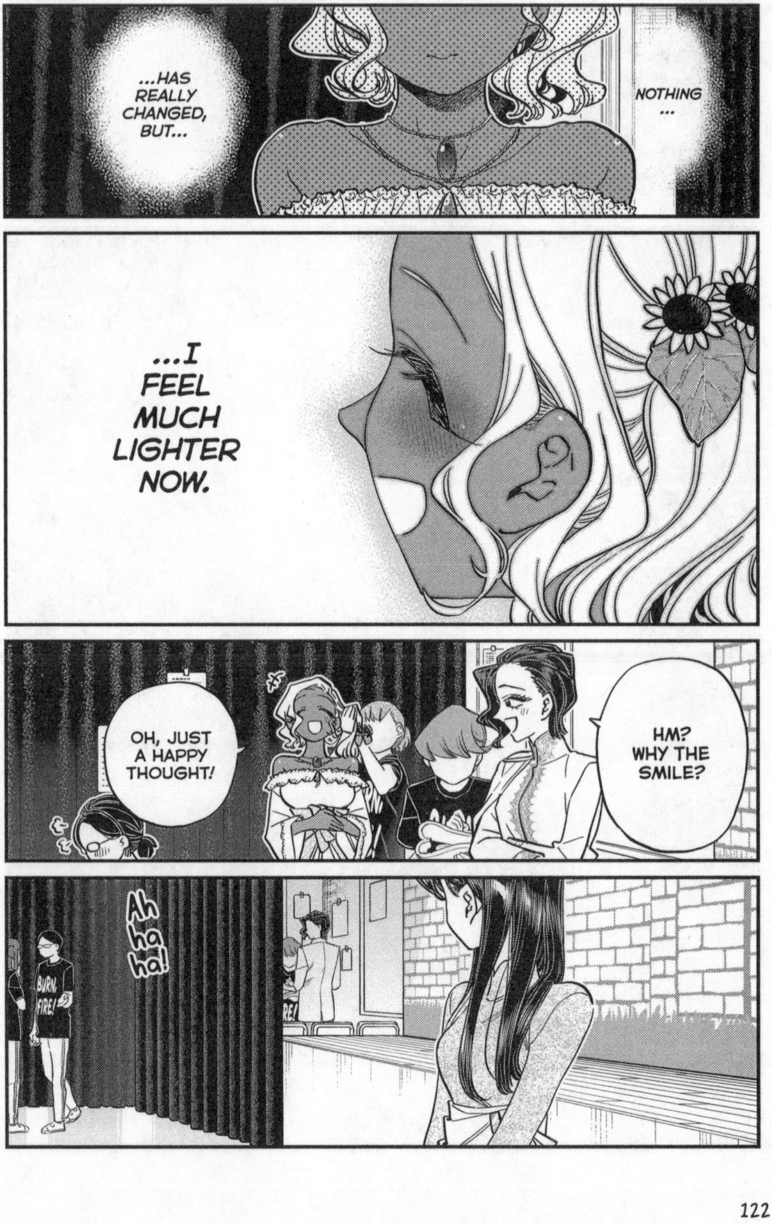
NOTHING ...
...HAS REALLY CHANGED, BUT...
...I FEEL MUCH LIGHTER NOW.
HM? WHY THE SMILE?
OH, JUST A HAPPY THOUGHT!
Ah ha ha!
BURN, FIRE!

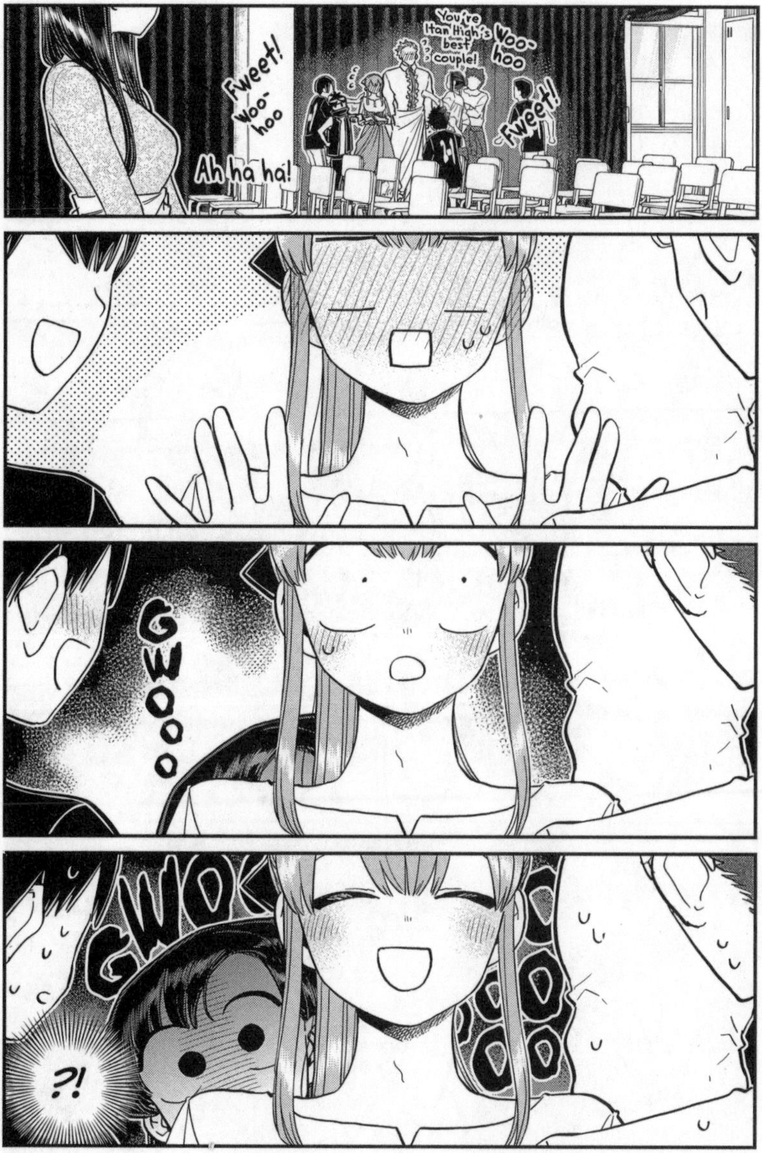
Fweet!
Woo-hoo
You're Itan High's best couple!
Fweet!
Woo-hoo
Ah ha ha!
GWOOO
GWOOOOOOOO
?!

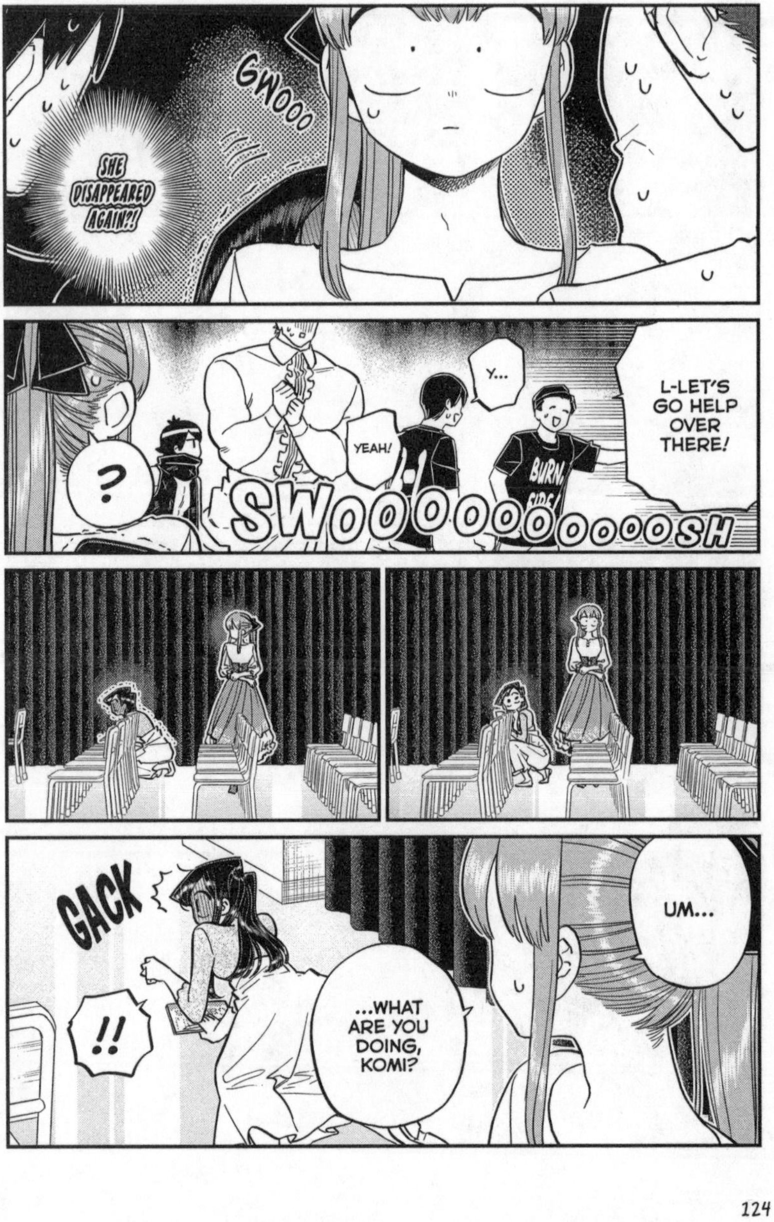
GWOOO
SHE DISAPPEARED AGAIN?!
L-LET'S GO HELP OVER THERE!
Y...
YEAH!
SWOOOOOOOOOOSH
?
UM...
...WHAT ARE YOU DOING, KOMI?
GACK
!!

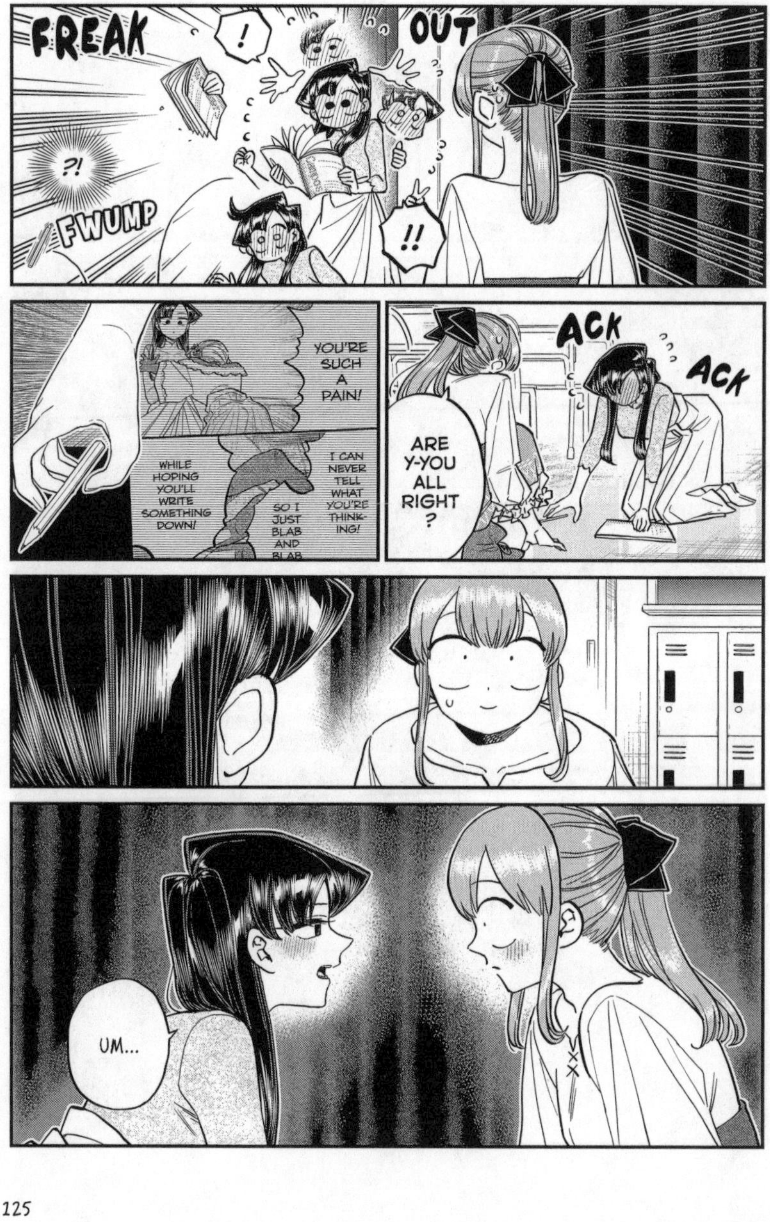
FREAK OUT
!
!!
?!
FWUMP
ACK
ACK
ARE Y-YOU ALL RIGHT?
YOU'RE SUCH A PAIN!
I CAN NEVER TELL WHAT YOU'RE THINKING!
SO I JUST BLAB AND BLAB
WHILE HOPING YOU'LL WRITE SOMETHING DOWN!
UM...

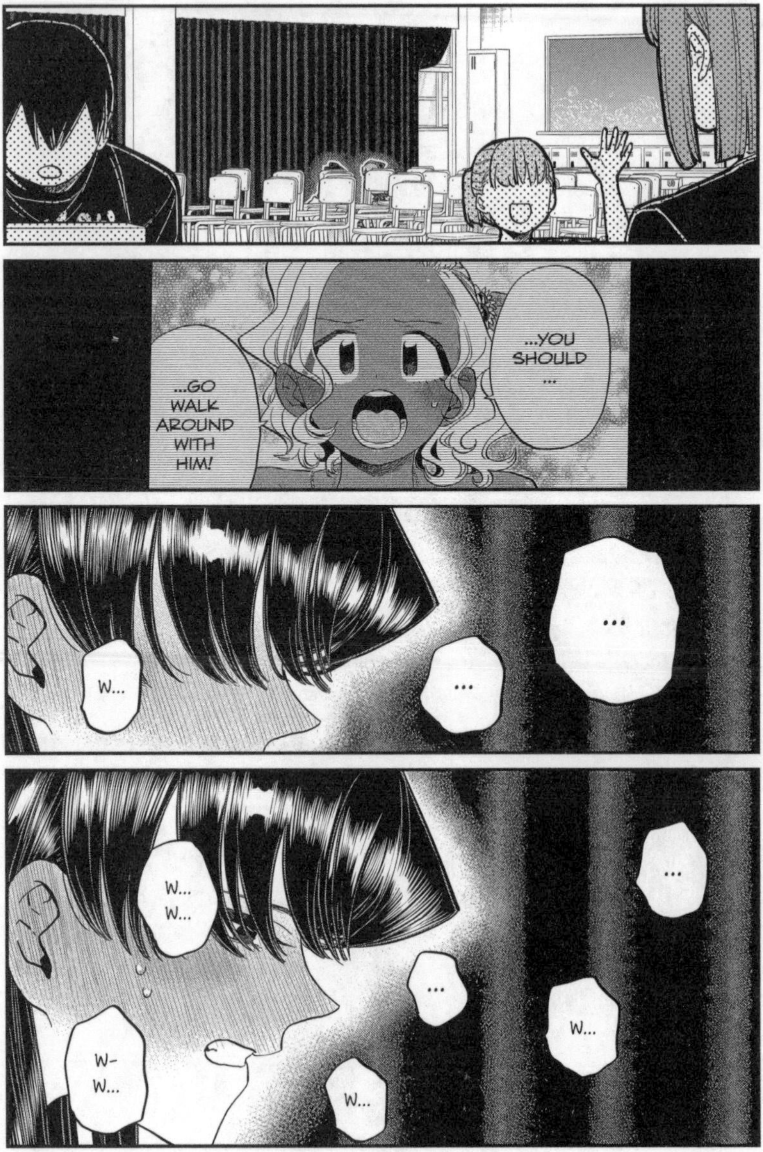
...YOU SHOULD ...
...GO WALK AROUND WITH HIM!
...
...
W...
...
W...
...
W... W...
W...
W- W...

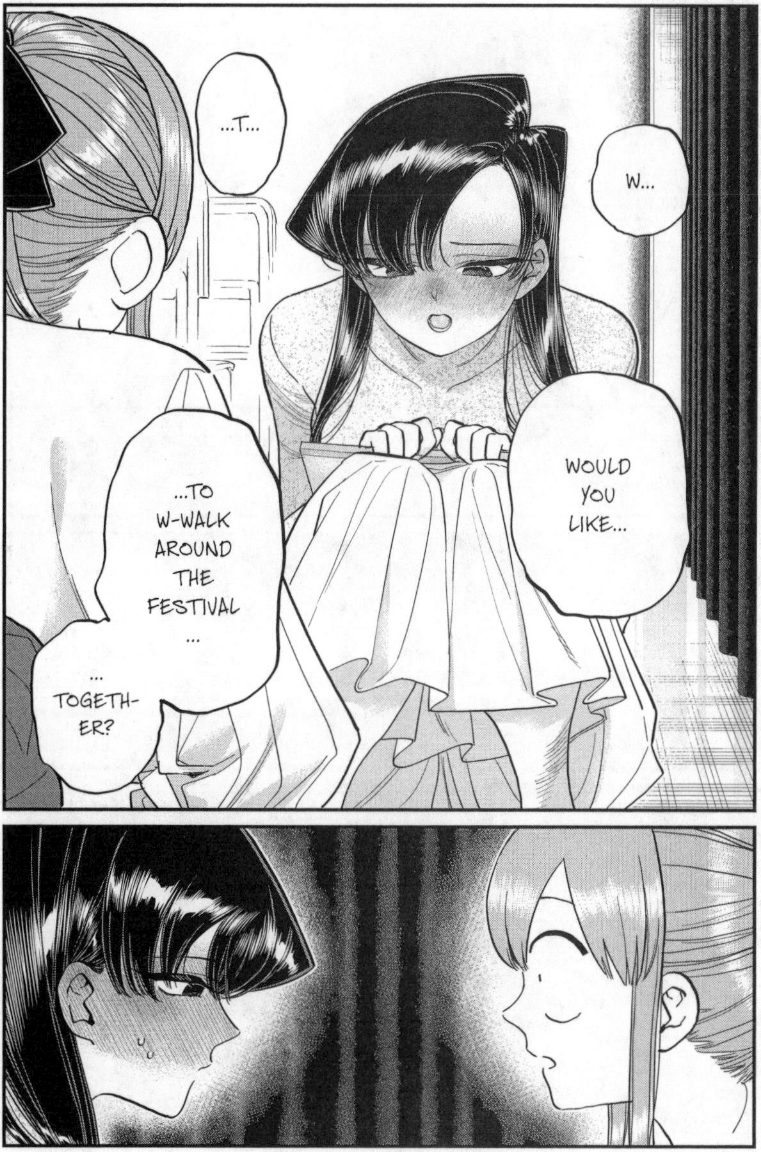
W...
...T...
WOULD YOU LIKE...
...TO W-WALK AROUND THE FESTIVAL ...
... TOGETH-ER?

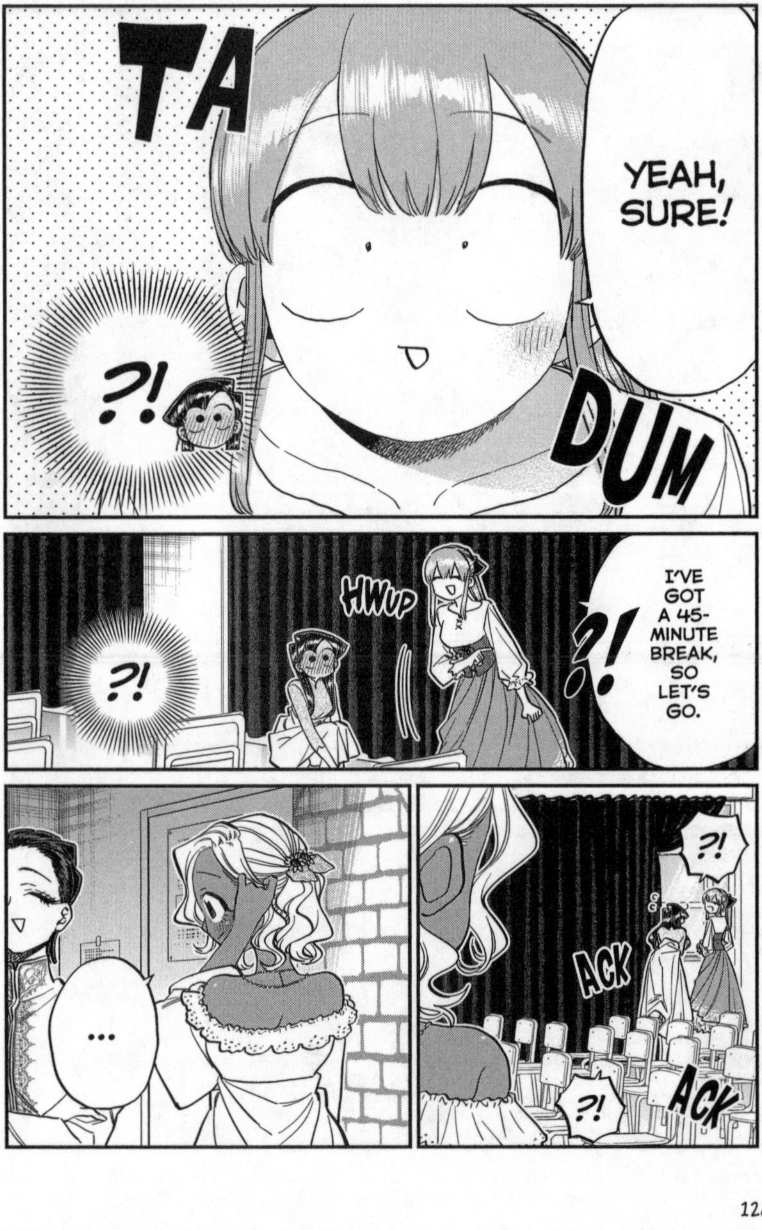
YEAH, SURE!
TA
DUM
?!
I'VE GOT A 45-MINUTE BREAK, SO LET'S GO.
?!
HWUP
?!
?!
ACK
ACK
?!
...

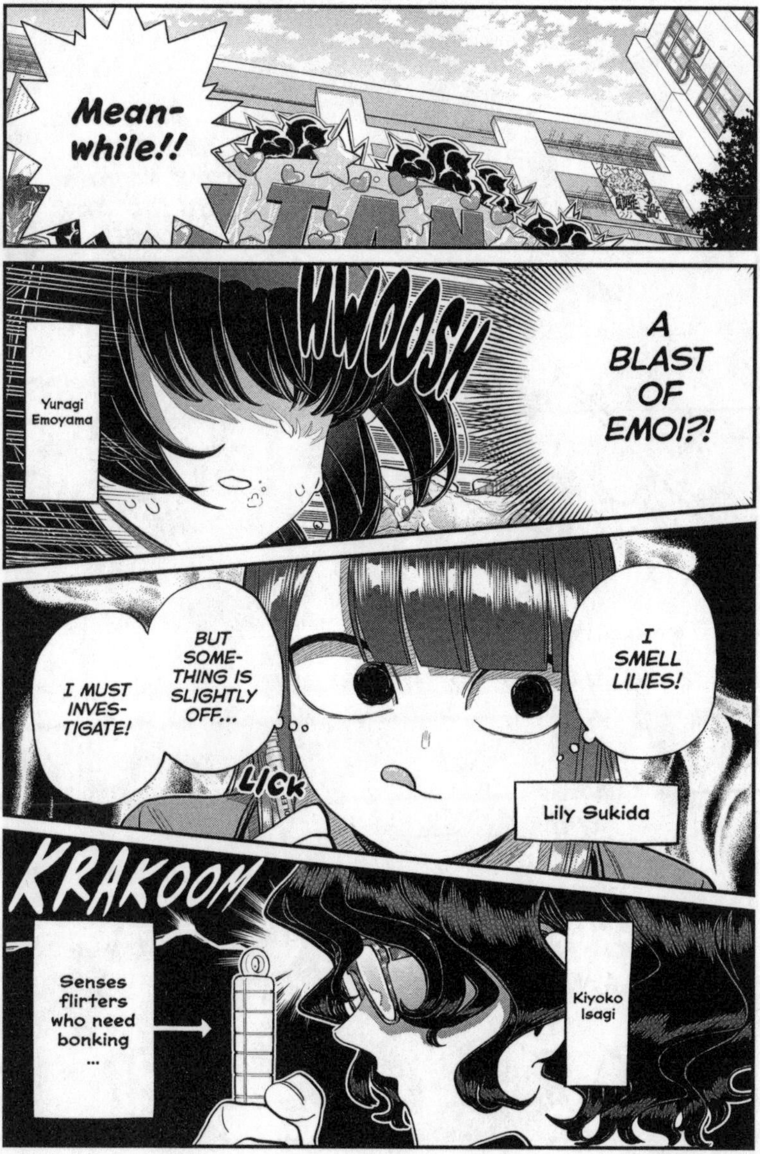
Mean-while!!
A BLAST OF EMOI?!
WHOOSH
Yuragi Emoyama
I SMELL LILIES!
Lily Sukida
BUT SOME-THING IS SLIGHTLY OFF...
LICK
I MUST INVES-TIGATE!
Kiyoko Isagi
KRAKOOM
Senses flirters who need bonking ...

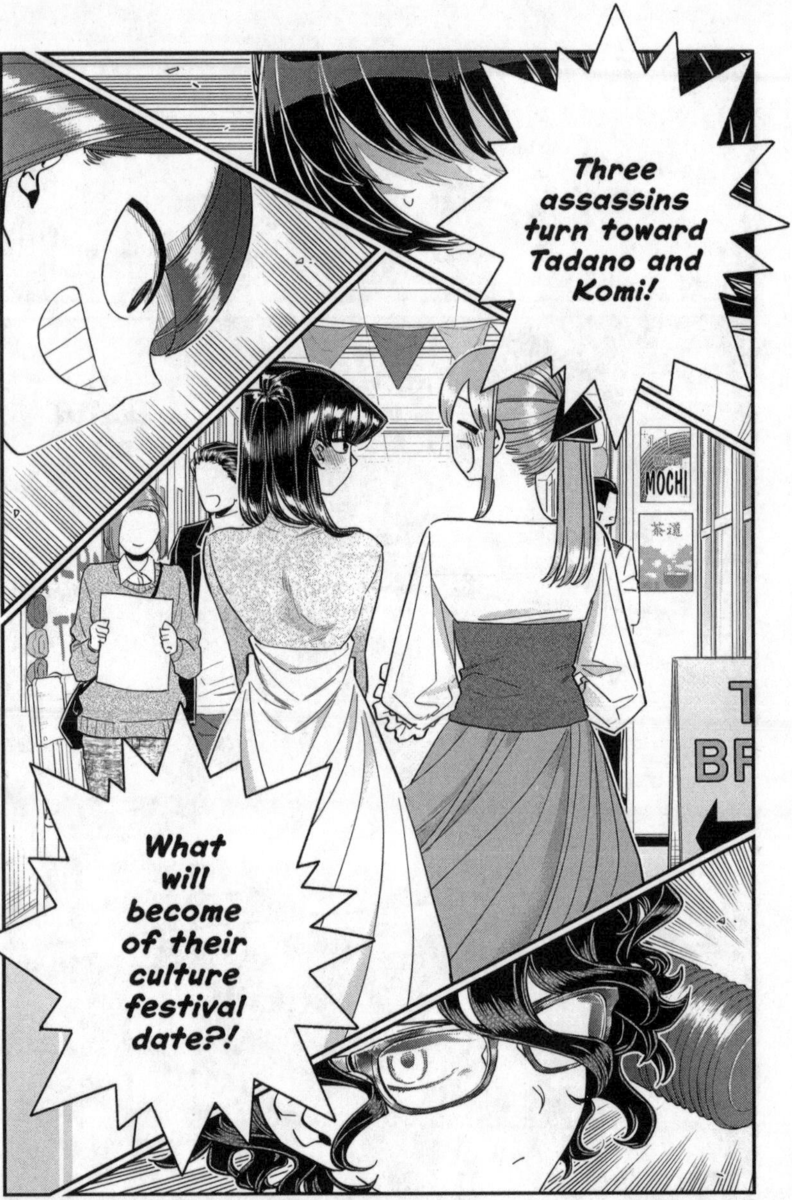
Three assassins turn toward Tadano and Komi!
MOCHI
茶道
What will become of their culture festival date?!

Communication 231 — The End

Komi Can't Communicate

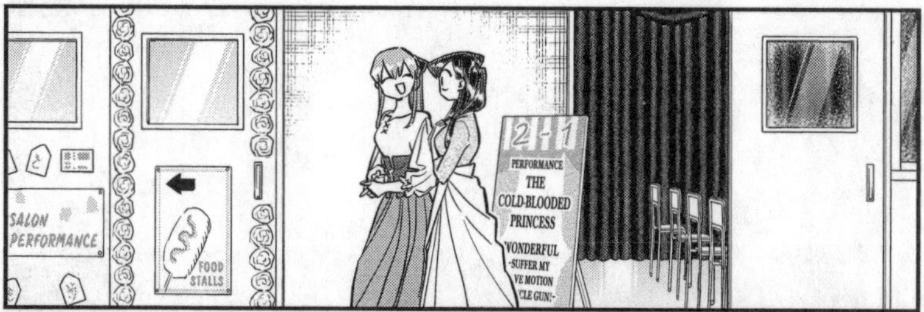
2-1
PERFORMANCE
THE
COLD-BLOODED
PRINCESS
'WONDERFUL
-SUFFER MY
SALON
PERFORMANCE
FOOD
STALLS

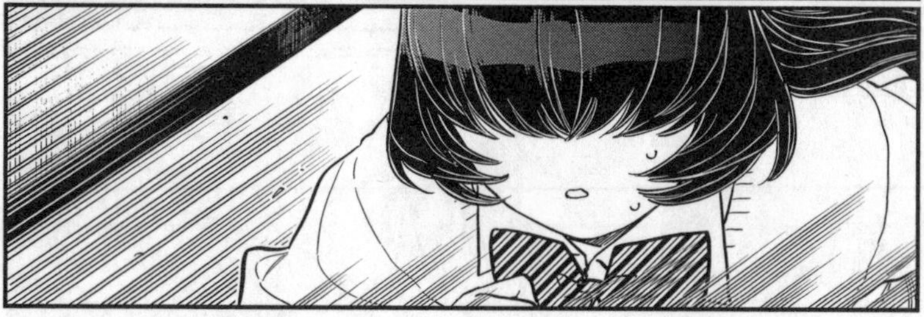

Communication 232: Secret

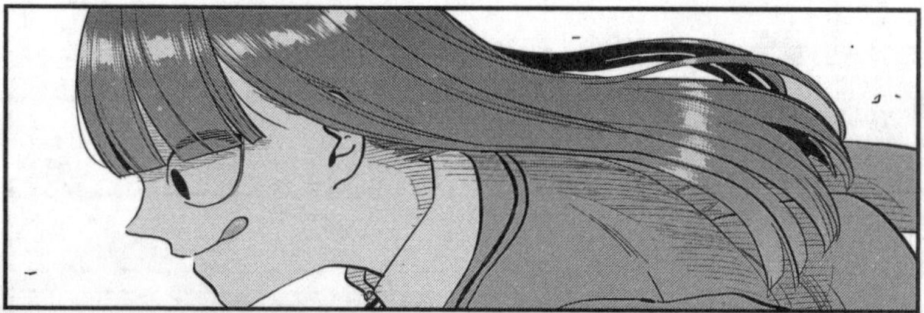

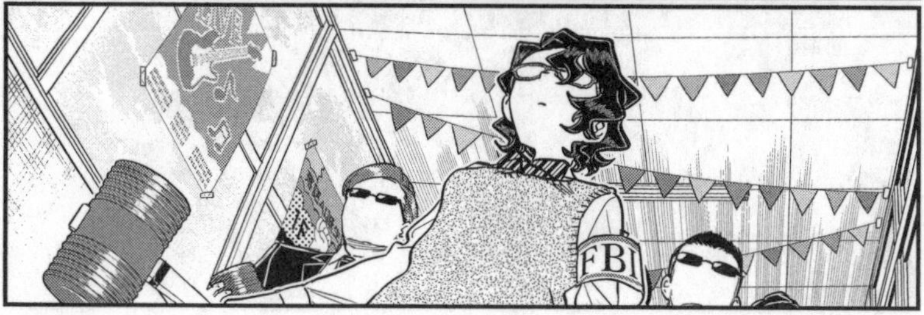
FBI

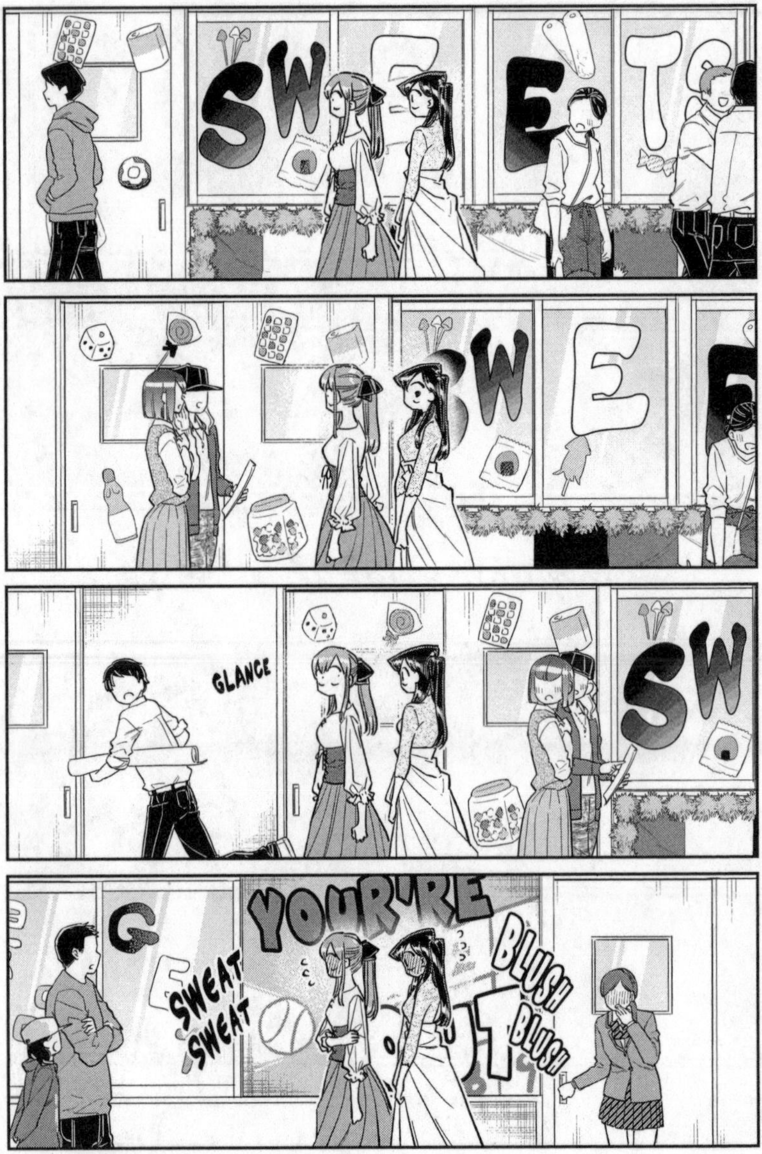
GLANCE
YOUR'RE
BLUSH BLUSH
SWEAT SWEAT

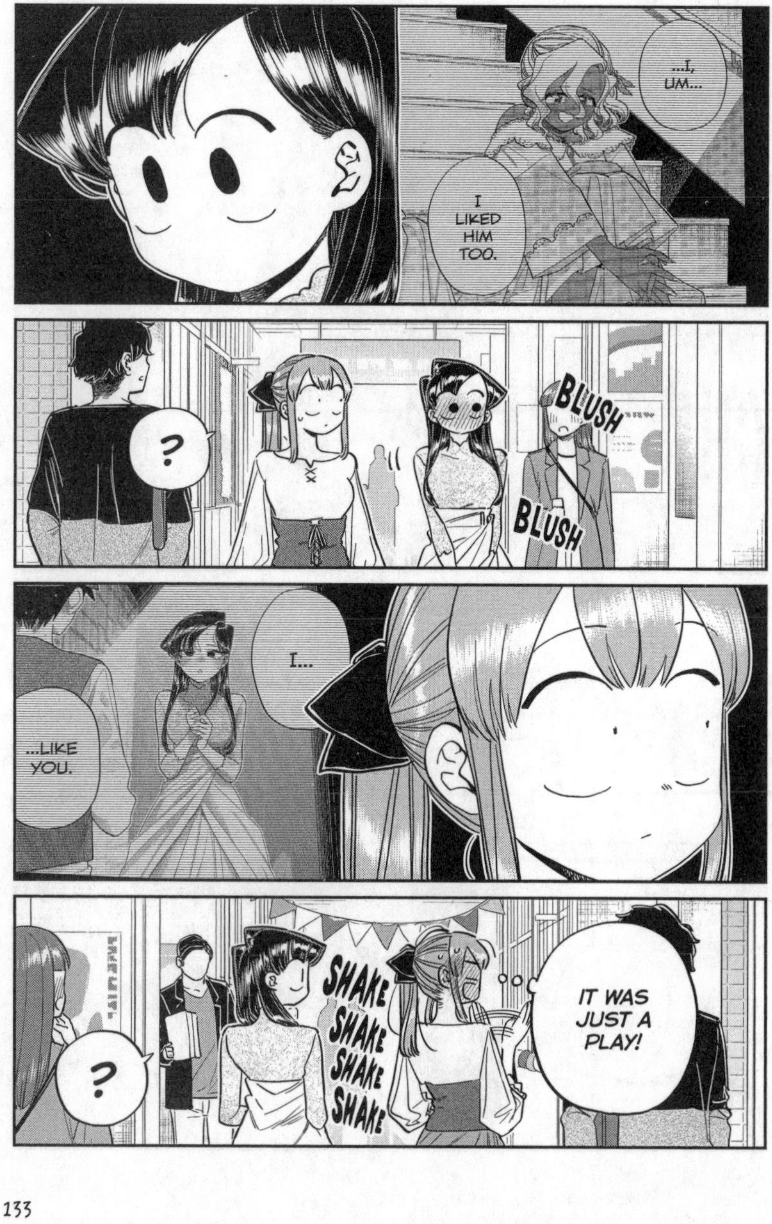
...I, UM...
I LIKED HIM TOO.
BLUSH
BLUSH
?
I...
...LIKE YOU.
IT WAS JUST A PLAY!
SHAKE SHAKE SHAKE SHAKE
?

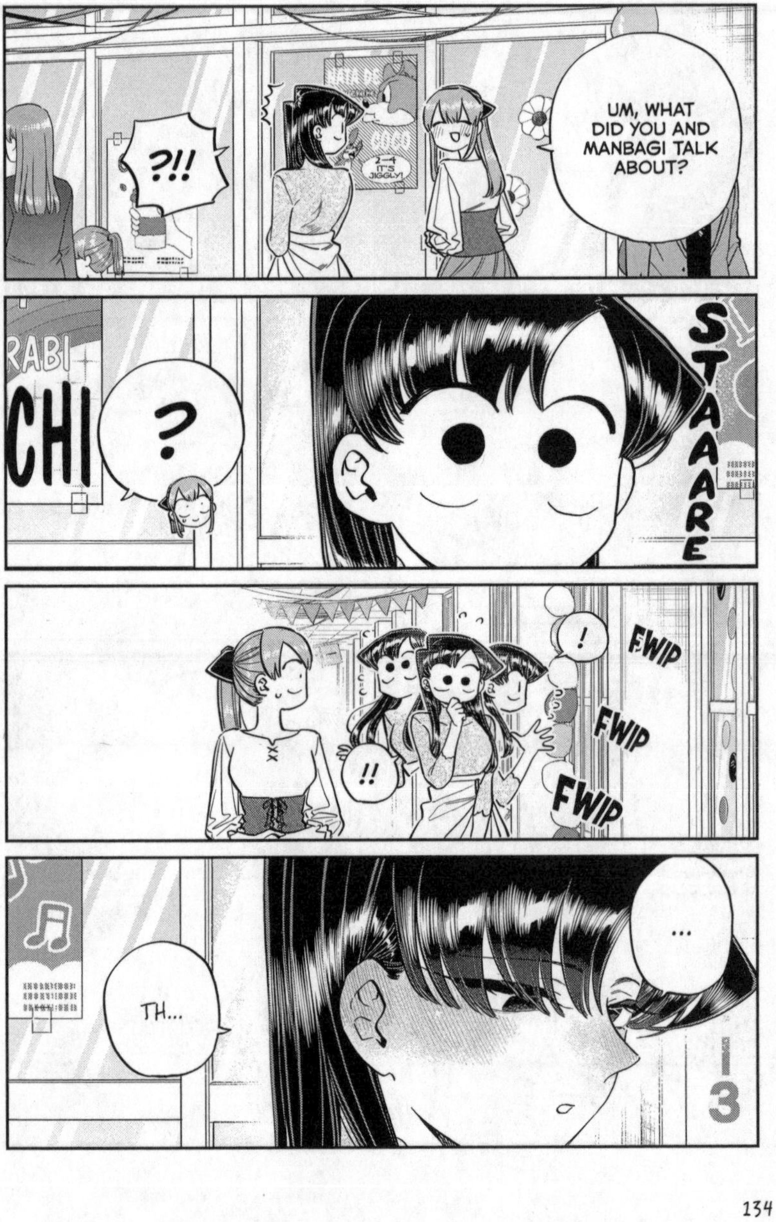
UM, WHAT DID YOU AND MANBAGI TALK ABOUT?
COCO
2-4 IT'S JIGGLY!
?!!
STAAARE
?
RABI
CHI
!
FWIP
FWIP
FWIP
!!
...
TH...
13

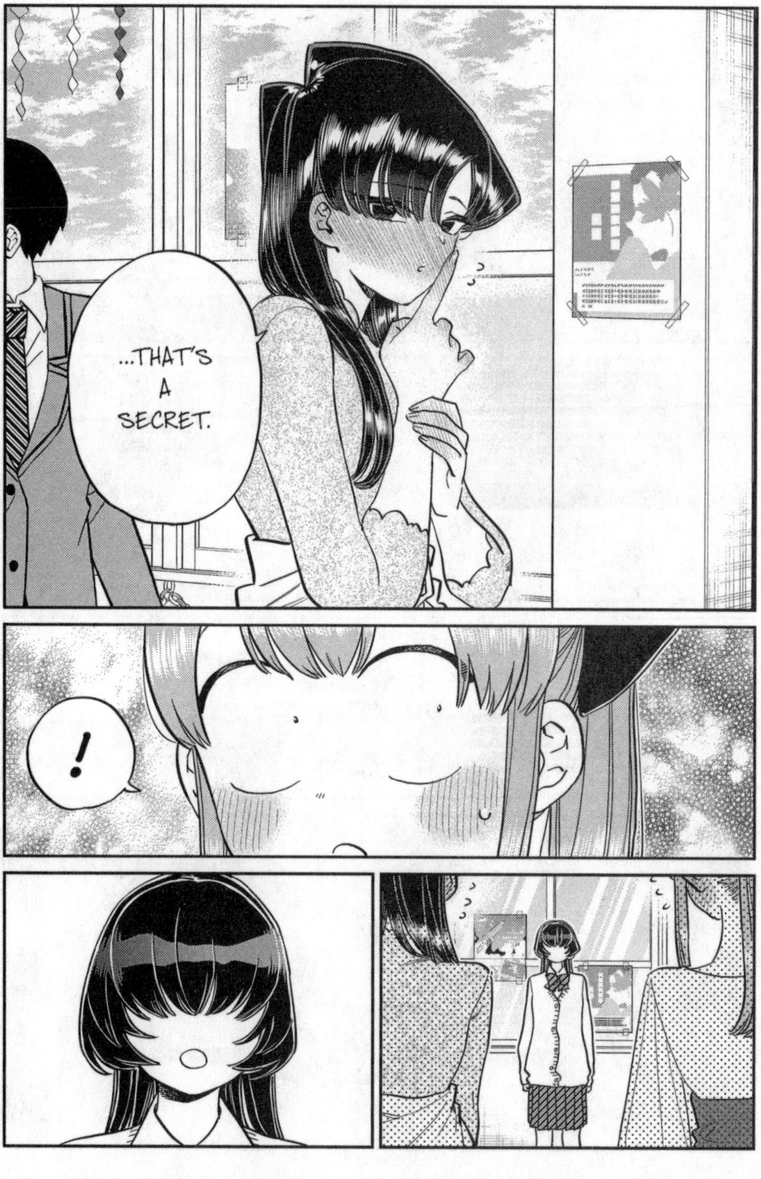
...THAT'S A SECRET.
!

*All becomes clear.

HUFF
HUFF

TRMBL
TRMBL

BAM

GASP!

...

THUD

?!

EMOI...

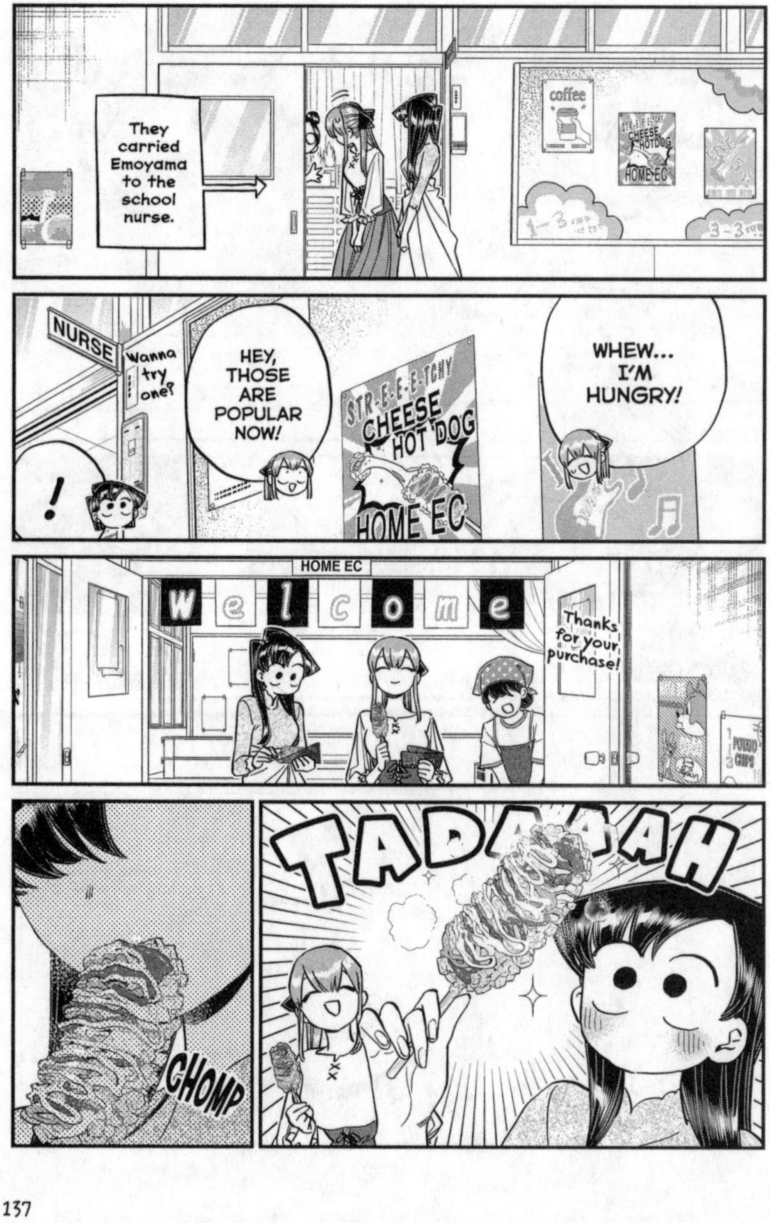

They carried Emoyama to the school nurse.
coffee
CHEESE HOTDOG
HOME EC
WHEW... I'M HUNGRY!
STR-E-E-E-TCHY
CHEESE HOT DOG
HOME EC
HEY, THOSE ARE POPULAR NOW!
Wanna try one?
NURSE
!
HOME EC
welcome
Thanks for your purchase!
TADAAAH
CHOMP

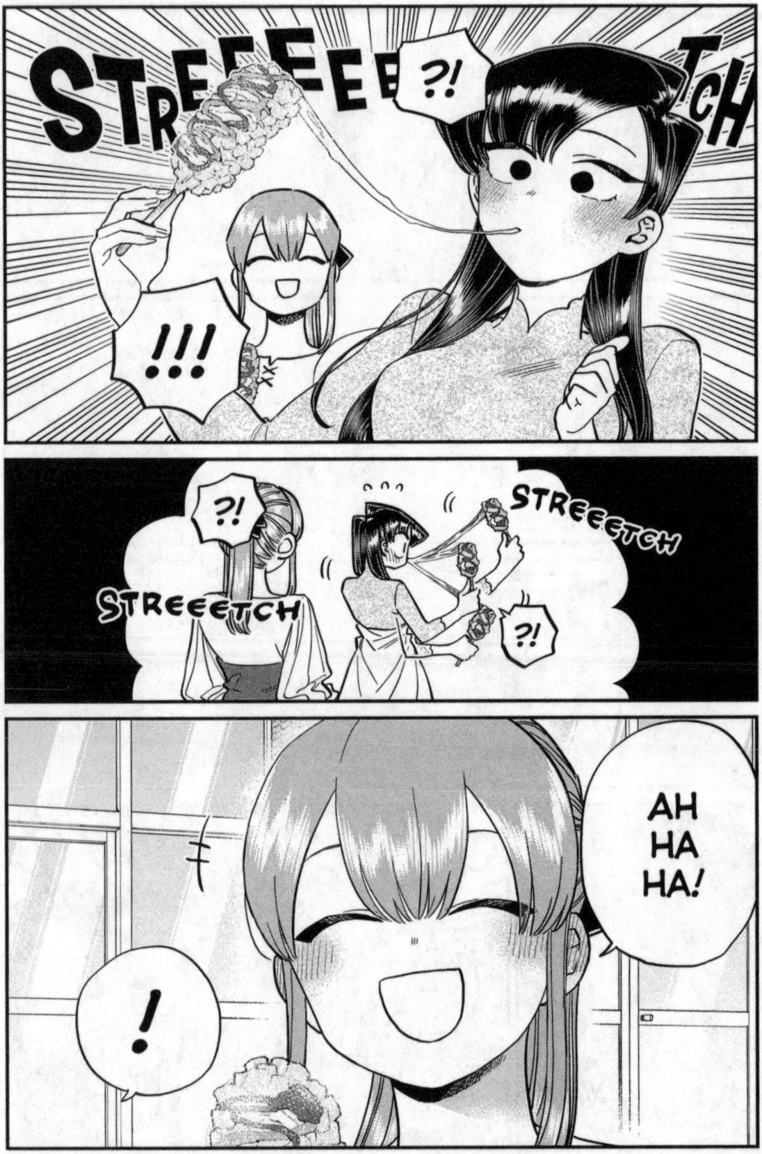
?!
STREEEEETCH
!!!
STREEEETCH
?!
?!
STREEEETCH
AH HA HA!
!

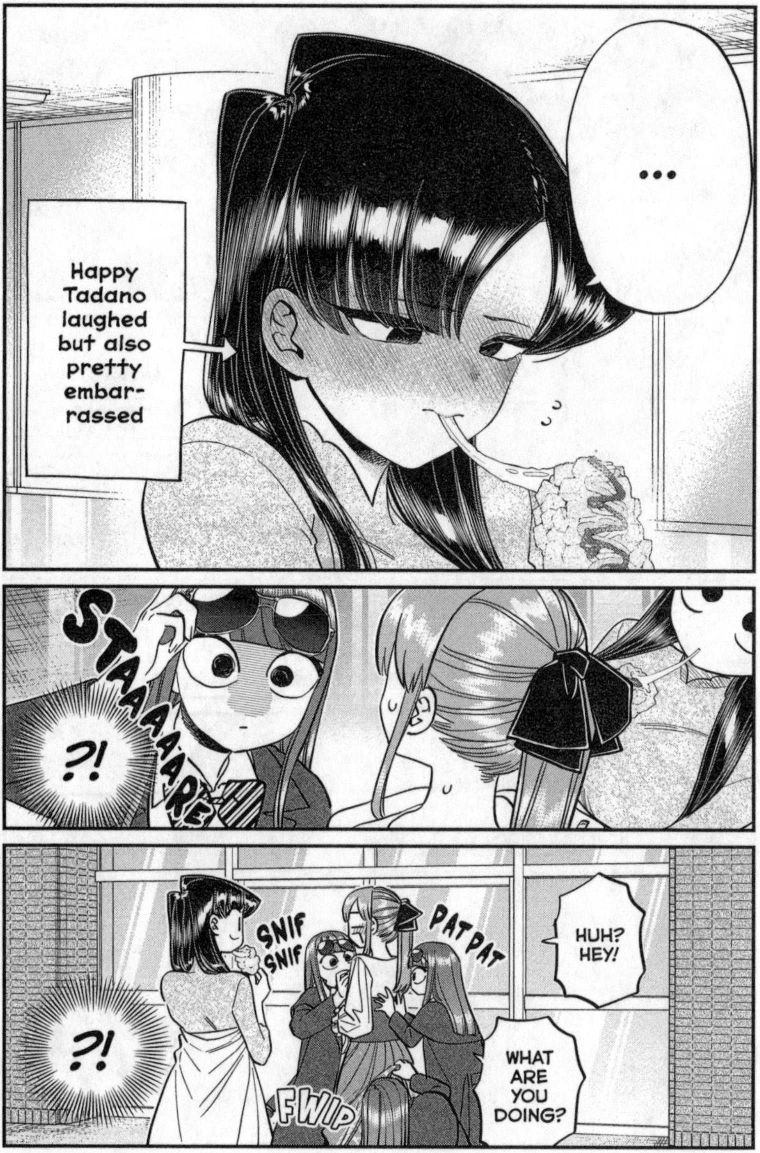
...
Happy Tadano laughed but also pretty embarrassed
STAAAAARE
?!
HUH? HEY!
WHAT ARE YOU DOING?
PAT PAT
SNIF SNIF
?!
FWIP

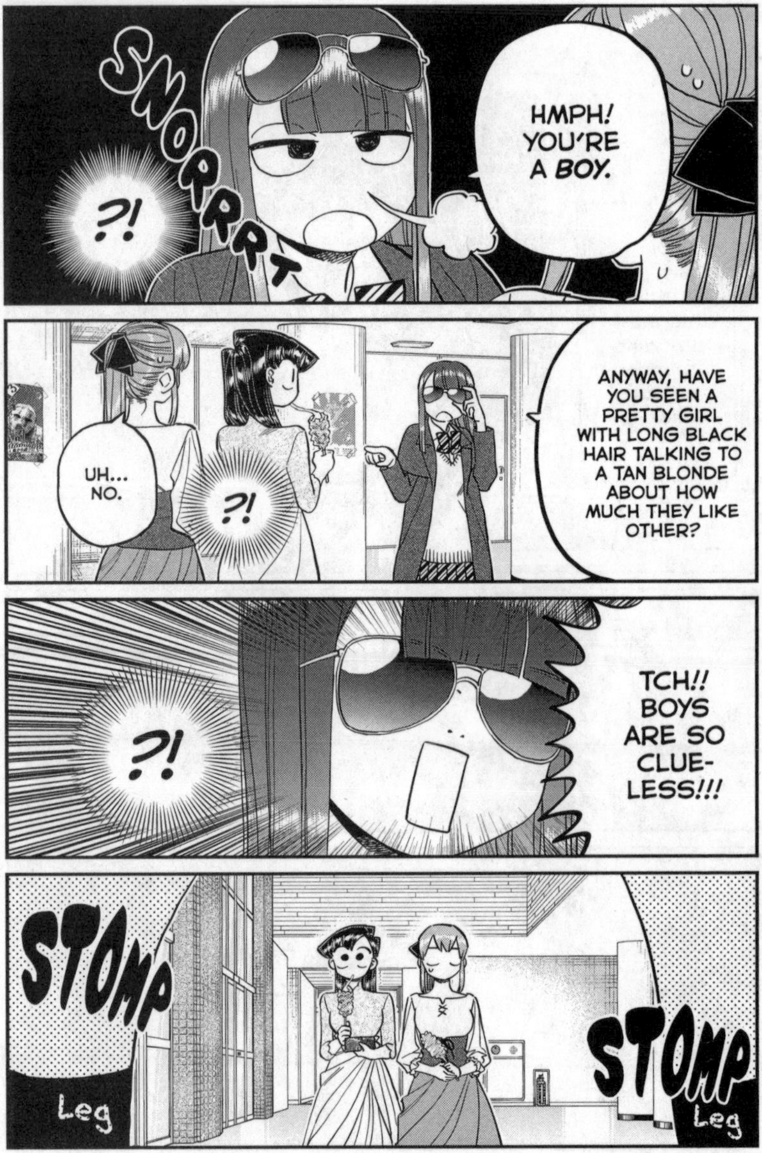

HMPH! YOU'RE A *BOY*.
SNORRRT
?!
ANYWAY, HAVE YOU SEEN A PRETTY GIRL WITH LONG BLACK HAIR TALKING TO A TAN BLONDE ABOUT HOW MUCH THEY LIKE OTHER?
?!
UH... NO.
TCH!! BOYS ARE SO CLUELESS!!!
?!
STOMP
Leg
STOMP
Leg

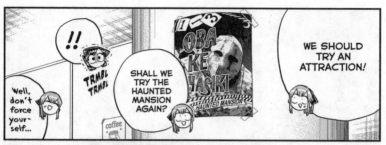

WE SHOULD TRY AN ATTRACTION!
OBAKE YASIKI
HAUNTED MANSION
SHALL WE TRY THE HAUNTED MANSION AGAIN?
!!
TRMBL TRMBL
Well, don't force your-self...
coffee
THE GAME ENDS IF THE SERIAL KILLER'S RED LIGHT HITS YOU...
...SO HIDE BEHIND THINGS!
THING
STAY
Decided to go
Inside the haunted man-sion
DRIP
DRIP
WHOA... IT'S PRETTY CREEPY...
Kon-nyaku noodles
SPLAP
...?!?!
?!?!?!
(a silent scream)
THAT HAP-PENED LAST YEAR TOO.

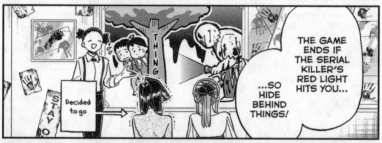

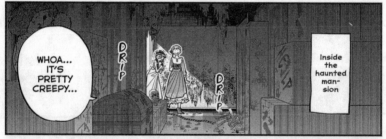

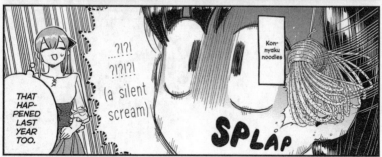

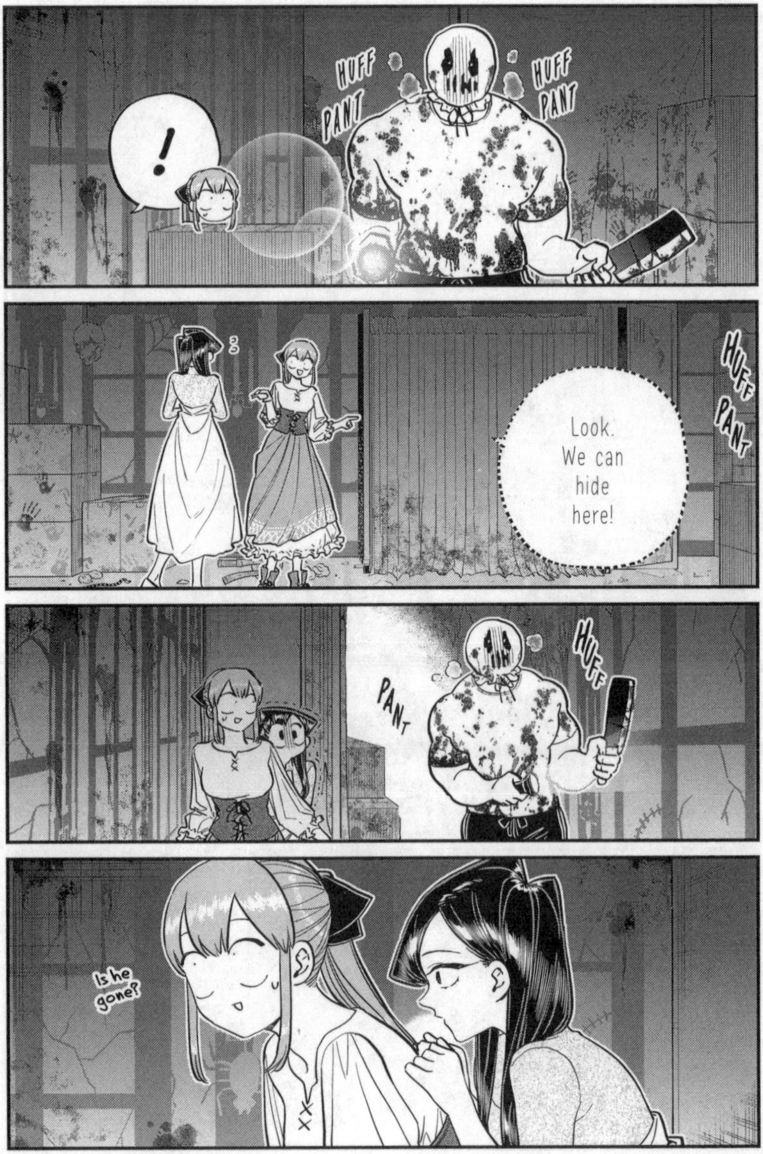
HUFF
PANT
HUFF
PANT
!
HUFF
PANT
Look. We can hide here!
HUFF
PANT
Is he gone?

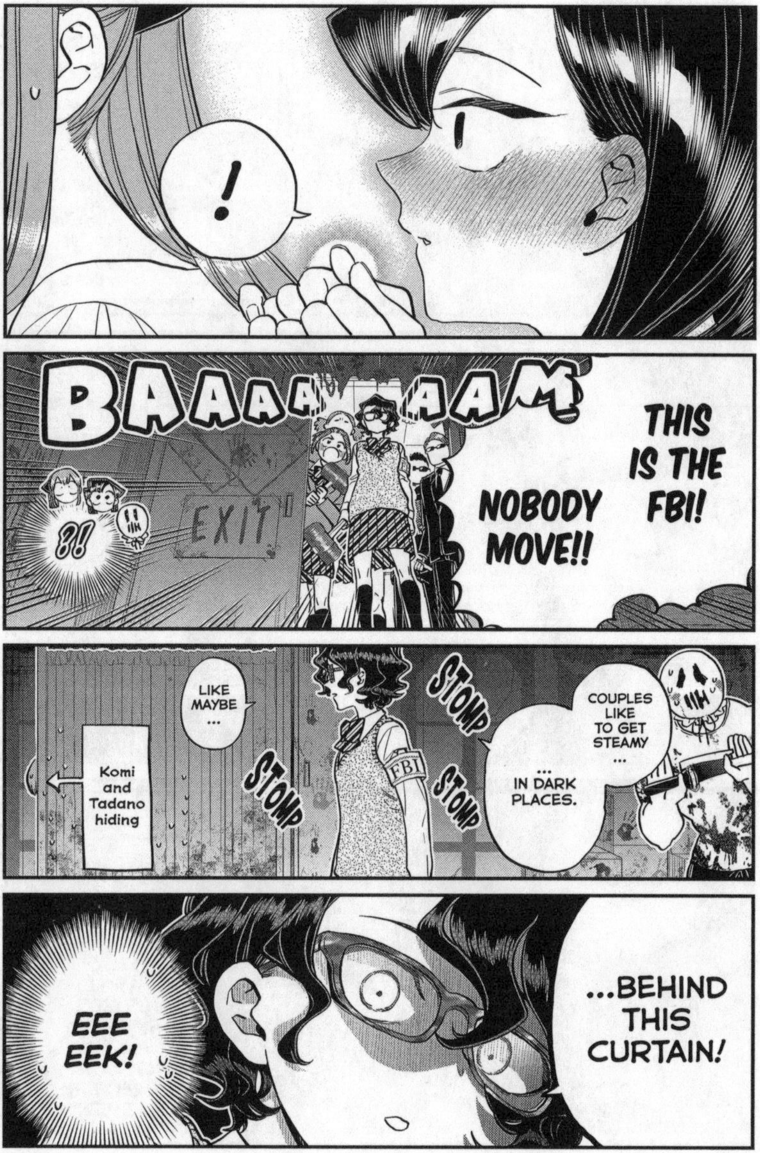
!
THIS IS THE FBI!
NOBODY MOVE!!
BAAAA AAM
?!
COUPLES LIKE TO GET STEAMY ...
... IN DARK PLACES.
STOMP
STOMP
LIKE MAYBE ...
STOMP
Komi and Tadano hiding
...BEHIND THIS CURTAIN!
EEE EEK!

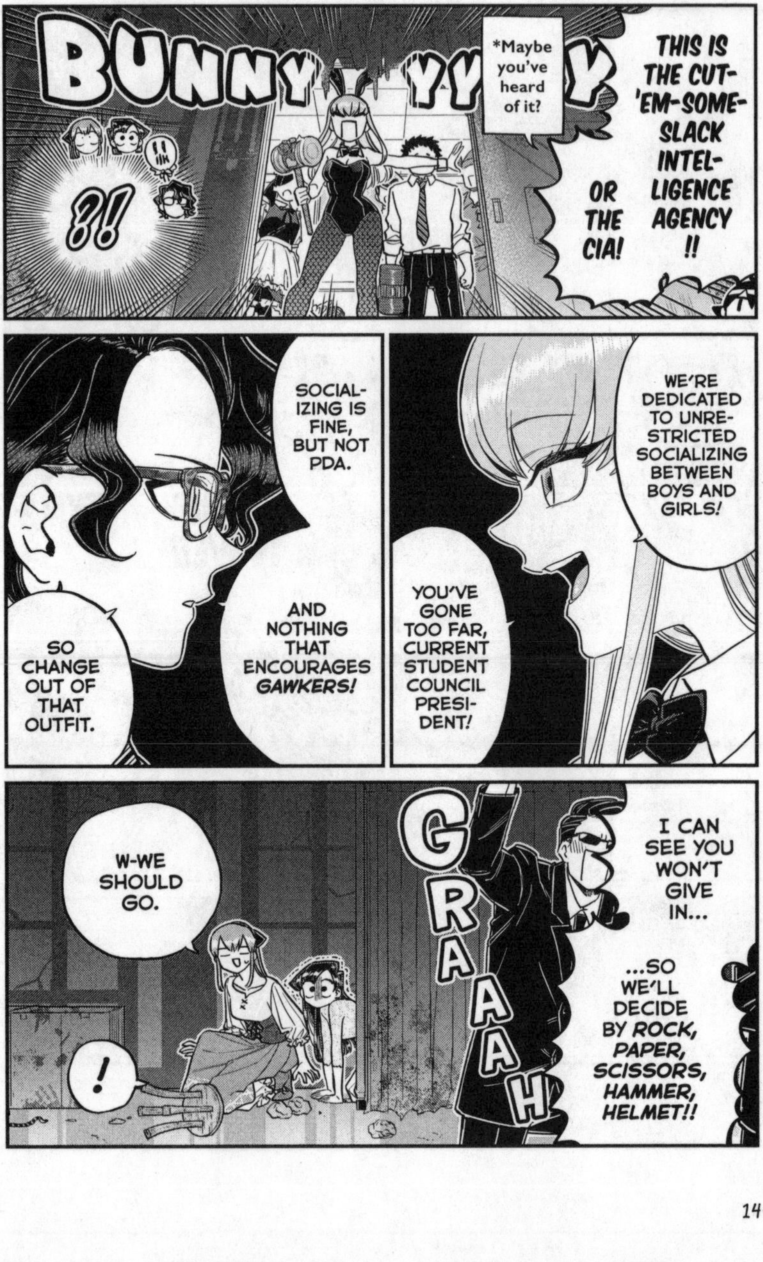

THIS IS THE CUT-'EM-SOME-SLACK INTELLIGENCE AGENCY!!
OR THE CIA!
*Maybe you've heard of it?
BUNNYYYYY
?!
WE'RE DEDICATED TO UNRESTRICTED SOCIALIZING BETWEEN BOYS AND GIRLS!
YOU'VE GONE TOO FAR, CURRENT STUDENT COUNCIL PRESIDENT!
SOCIALIZING IS FINE, BUT NOT PDA.
AND NOTHING THAT ENCOURAGES *GAWKERS!*
SO CHANGE OUT OF THAT OUTFIT.
I CAN SEE YOU WON'T GIVE IN...
...SO WE'LL DECIDE BY *ROCK, PAPER, SCISSORS, HAMMER, HELMET!!*
GRAAAAH
W-WE SHOULD GO.
!

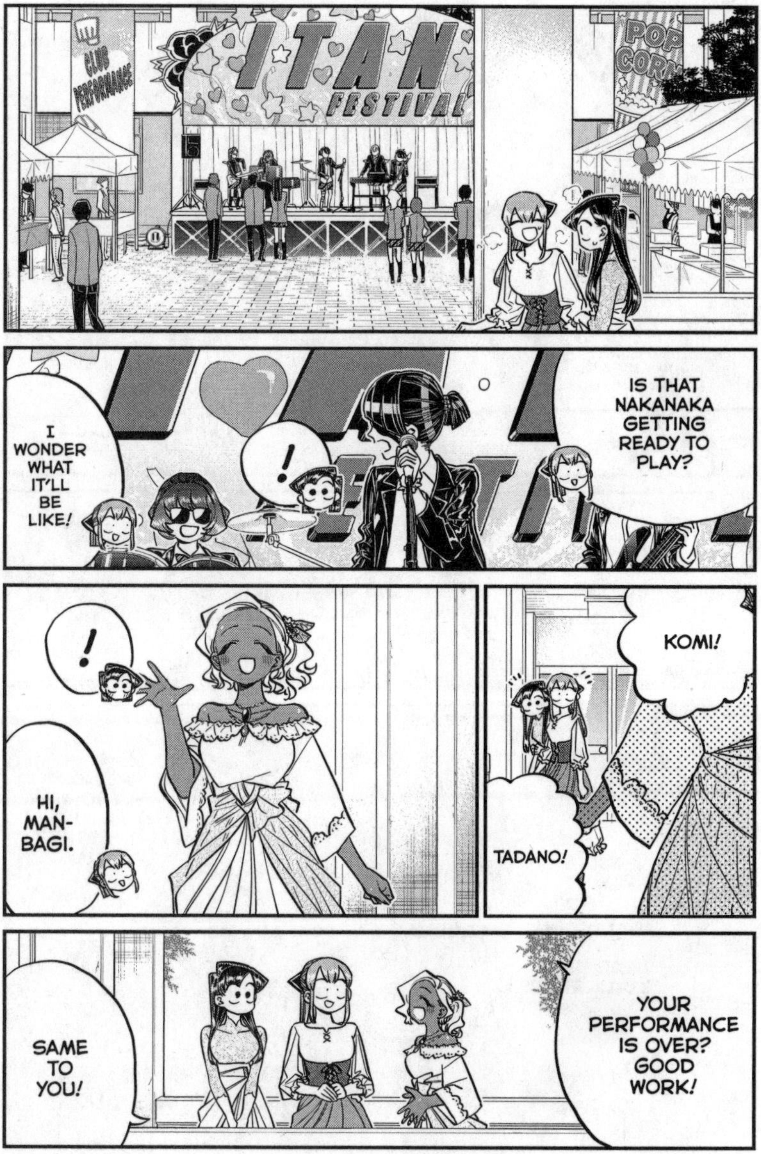
CLUB PERFORMANCE
ITAN FESTIVAL
POP
IS THAT NAKANAKA GETTING READY TO PLAY?
!
I WONDER WHAT IT'LL BE LIKE!
KOMI!
TADANO!
!
HI, MAN-BAGI.
YOUR PERFORMANCE IS OVER? GOOD WORK!
SAME TO YOU!

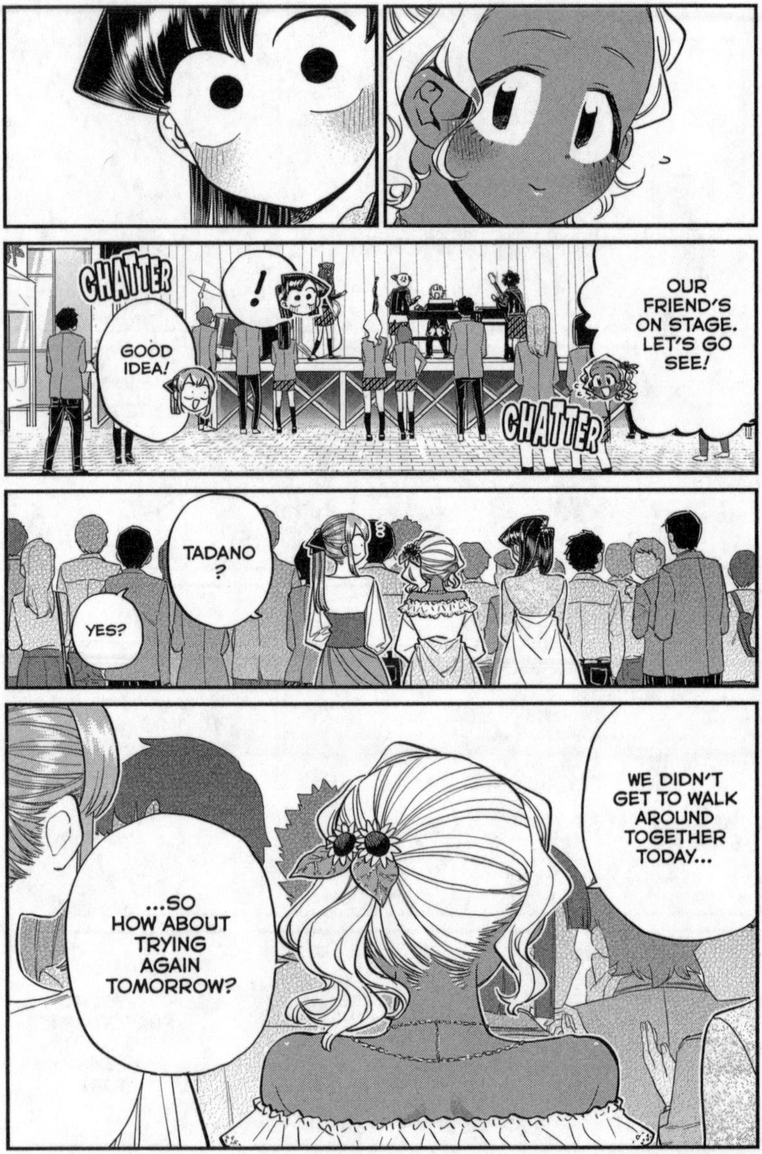
OUR FRIEND'S ON STAGE. LET'S GO SEE!
CHATTER
!
GOOD IDEA!
CHATTER
TADANO?
YES?
WE DIDN'T GET TO WALK AROUND TOGETHER TODAY...
...SO HOW ABOUT TRYING AGAIN TOMORROW?

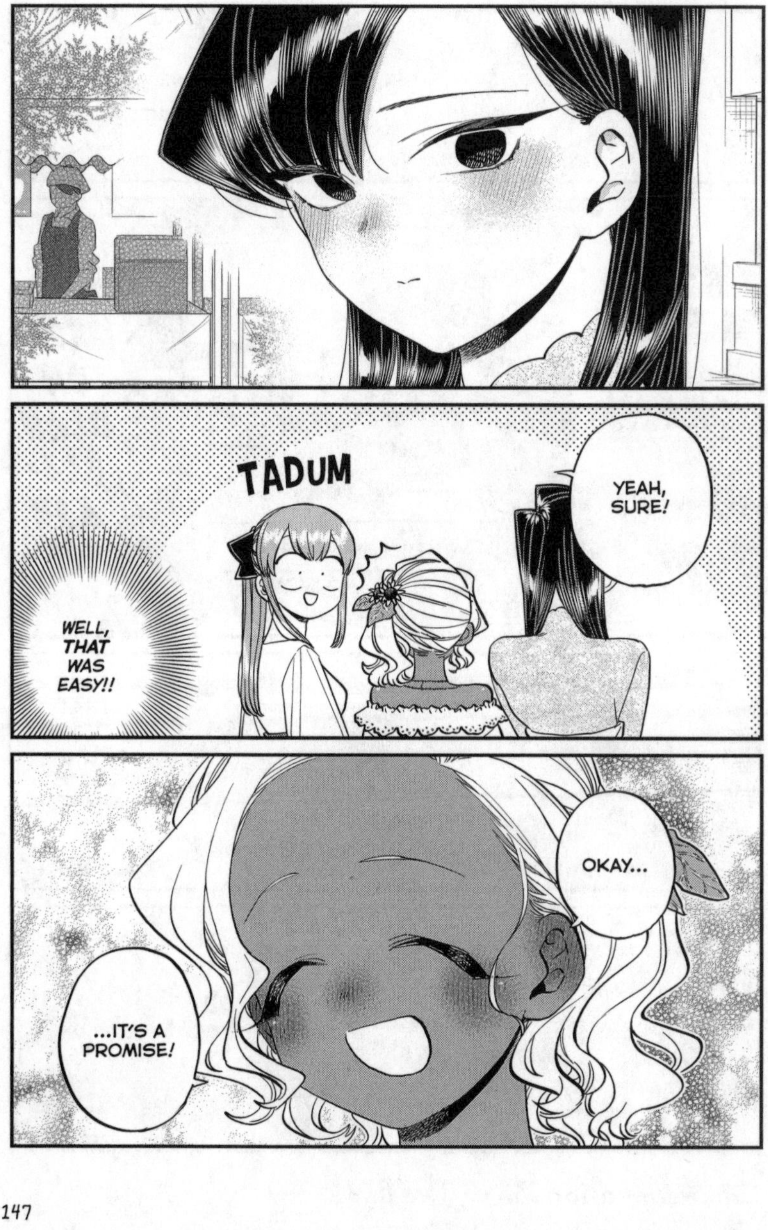
YEAH, SURE!
TADUM
WELL, THAT WAS EASY!!
OKAY...
...IT'S A PROMISE!

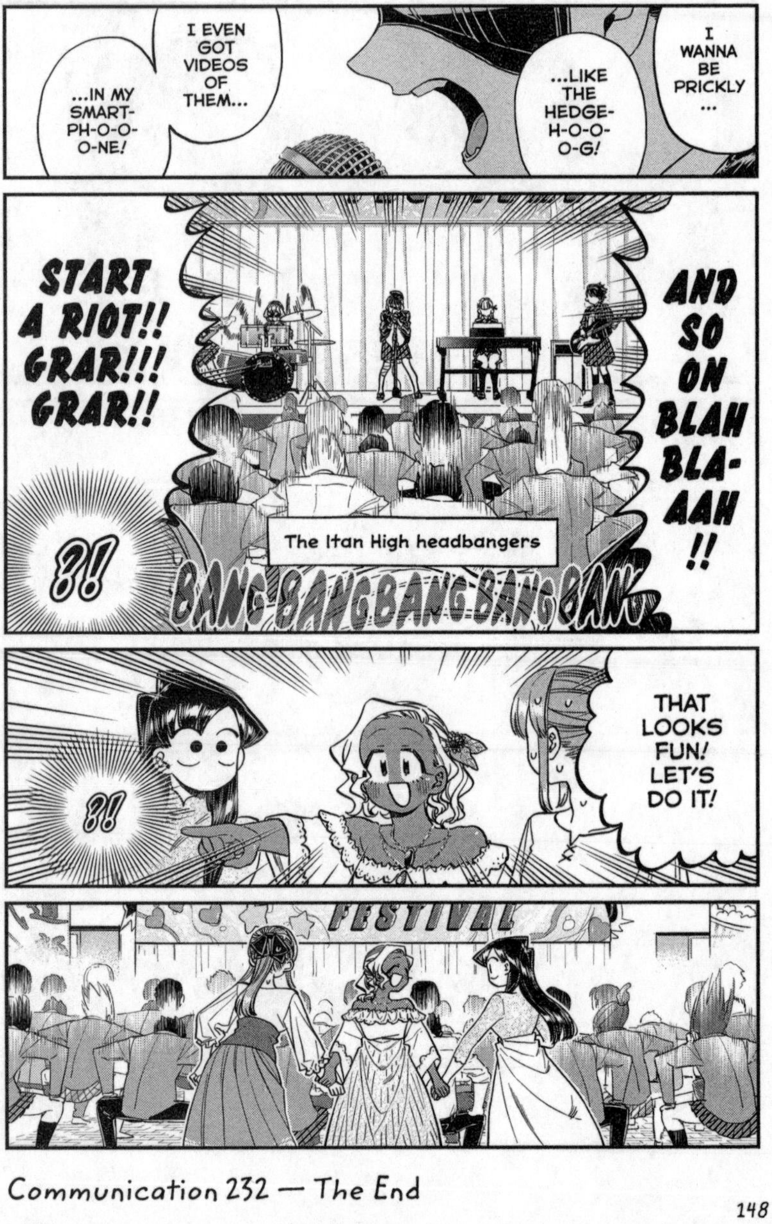
I WANNA BE PRICKLY...
...LIKE THE HEDGE-H-O-O-O-G!
I EVEN GOT VIDEOS OF THEM...
...IN MY SMART-PH-O-O-O-NE!
AND SO ON BLAH BLA-AAH!!
START A RIOT!! GRAR!!! GRAR!!
The Itan High headbangers
?!
BANG BANG BANG BANG BANG
THAT LOOKS FUN! LET'S DO IT!
?!
FESTIVAL

Communication 232 — The End

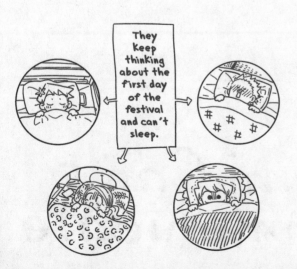

They keep thinking about the first day of the festival and can't sleep.

Komi Can't
Communicate

Komi Can't Communicate

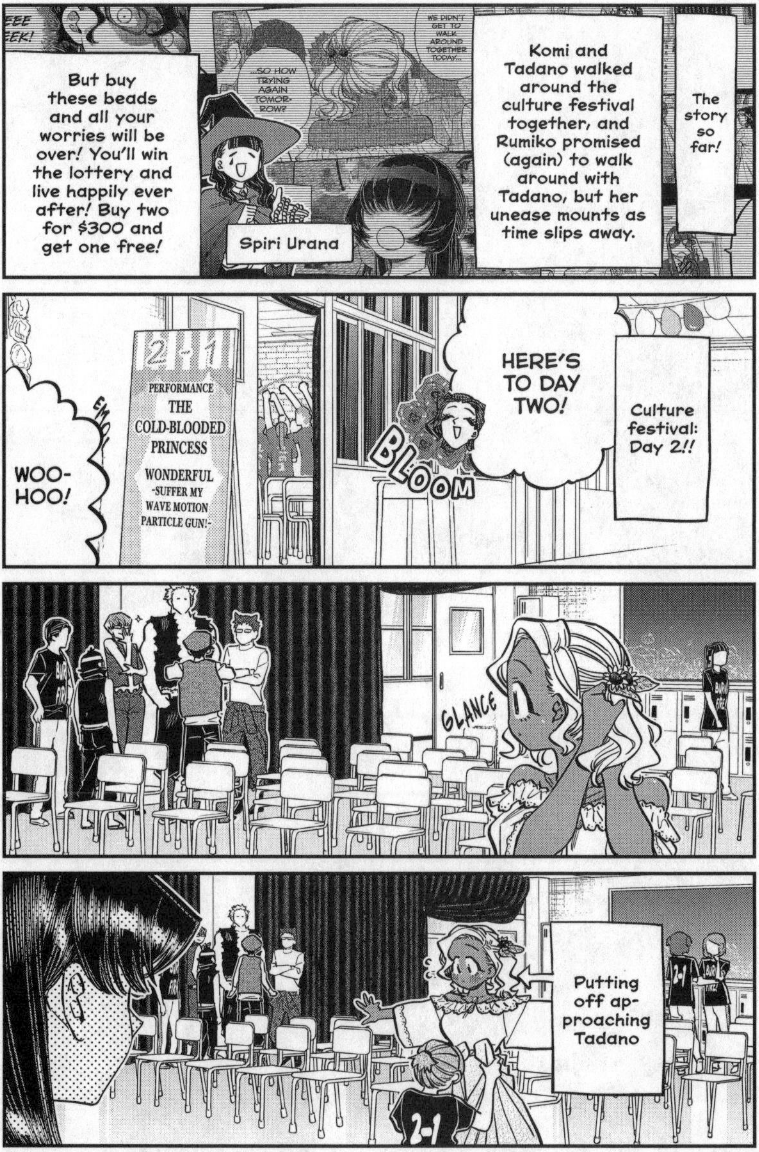

The story so far!
Komi and Tadano walked around the culture festival together, and Rumiko promised (again) to walk around with Tadano, but her unease mounts as time slips away.
WE DIDN'T GET TO WALK AROUND TOGETHER TODAY...
...SO HOW TRYING AGAIN TOMORROW?
Spiri Urana
But buy these beads and all your worries will be over! You'll win the lottery and live happily ever after! Buy two for $300 and get one free!
Culture festival: Day 2!!
HERE'S TO DAY TWO!
BLOOM
2-1
PERFORMANCE
THE COLD-BLOODED PRINCESS
WONDERFUL
-SUFFER MY WAVE MOTION PARTICLE GUN!-
WOO-HOO!
GLANCE
Putting off ap-proaching Tadano
2-1

SWUF

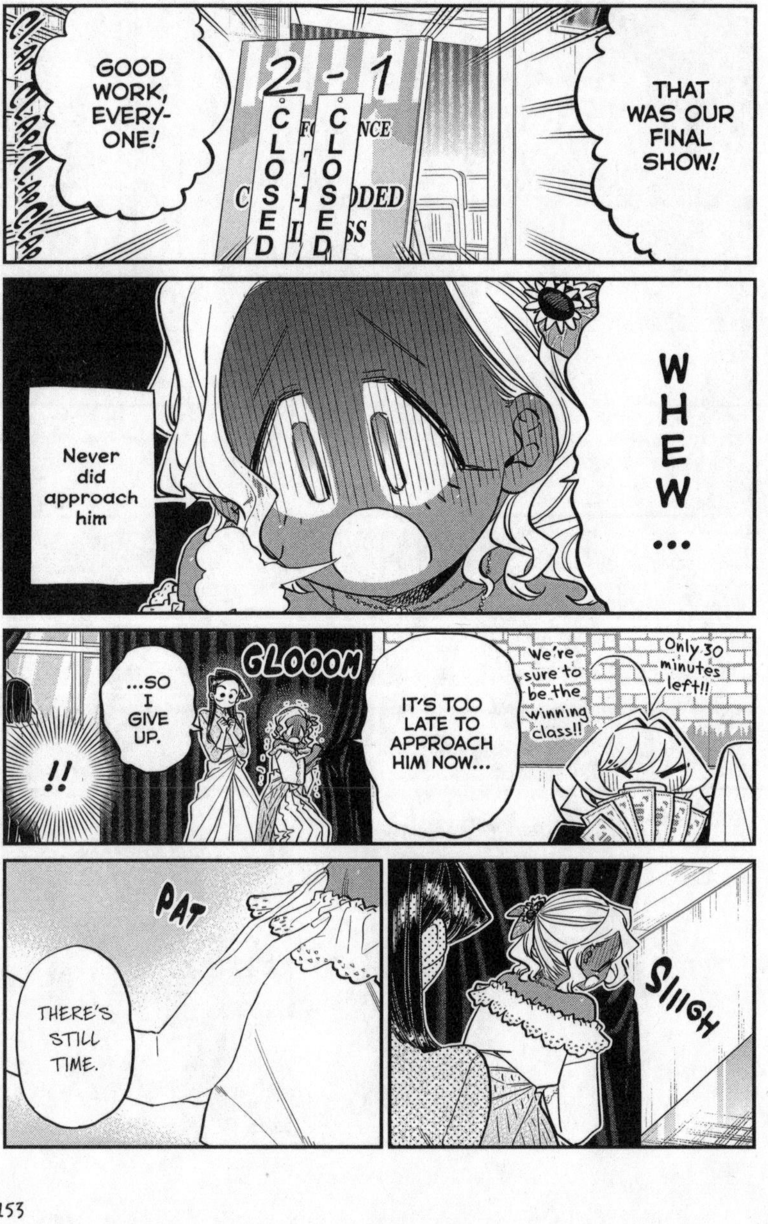
THAT WAS OUR FINAL SHOW!
2-1
CLOSED
CLOSED
GOOD WORK, EVERY-ONE!
CLAP CLAP CLAP CLAP CLAP
WHEW...
Never did approach him
Only 30 minutes left!!
We're sure to be the winning class!!
IT'S TOO LATE TO APPROACH HIM NOW...
GLOOOM
...SO I GIVE UP.
!!
SIIIGH
PAT
THERE'S STILL TIME.

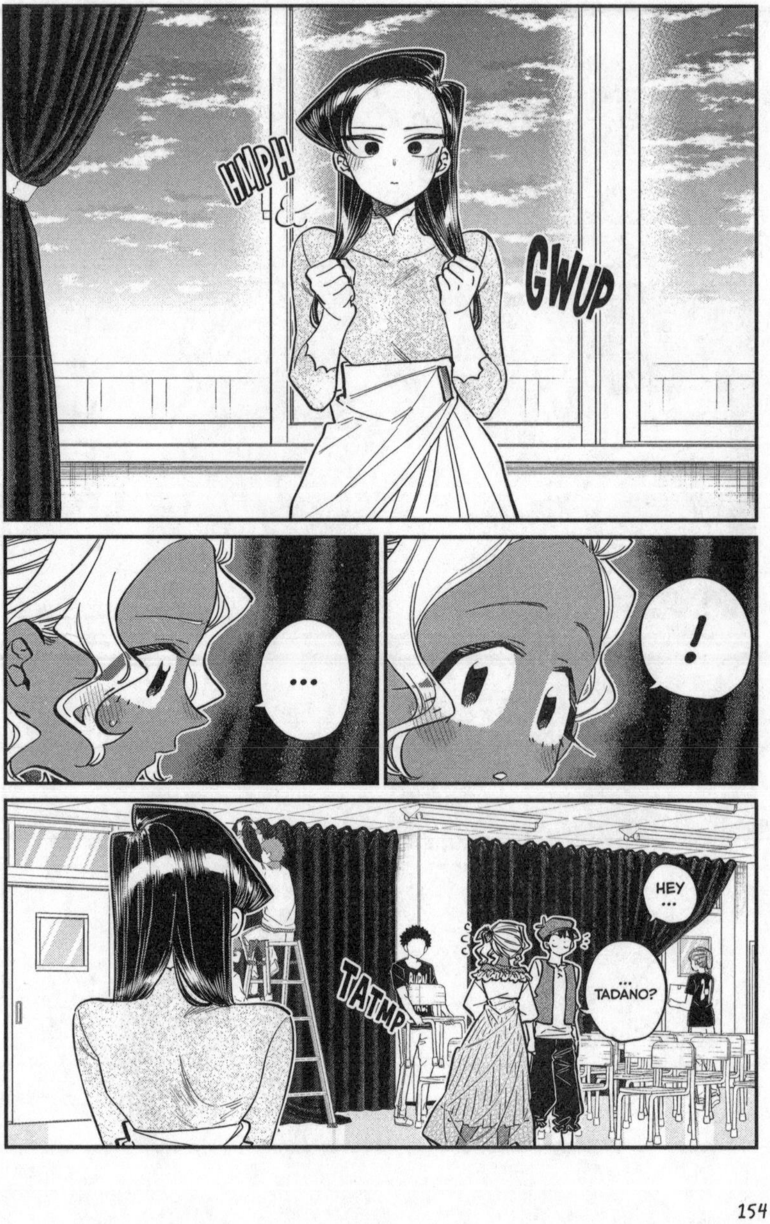
HMPH
GWUP
!
...
HEY ...
... TADANO?
TATMP

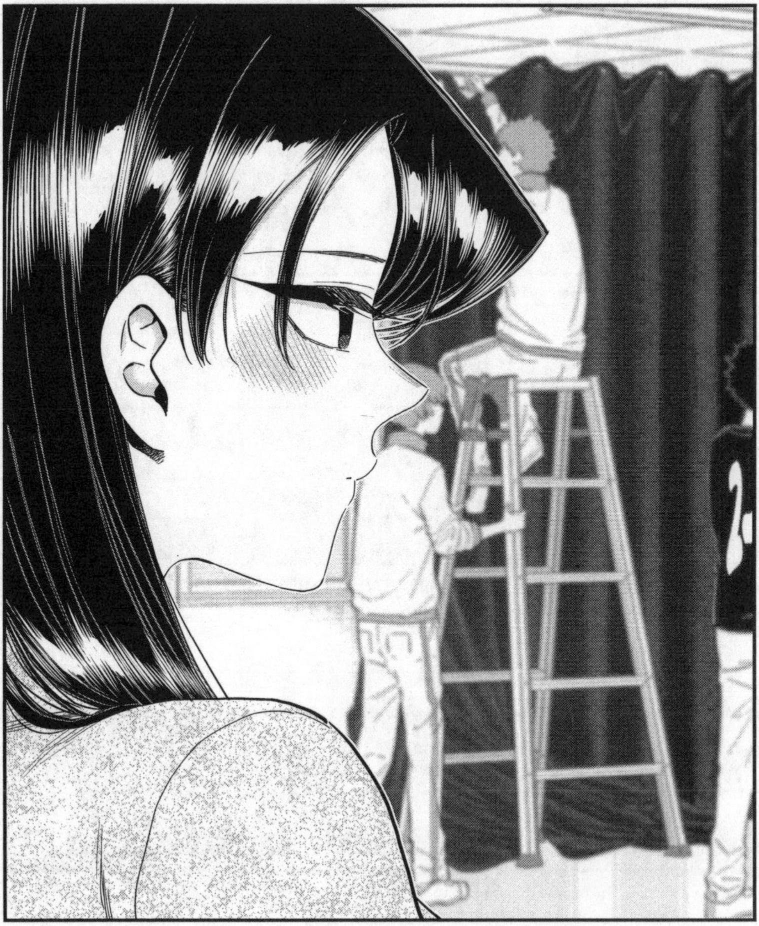

Komi Can't Communicate

Communication 233: Culture Festival Date

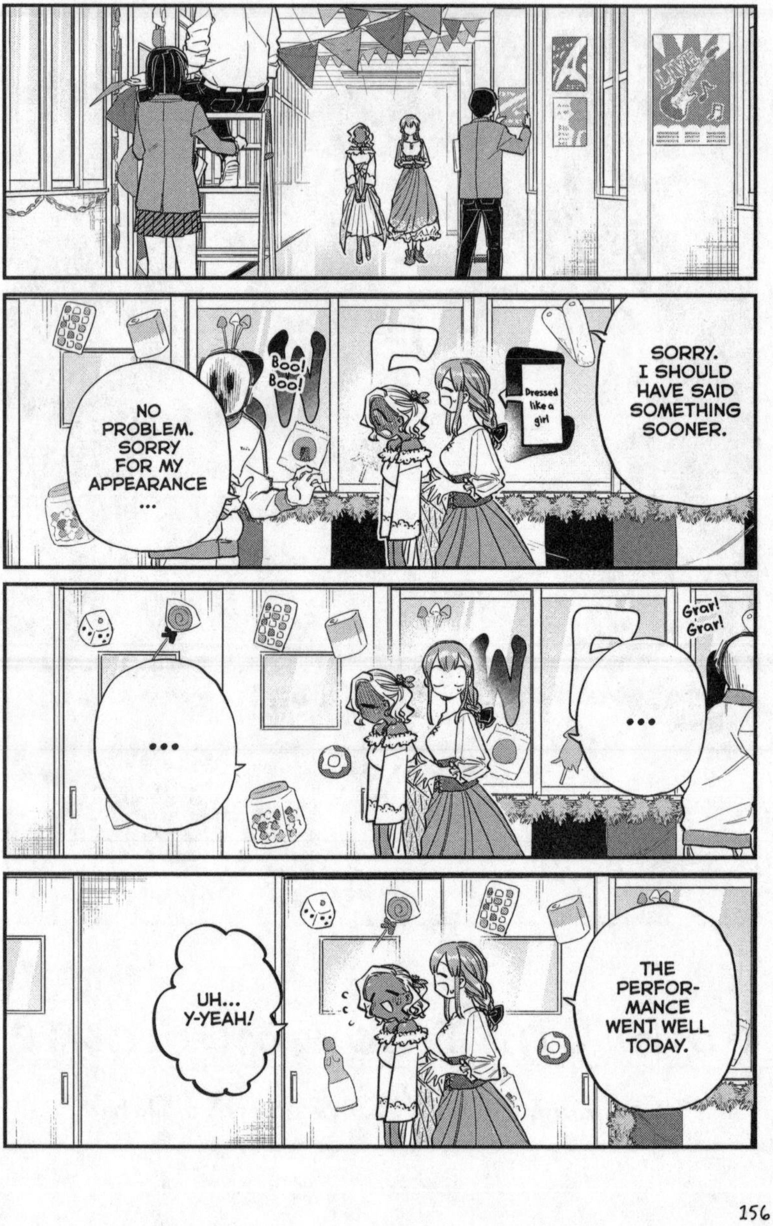
SORRY. I SHOULD HAVE SAID SOMETHING SOONER.
Dressed like a girl
Boo! Boo!
NO PROBLEM. SORRY FOR MY APPEARANCE ...
Grar! Grar!
...
...
THE PERFORMANCE WENT WELL TODAY.
UH... Y-YEAH!

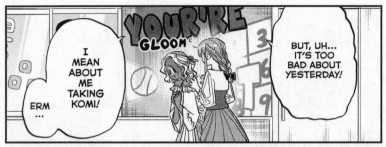

BUT, UH... IT'S TOO BAD ABOUT YESTERDAY!
YOUR'RE
GLOOM
I MEAN ABOUT ME TAKING KOMI!
ERM ...
...
Aw, the festival's ending!
BONK
!!
DID KOMI TELL YOU ANYTHING?
NO, SHE SAID IT WAS A SECRET.
...
OH, RIGHT.
...

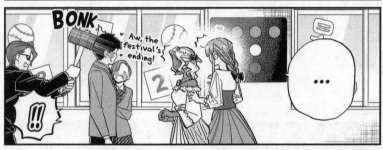

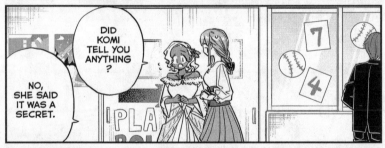

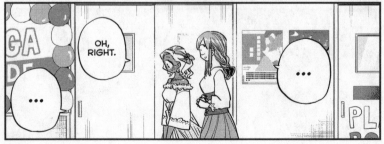

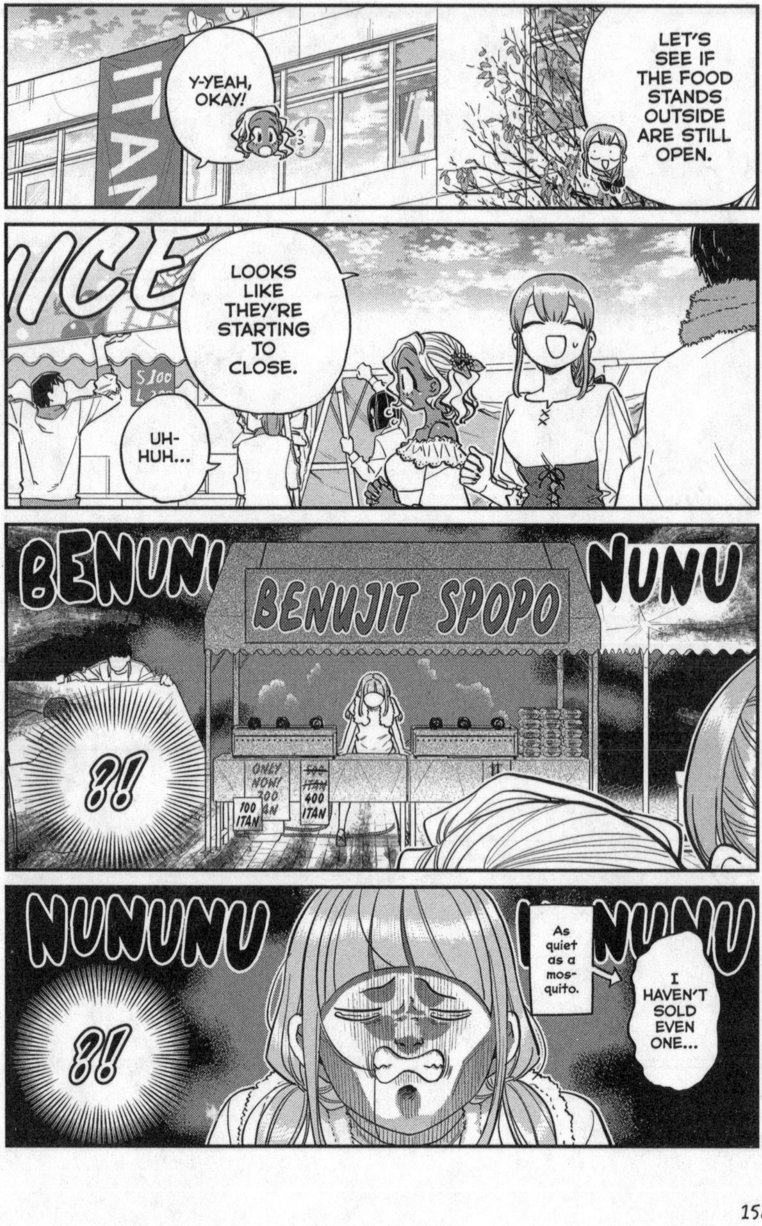
LET'S SEE IF THE FOOD STANDS OUTSIDE ARE STILL OPEN.
Y-YEAH, OKAY!
LOOKS LIKE THEY'RE STARTING TO CLOSE.
UH-HUH...
NUNU
BENUJIT SPOPO
BENUNU
500 ITAN
400 ITAN
ONLY NOW!
100 ITAN
?!
I HAVEN'T SOLD EVEN ONE...
As quiet as a mosquito.
NUNUNU
?!

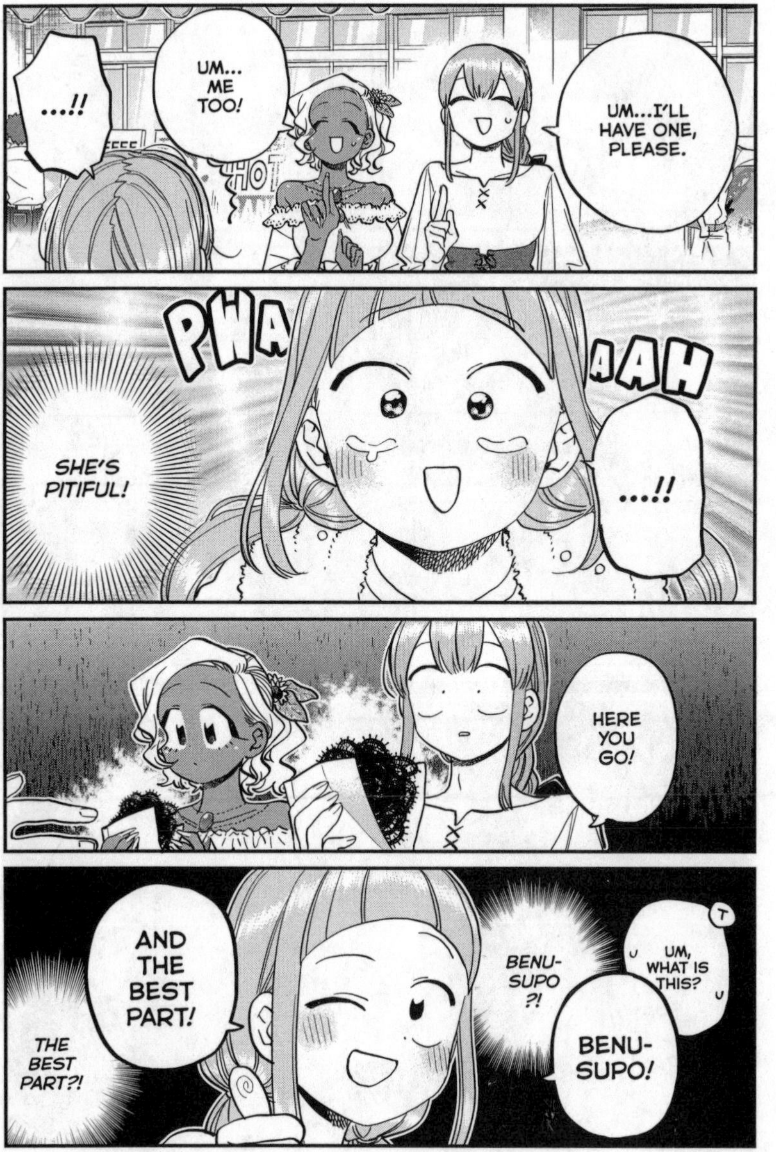
UM...I'LL HAVE ONE, PLEASE.
UM... ME TOO!
...!!
PWAAAH
...!!
SHE'S PITIFUL!
HERE YOU GO!
UM, WHAT IS THIS?
BENU-SUPO!
BENU-SUPO?!
AND THE BEST PART!
THE BEST PART?!

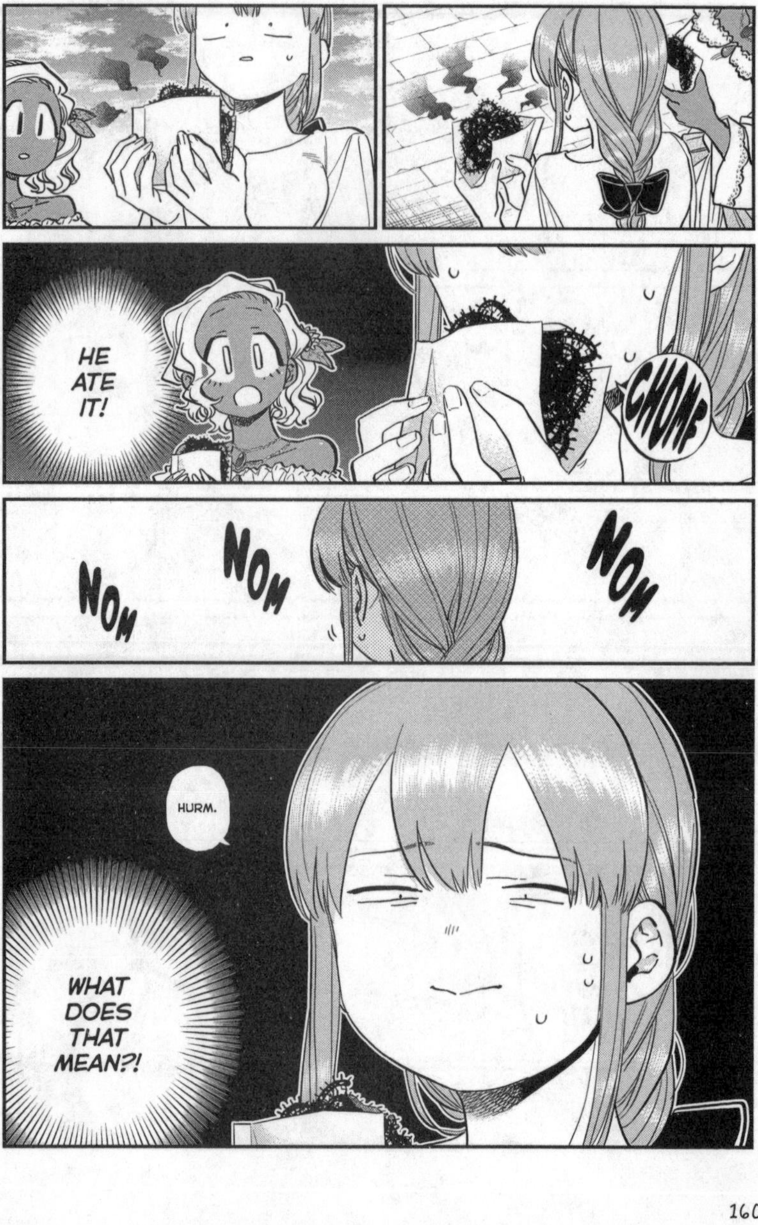
CHOMP
HE ATE IT!
NOM
NOM
NOM
HURM.
WHAT DOES THAT MEAN?!

IT'S, UM... NOT... AWFUL?
RUMIKO, IT *IS* EDIBLE... SORTA.
S-SERIOUSLY?!
W-WELL, HERE GOES...
CHOMP
YAY YAY
NOM
NOM
NOM
IT'S SURPRISINGLY...
... HURM.
SHOULD I HAVE STOPPED HER?

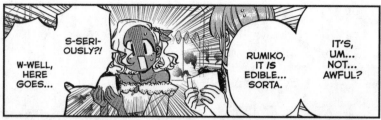

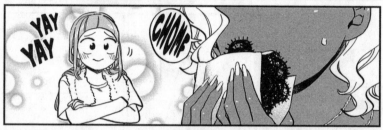

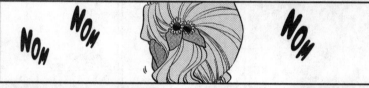

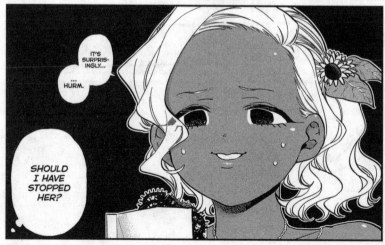

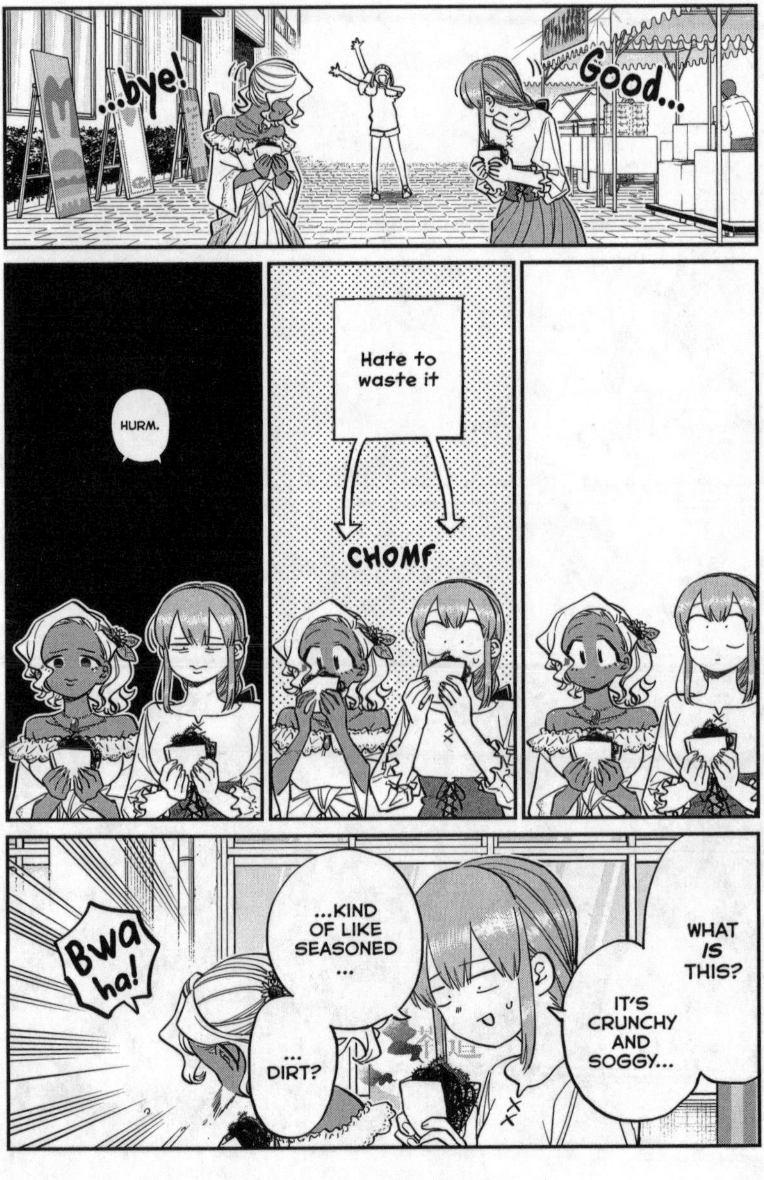
Good...
...bye!
Hate to waste it
CHOMF
HURM.
WHAT IS THIS?
IT'S CRUNCHY AND SOGGY...
...KIND OF LIKE SEASONED ...
... DIRT?
Bwa ha!

AH HA HA HA! YOUR FACIAL EXPRESSION!!

BUT I KNOW HOW YOU FEEL!

HA HA...

!

HUH? OKAY...

TAKE ANOTHER BITE! FOR A SO-ME-FO-PO!*

WA HA HA HA!

CHOMF

*Social Media Food Post.

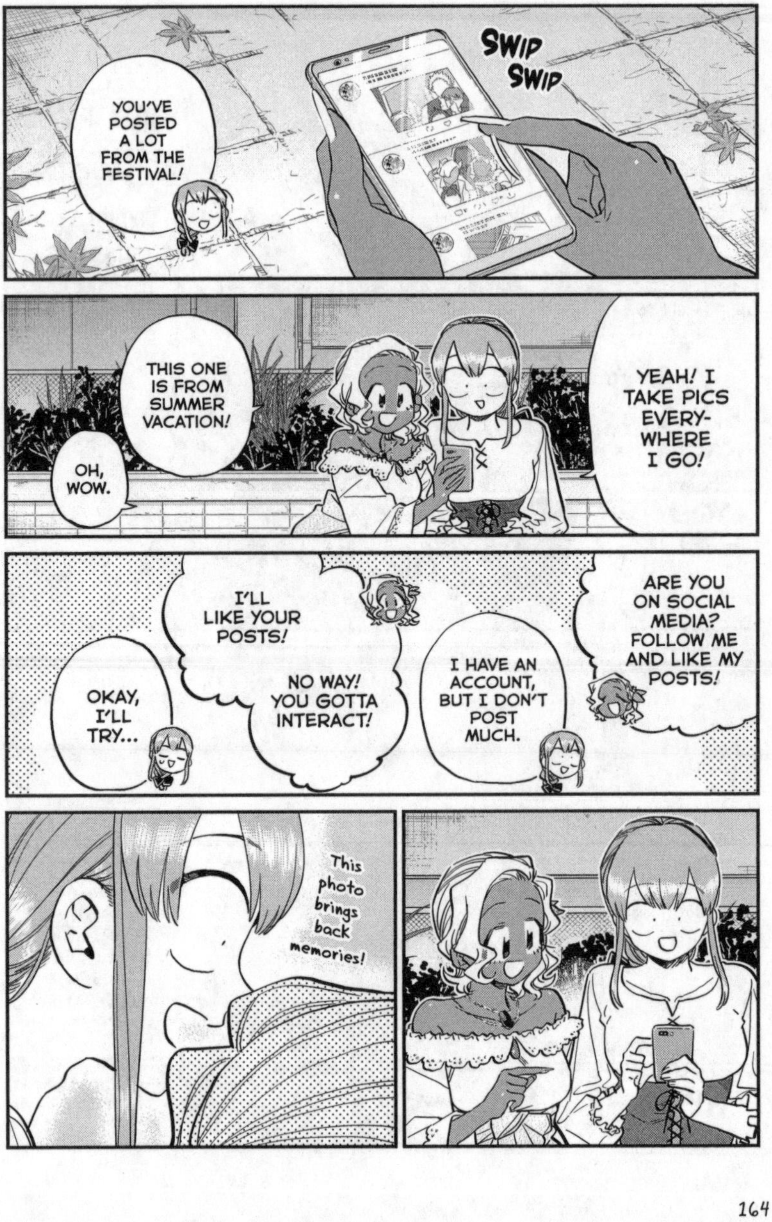
SWIP SWIP
YOU'VE POSTED A LOT FROM THE FESTIVAL!
YEAH! I TAKE PICS EVERY-WHERE I GO!
THIS ONE IS FROM SUMMER VACATION!
OH, WOW.
ARE YOU ON SOCIAL MEDIA? FOLLOW ME AND LIKE MY POSTS!
I HAVE AN ACCOUNT, BUT I DON'T POST MUCH.
I'LL LIKE YOUR POSTS!
NO WAY! YOU GOTTA INTERACT!
OKAY, I'LL TRY...
This photo brings back memories!

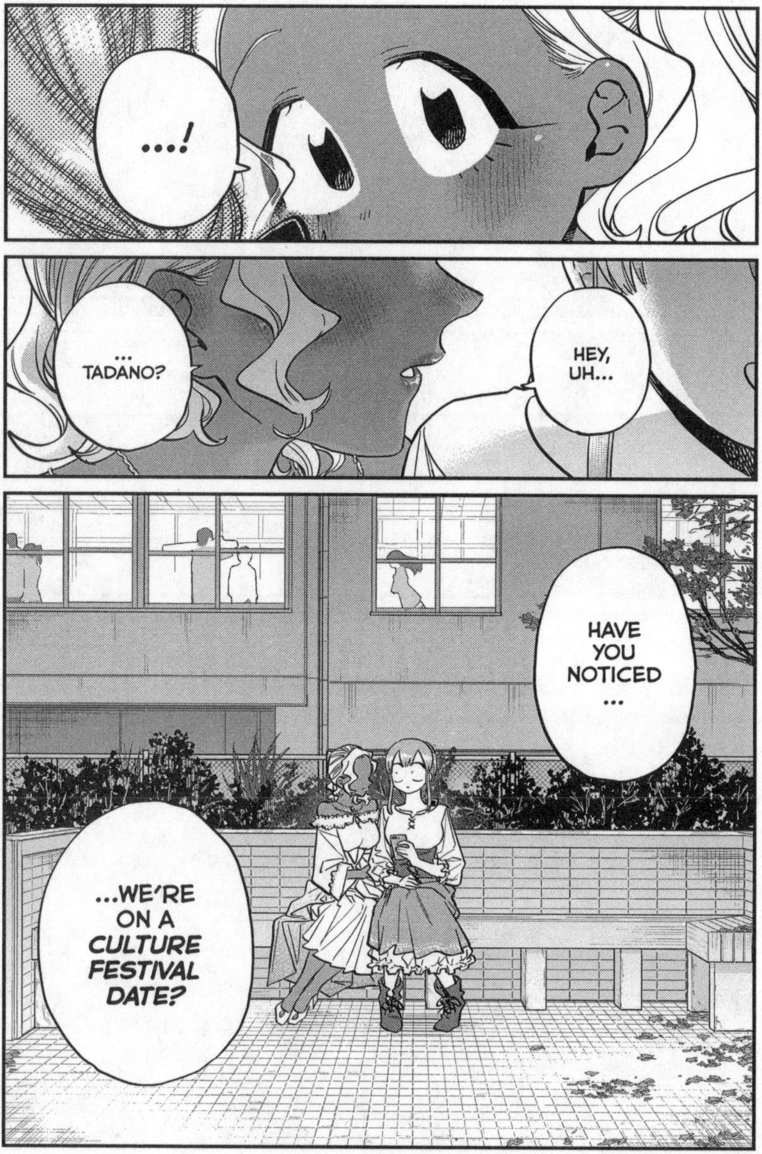
...!
HEY, UH...
...TADANO?
HAVE YOU NOTICED...
...WE'RE ON A CULTURE FESTIVAL DATE?

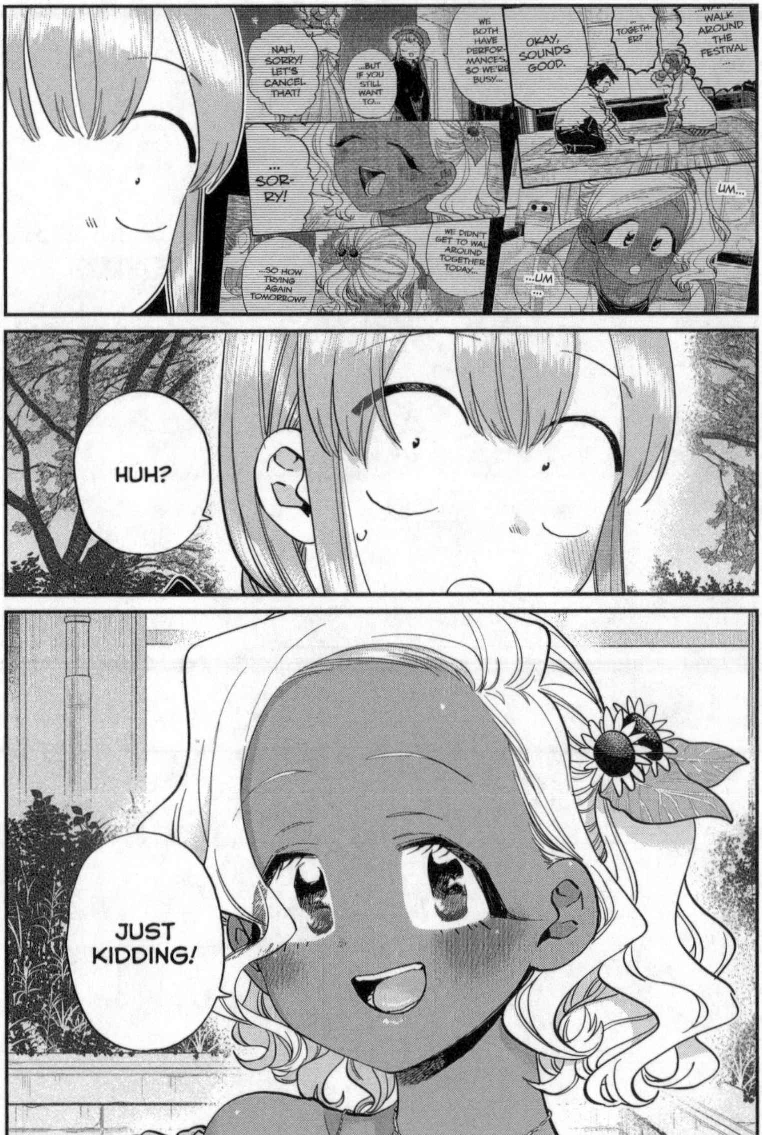

WALK AROUND THE FESTIVAL ...
... TOGETHER?
OKAY, SOUNDS GOOD.
UM...
...UM ...
WE BOTH HAVE PERFORMANCES, SO WE'RE BUSY...
...BUT IF YOU STILL WANT TO...
NAH, SORRY! LET'S CANCEL THAT!
... SORRY!
WE DIDN'T GET TO WAL AROUND TOGETHER TODAY...
...SO HOW TRYING AGAIN TOMORROW?
HUH?
JUST KIDDING!

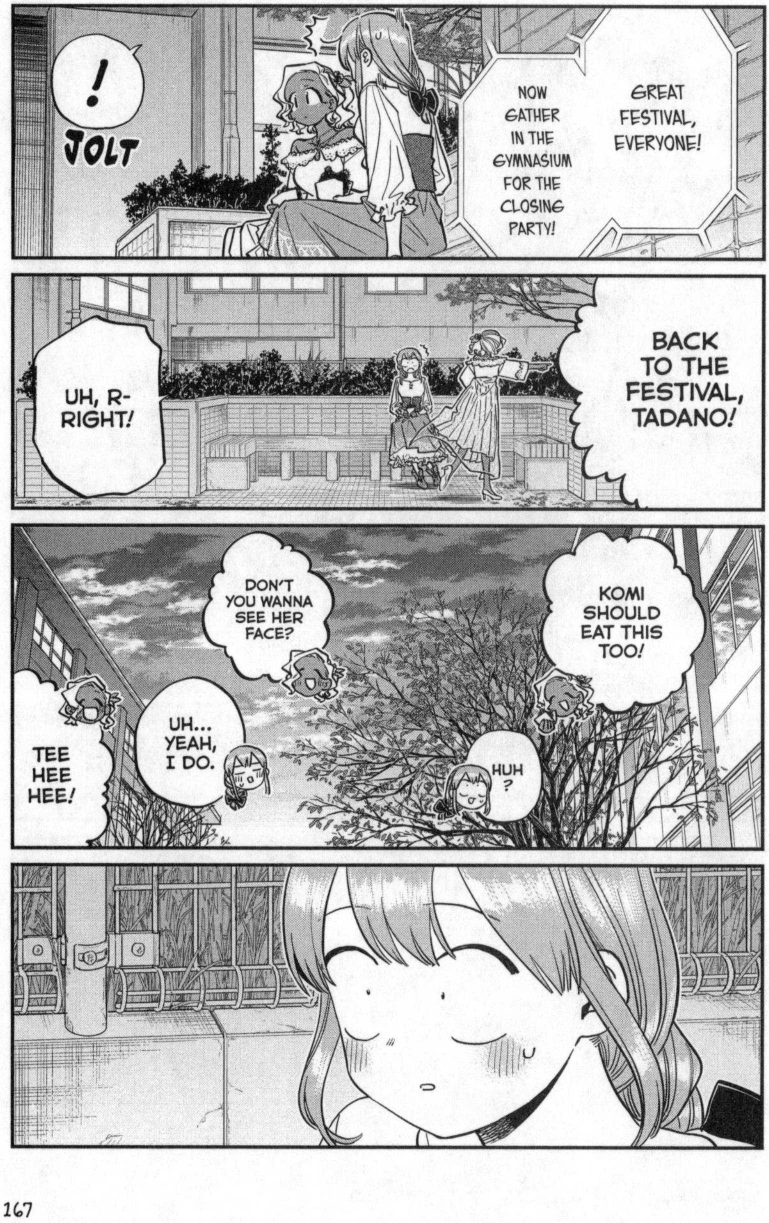
GREAT FESTIVAL, EVERYONE!
NOW GATHER IN THE GYMNASIUM FOR THE CLOSING PARTY!
!
JOLT
BACK TO THE FESTIVAL, TADANO!
UH, R-RIGHT!
KOMI SHOULD EAT THIS TOO!
HUH ?
DON'T YOU WANNA SEE HER FACE?
UH... YEAH, I DO.
TEE HEE HEE!

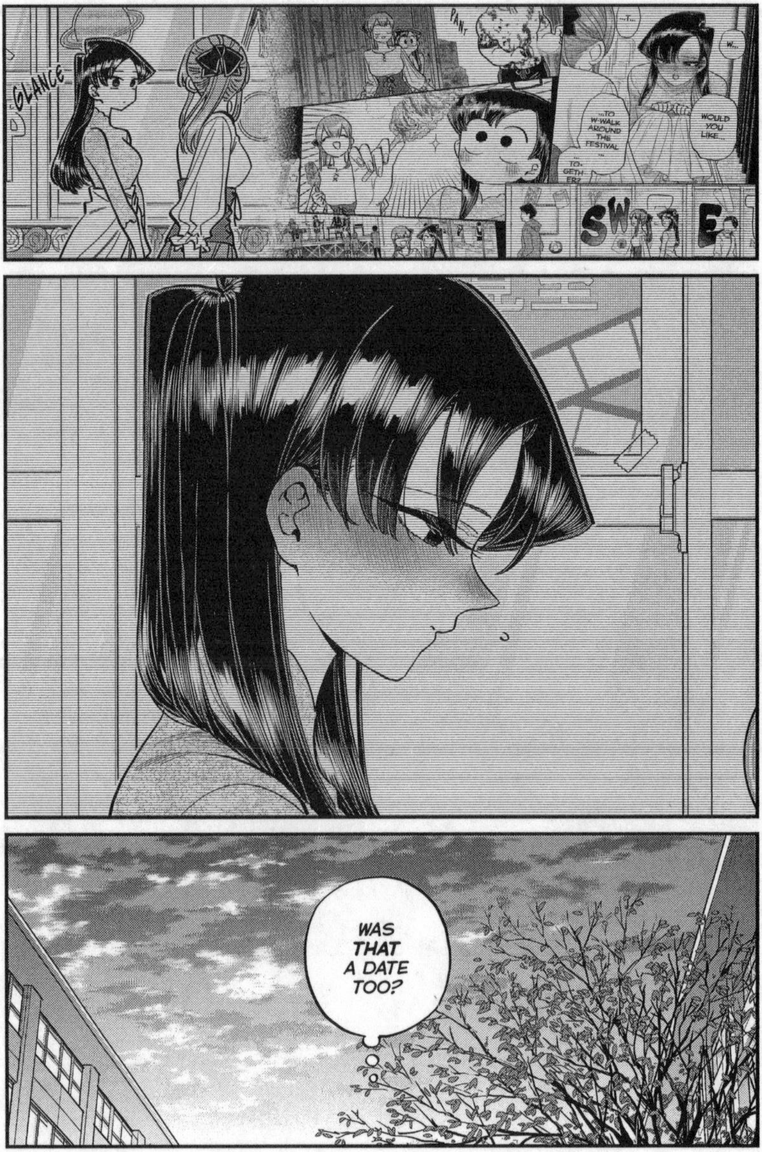
W...
...T...
WOULD YOU LIKE...
...TO W-WALK AROUND THE FESTIVAL ...
...TO-GETH-ER?
PANT
GLANCE
WAS THAT A DATE TOO?

Communication 233 — The End

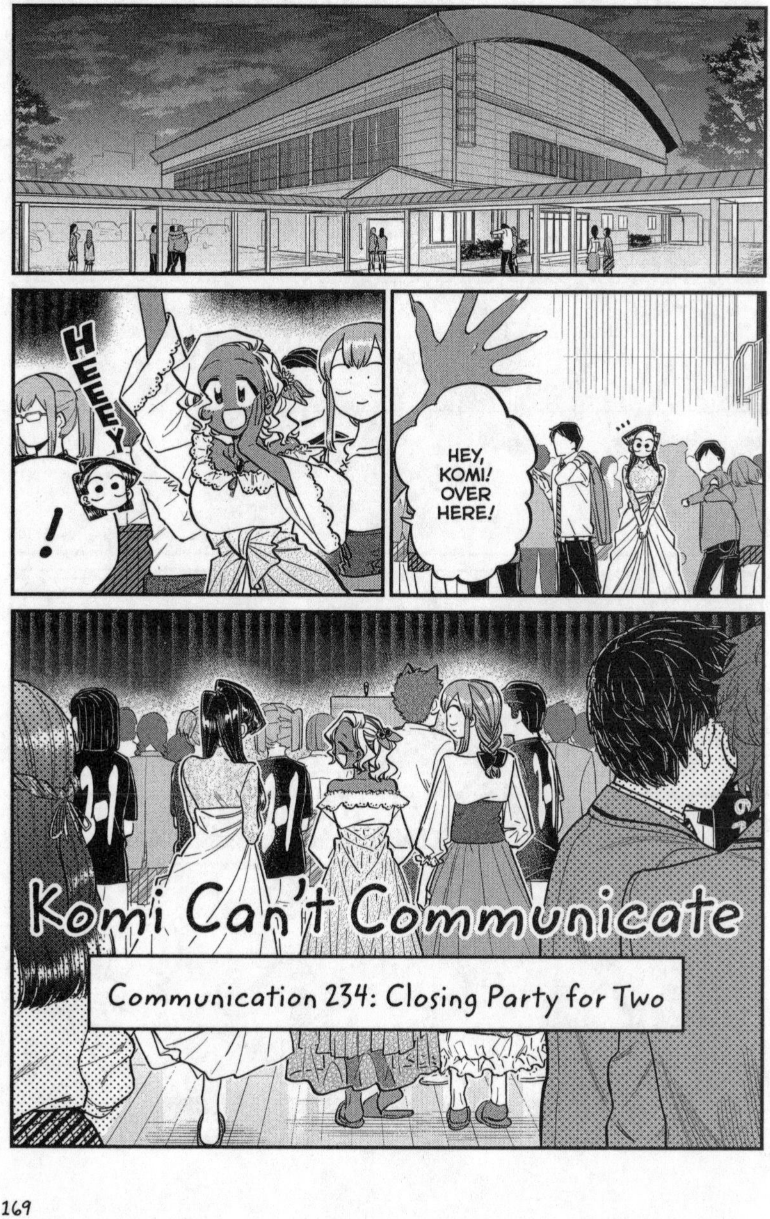
HEY, KOMI! OVER HERE!
HEEEY
!
Komi Can't Communicate
Communication 234: Closing Party for Two

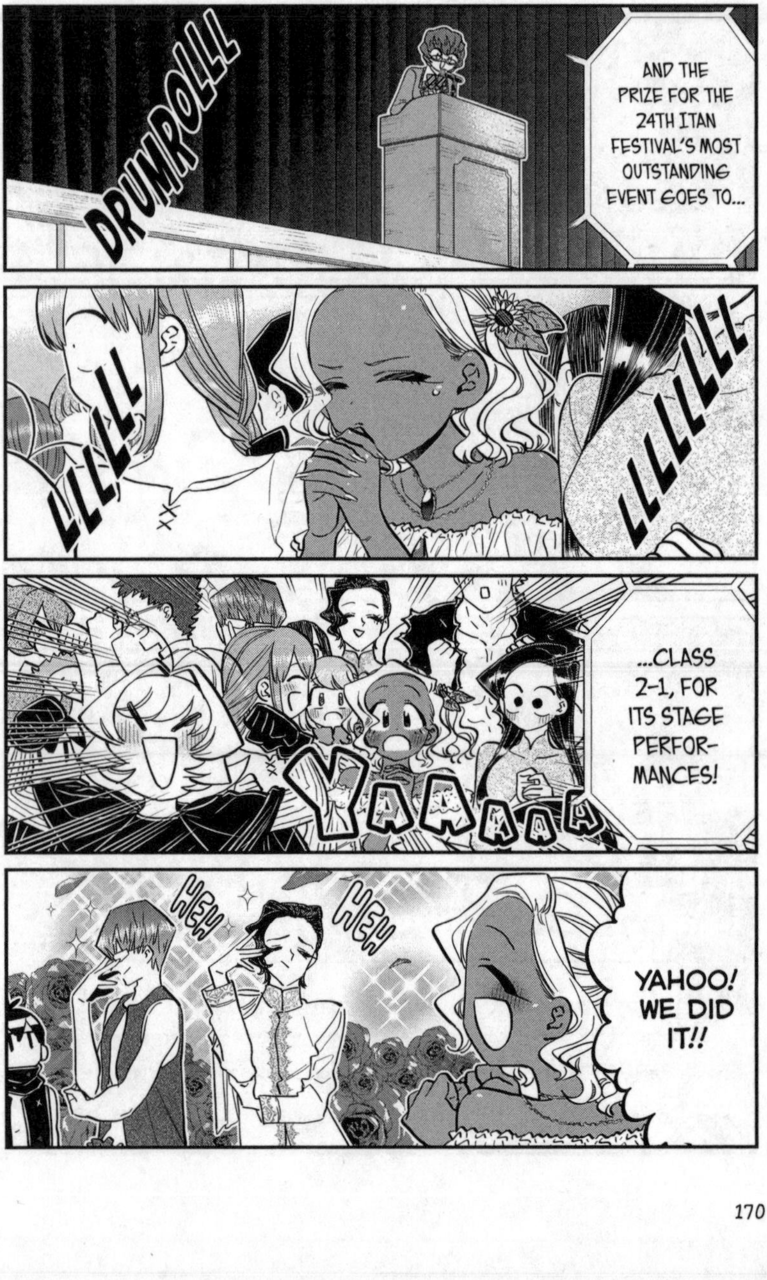
AND THE PRIZE FOR THE 24TH ITAN FESTIVAL'S MOST OUTSTANDING EVENT GOES TO...
DRUMROLLL
LLLLLLLL
LLLLL
...CLASS 2-1, FOR ITS STAGE PERFOR-MANCES!
YAAAAAH
YAHOO! WE DID IT!!
HEH
HEH

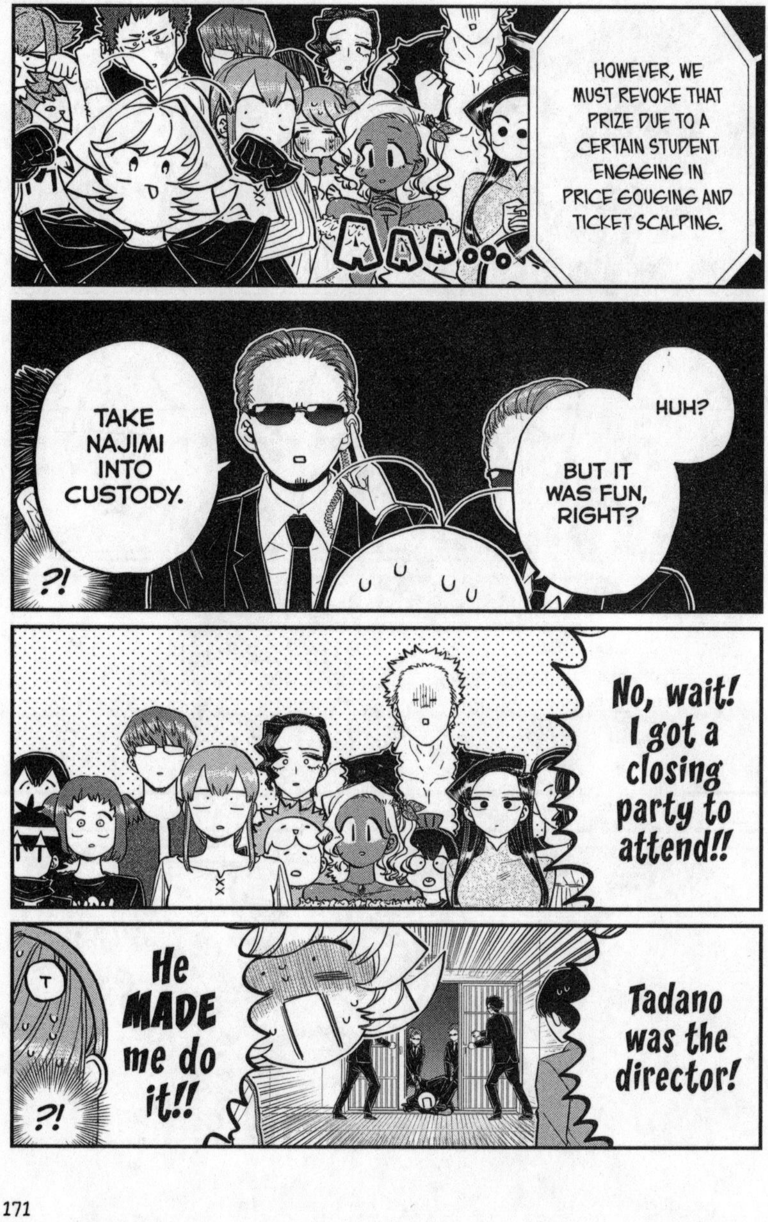
HOWEVER, WE MUST REVOKE THAT PRIZE DUE TO A CERTAIN STUDENT ENGAGING IN PRICE GOUGING AND TICKET SCALPING.
AAA...
HUH?
BUT IT WAS FUN, RIGHT?
TAKE NAJIMI INTO CUSTODY.
?!
No, wait! I got a closing party to attend!!
Tadano was the director!
He MADE me do it!!
?!

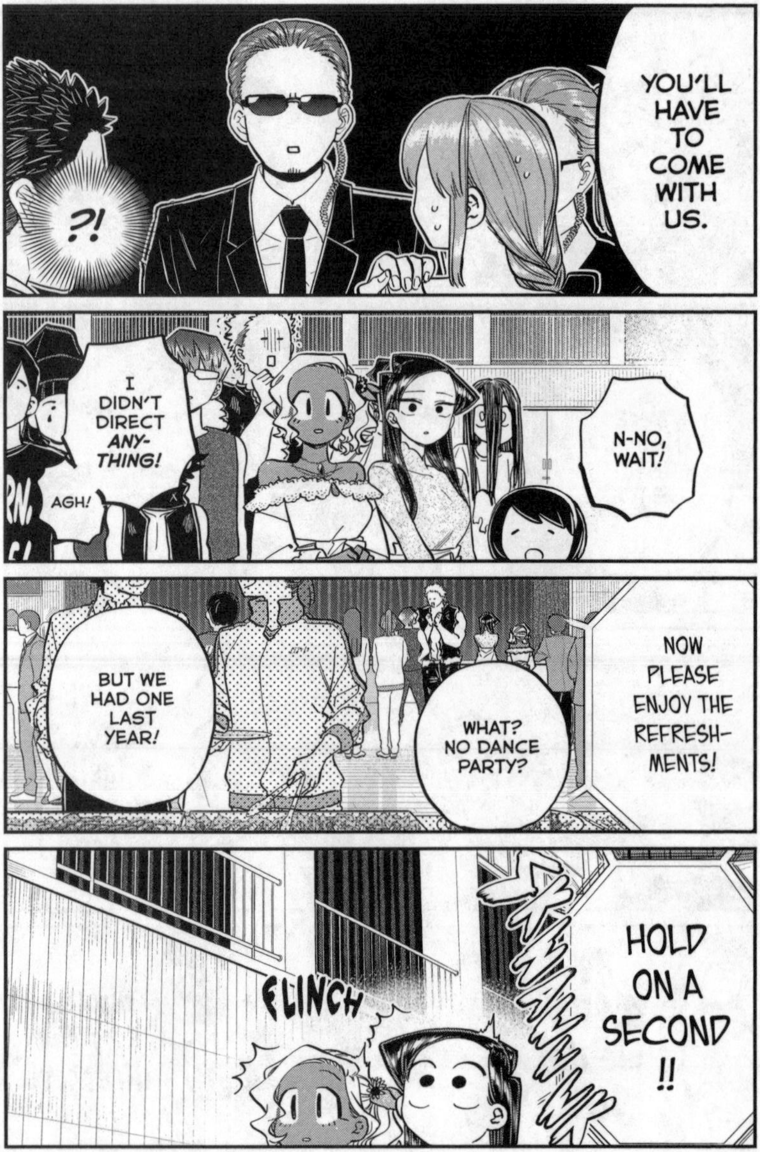
YOU'LL HAVE TO COME WITH US.
?!
N-NO, WAIT!
I DIDN'T DIRECT ANYTHING!
AGH!
NOW PLEASE ENJOY THE REFRESHMENTS!
WHAT? NO DANCE PARTY?
BUT WE HAD ONE LAST YEAR!
HOLD ON A SECOND!!
FLINCH

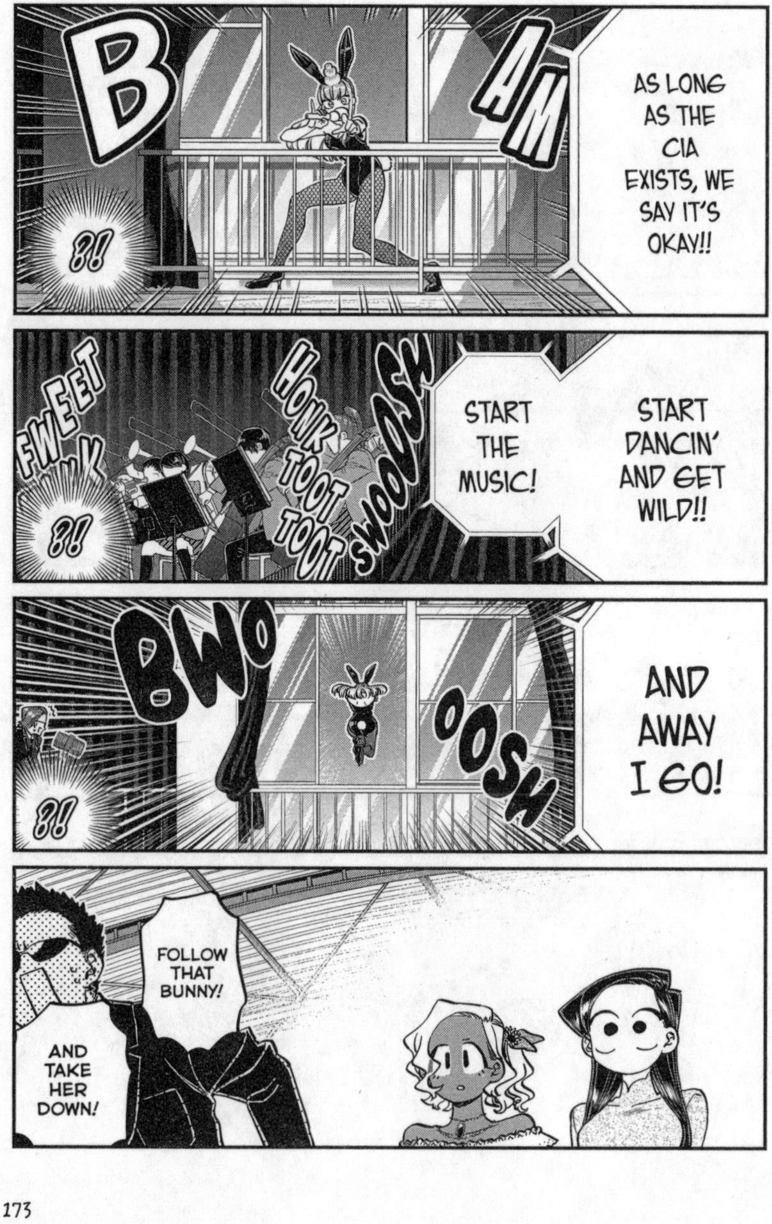
AS LONG AS THE CIA EXISTS, WE SAY IT'S OKAY!!
BAM
?!
START DANCIN' AND GET WILD!!
START THE MUSIC!
SWOOSH
HONK TOOT TOOT
FWEET
?!
AND AWAY I GO!
BWOOOSH
?!
FOLLOW THAT BUNNY!
AND TAKE HER DOWN!

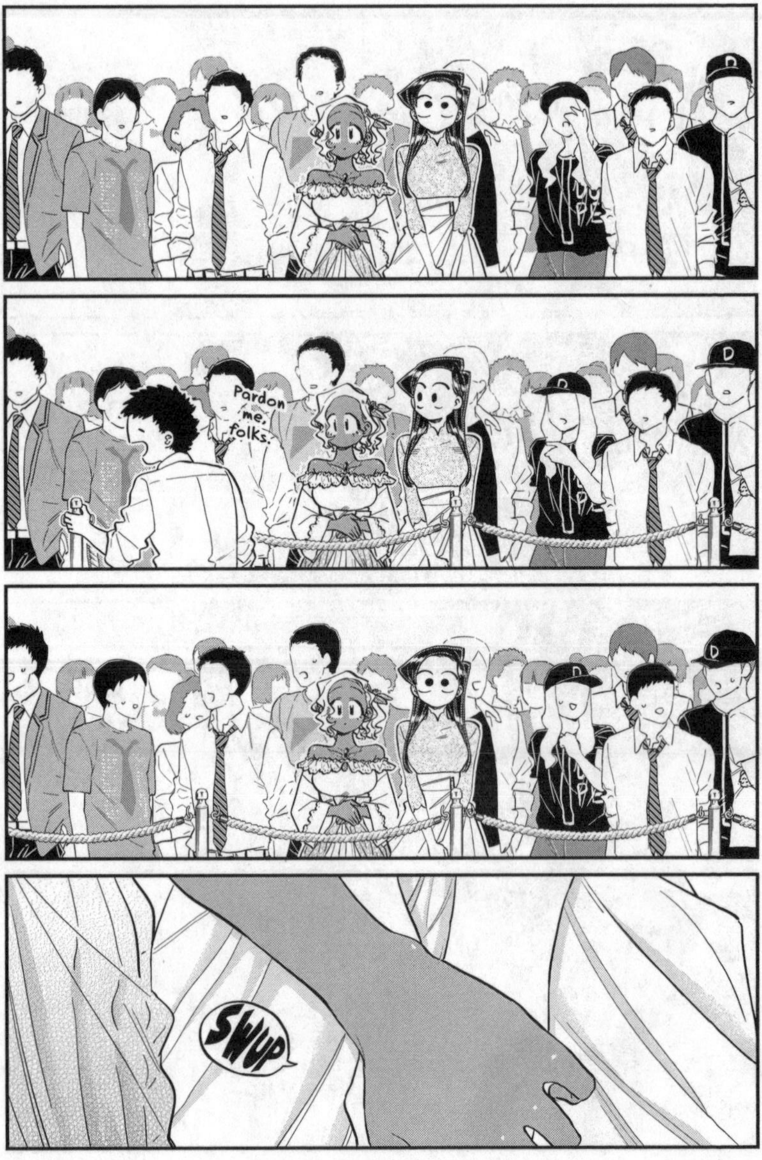
Pardon me, folks.
SWUP

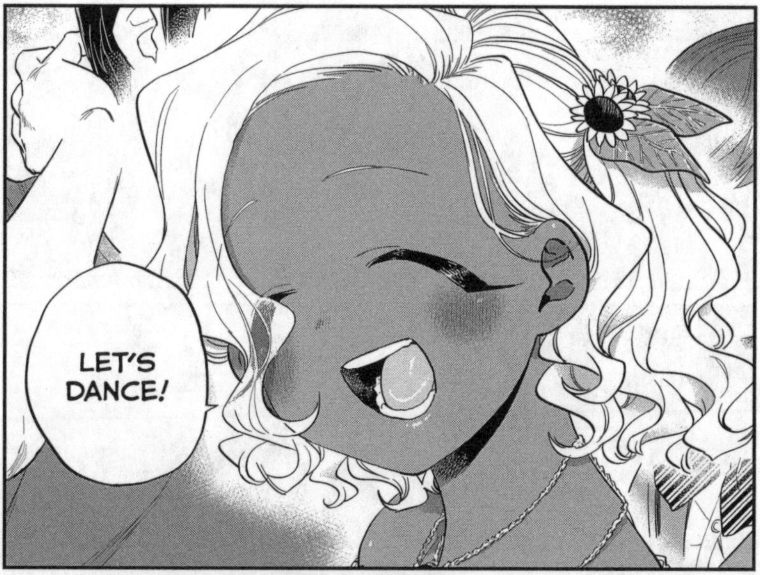
LET'S DANCE!

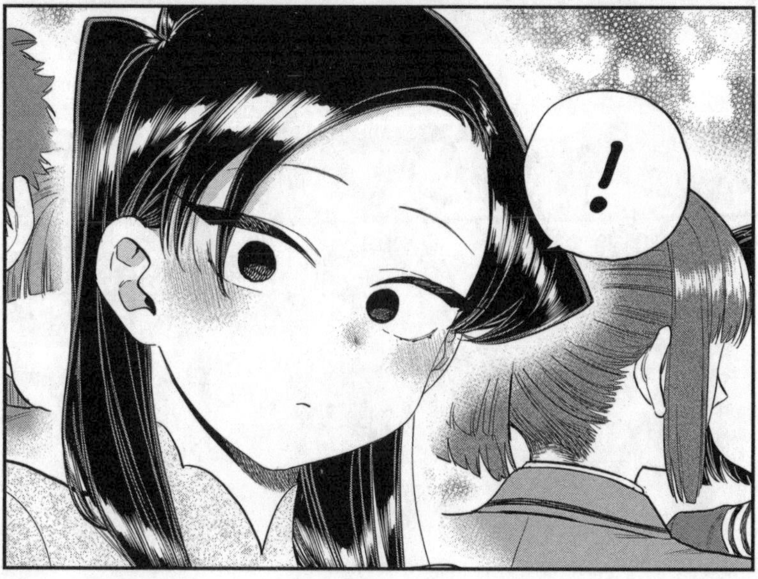
!

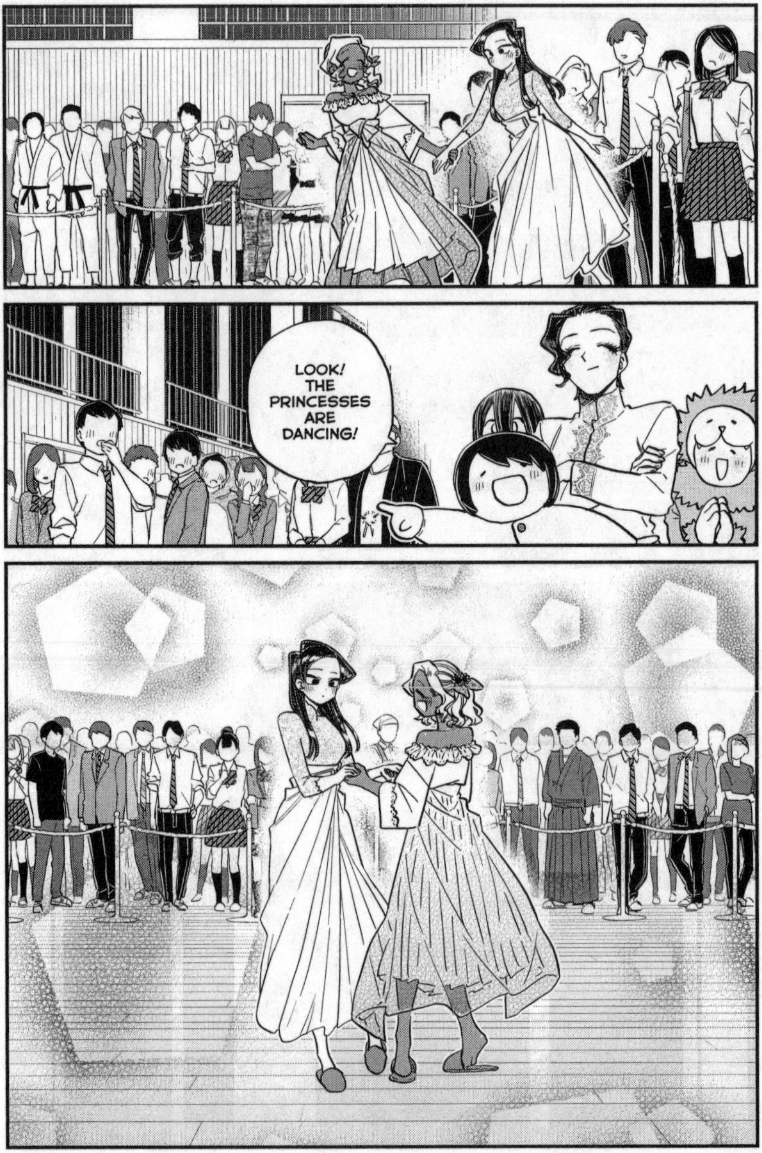
LOOK! THE PRINCESSES ARE DANCING!

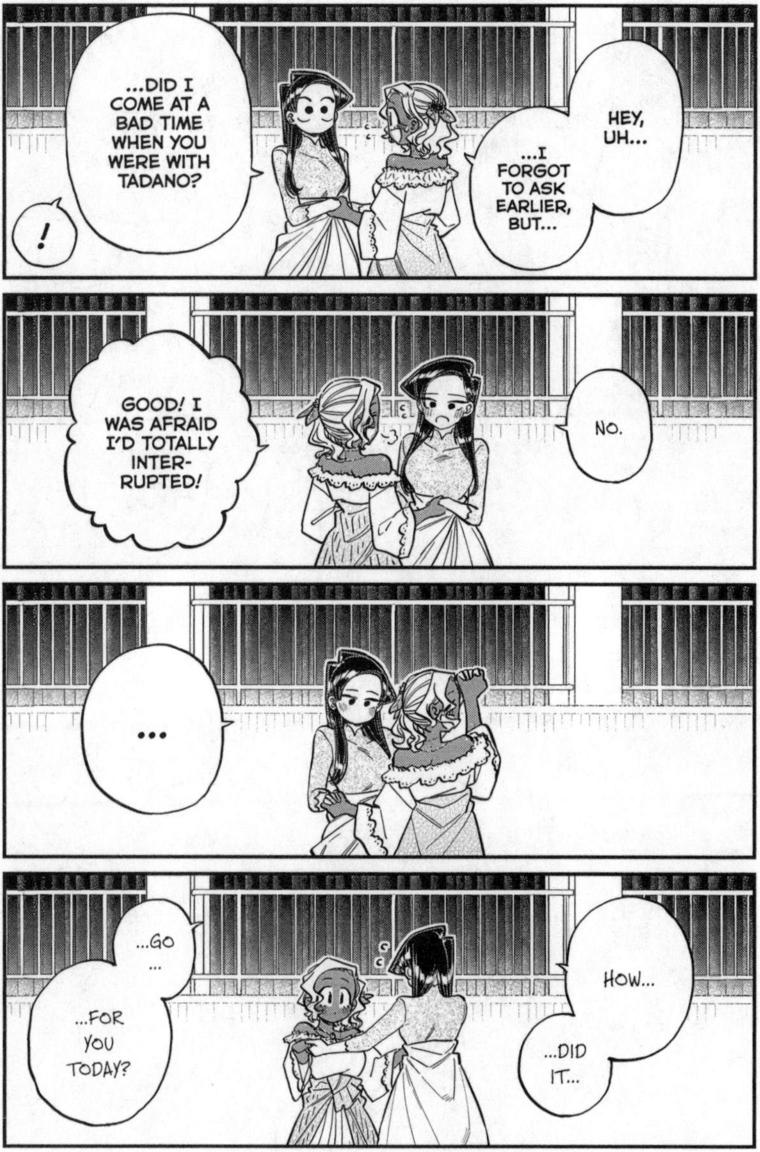
HEY, UH...
...I FORGOT TO ASK EARLIER, BUT...
...DID I COME AT A BAD TIME WHEN YOU WERE WITH TADANO?
!
NO.
GOOD! I WAS AFRAID I'D TOTALLY INTER-RUPTED!
...
HOW...
...DID IT...
...GO
...
...FOR YOU TODAY?

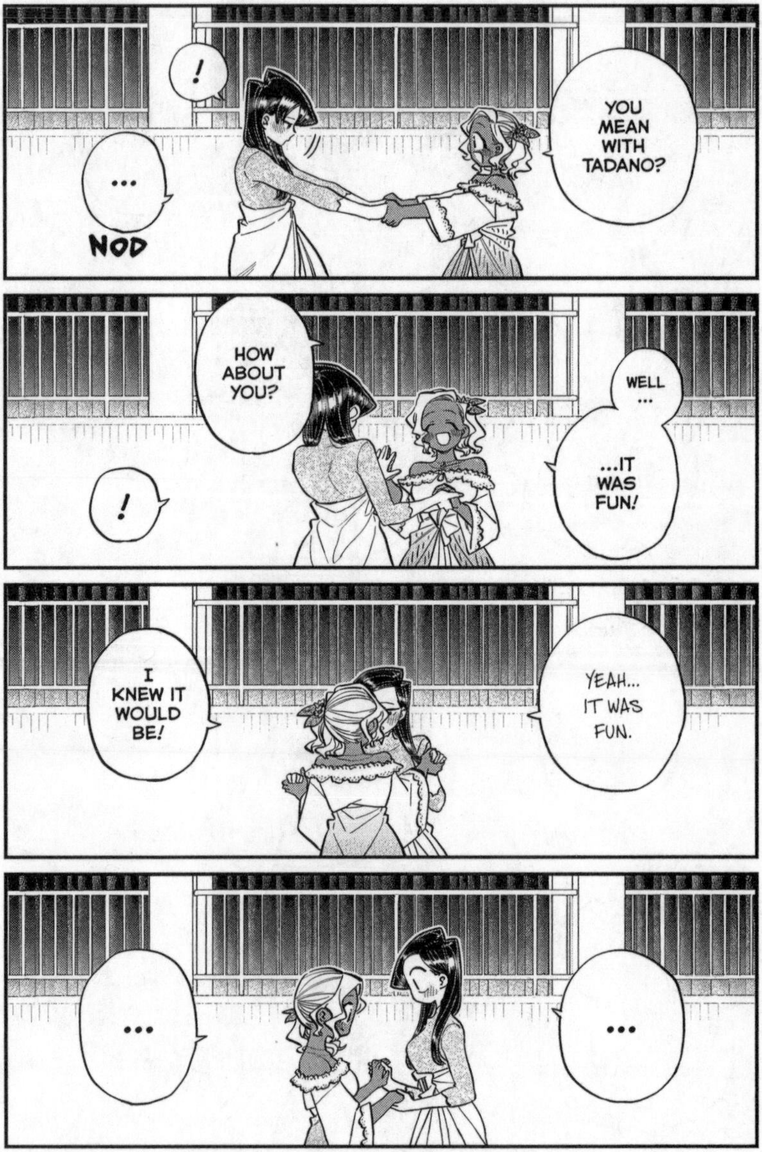
YOU MEAN WITH TADANO?
!
...
NOD
WELL ...
...IT WAS FUN!
HOW ABOUT YOU?
!
YEAH... IT WAS FUN.
I KNEW IT WOULD BE!
...
...

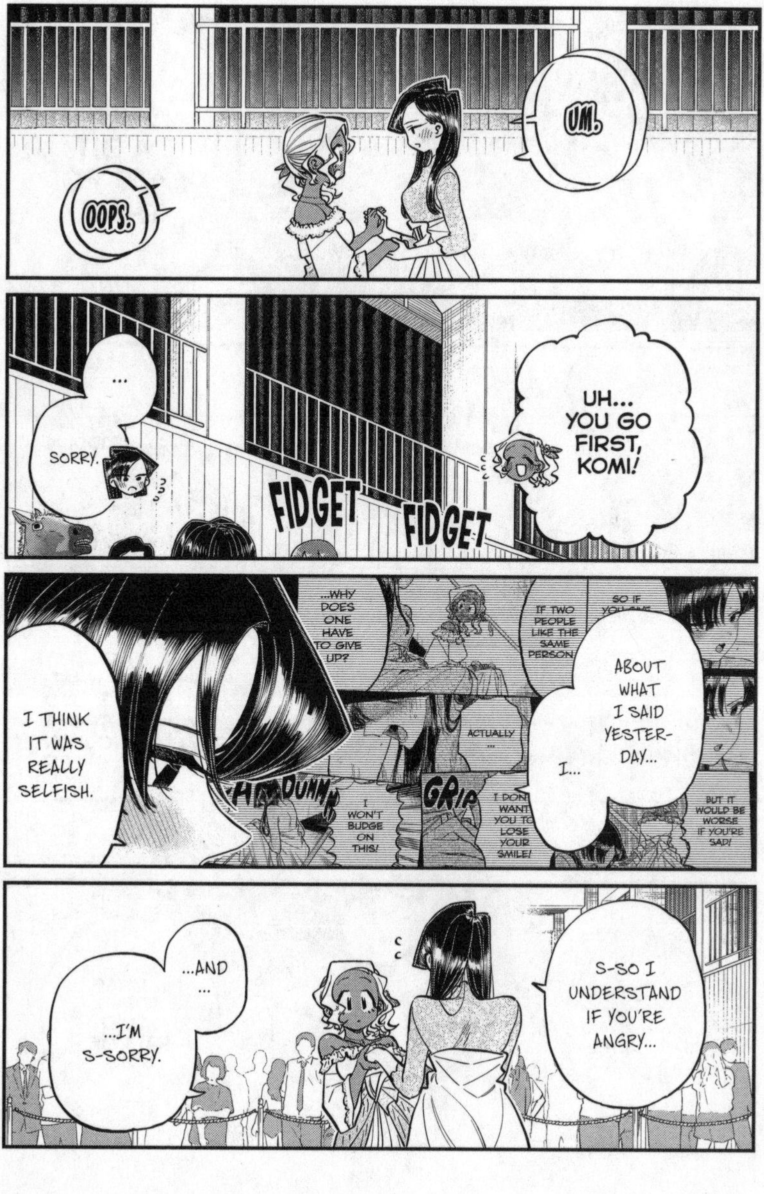
UM.
OOPS.
UH... YOU GO FIRST, KOMI!
FIDGET
FIDGET
...
SORRY.
I... ABOUT WHAT I SAID YESTERDAY...
BUT IT WOULD BE WORSE IF YOU'RE SAD!
IF TWO PEOPLE LIKE THE SAME PERSON
...WHY DOES ONE HAVE TO GIVE UP?
ACTUALLY ...
I DON WANT YOU TO LOSE YOUR SMILE!
GRIP
I WON'T BUDGE ON THIS!
DUNNN
I THINK IT WAS REALLY SELFISH.
S-SO I UNDERSTAND IF YOU'RE ANGRY...
...AND ...
...I'M S-SORRY.

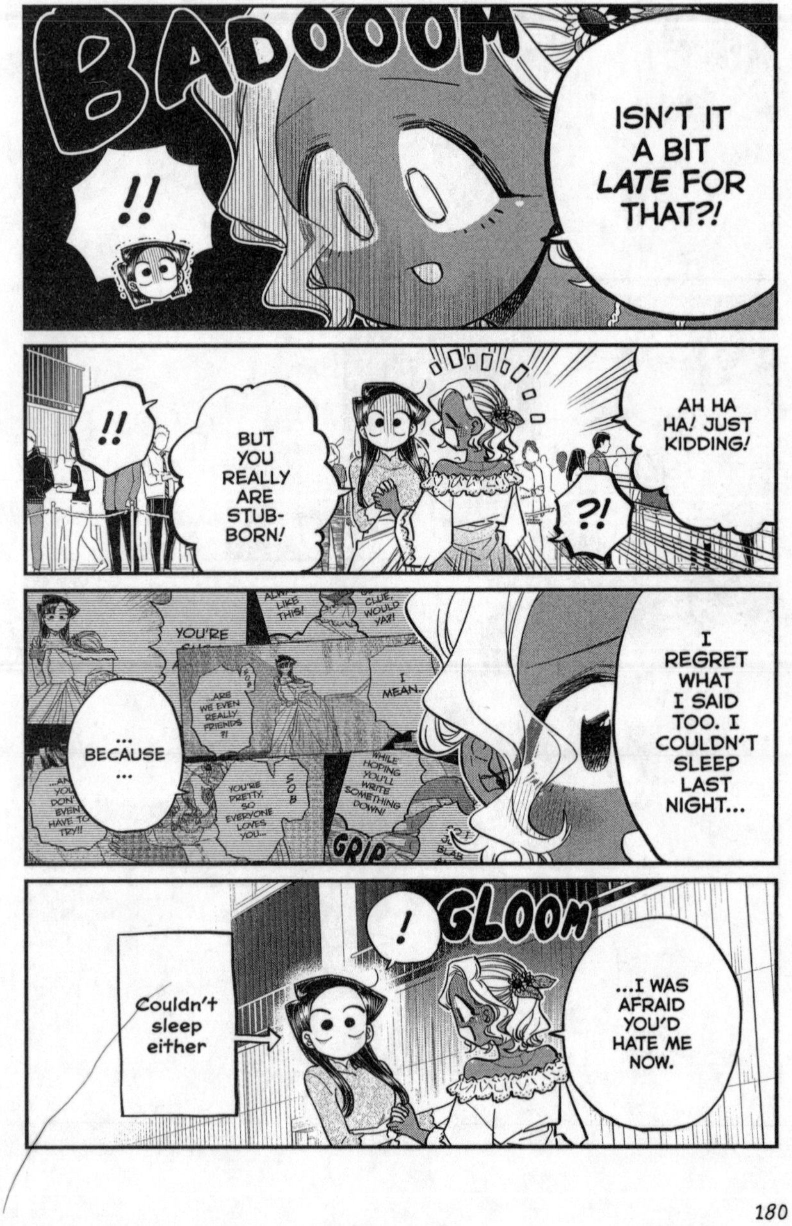
ISN'T IT A BIT *LATE* FOR THAT?!
BADOOOM
!!
AH HA HA! JUST KIDDING!
?!
BUT YOU REALLY ARE STUB-BORN!
!!
I REGRET WHAT I SAID TOO. I COULDN'T SLEEP LAST NIGHT...
I MEAN..
WHILE HOPING YOU'LL WRITE SOMETHING DOWN!
...ARE WE EVEN REALLY FRIENDS?!
SOB
YOU'RE PRETTY, SO EVERYONE LOVES YOU...
GRIP
... BECAUSE ...
...I WAS AFRAID YOU'D HATE ME NOW.
GLOOM
!
Couldn't sleep either

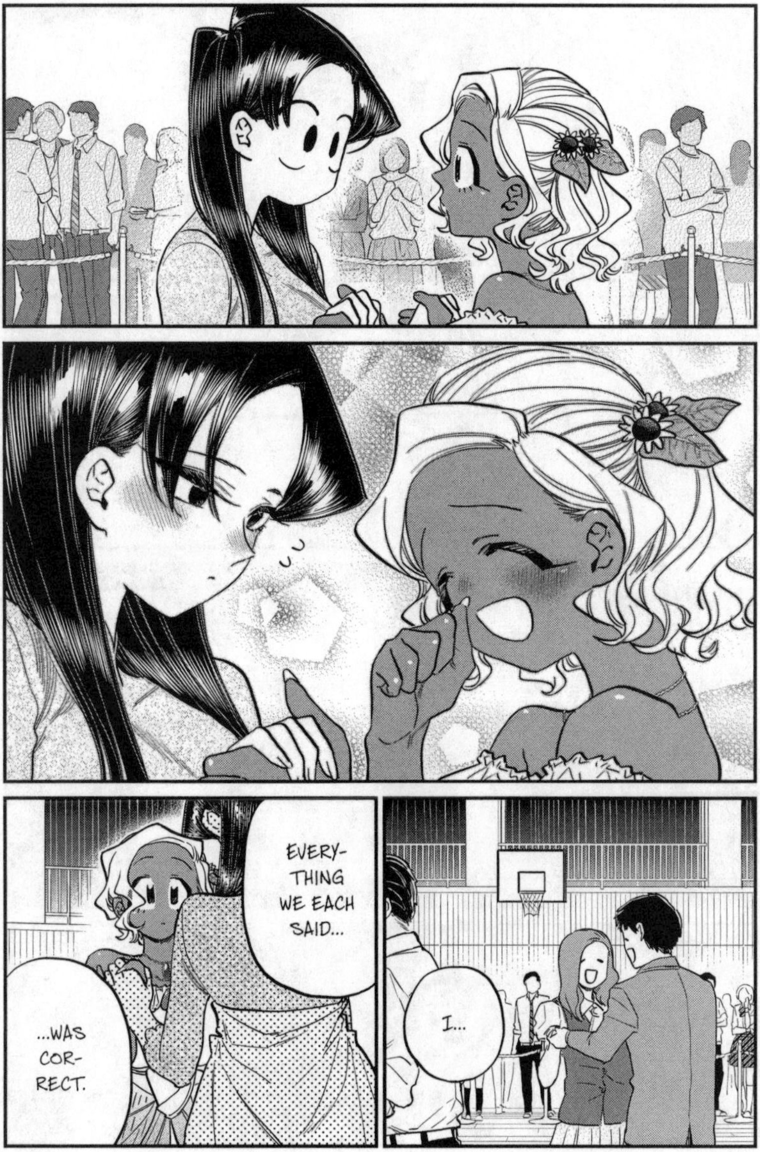
I...
EVERY-THING WE EACH SAID...
...WAS COR-RECT.

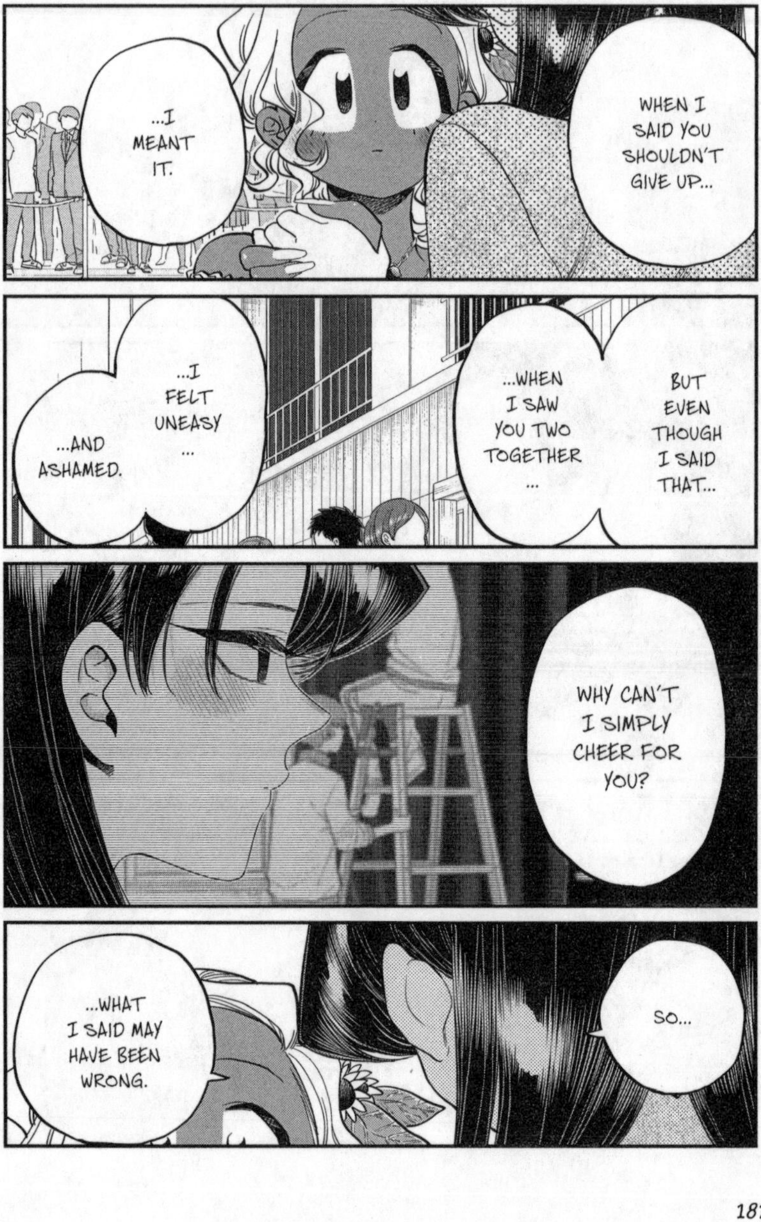
WHEN I SAID YOU SHOULDN'T GIVE UP...
...I MEANT IT.
BUT EVEN THOUGH I SAID THAT...
...WHEN I SAW YOU TWO TOGETHER ...
...I FELT UNEASY ...
...AND ASHAMED.
WHY CAN'T I SIMPLY CHEER FOR YOU?
SO...
...WHAT I SAID MAY HAVE BEEN WRONG.

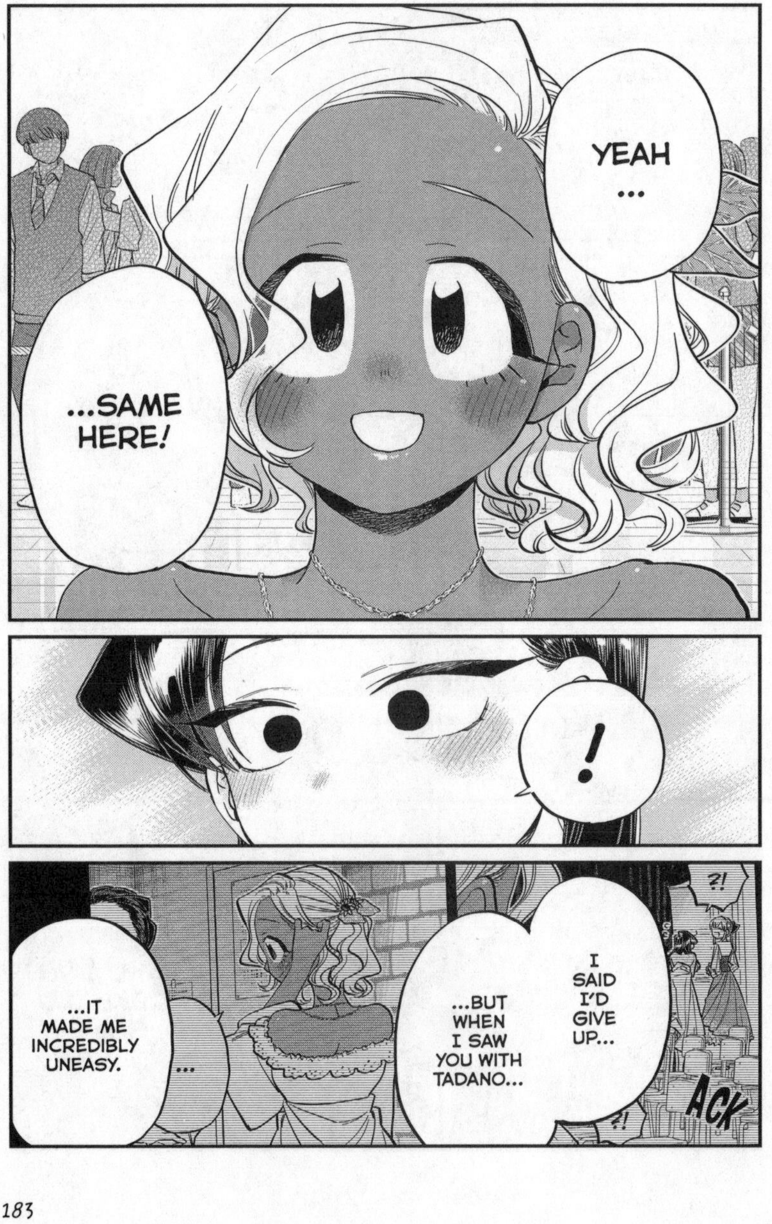
YEAH ...
...SAME HERE!
!
?!
I SAID I'D GIVE UP...
...BUT WHEN I SAW YOU WITH TADANO...
...
...IT MADE ME INCREDIBLY UNEASY.
ACK
?!

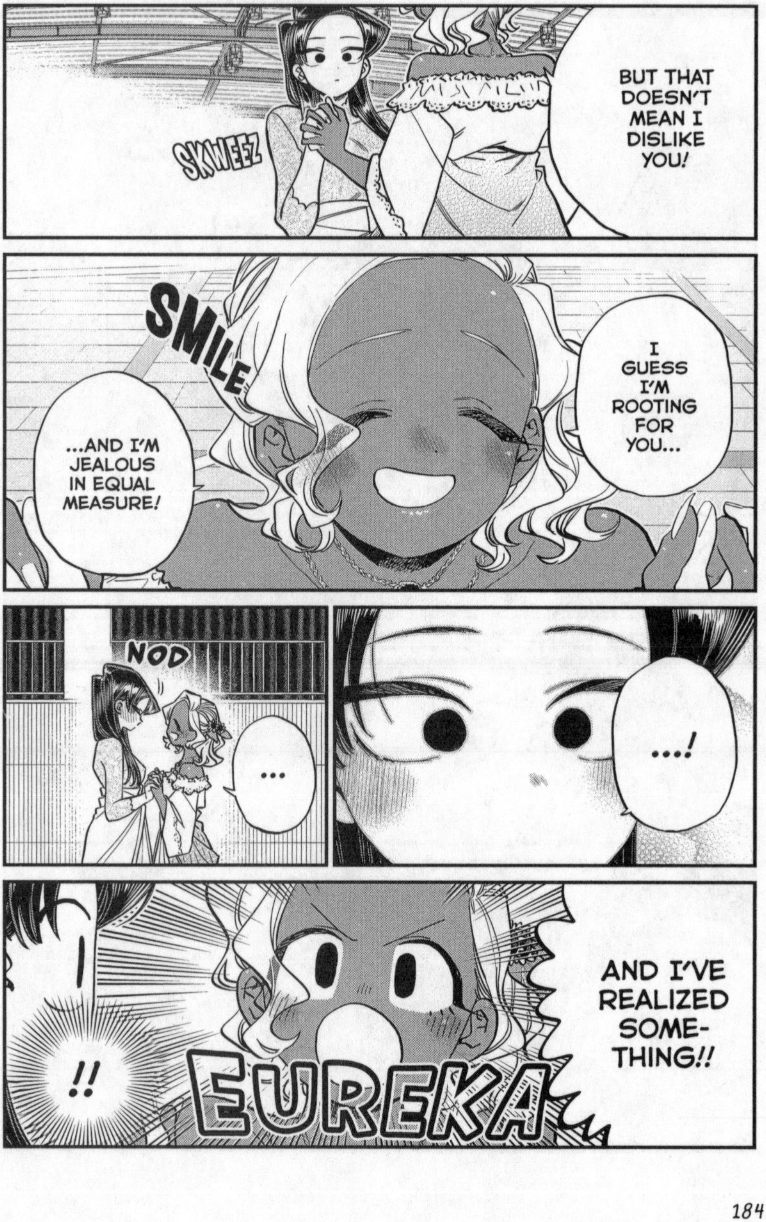
BUT THAT DOESN'T MEAN I DISLIKE YOU!
SKWEEZ
I GUESS I'M ROOTING FOR YOU...
SMILE
...AND I'M JEALOUS IN EQUAL MEASURE!
...!
NOD
...
AND I'VE REALIZED SOME-THING!!
EUREKA
!!

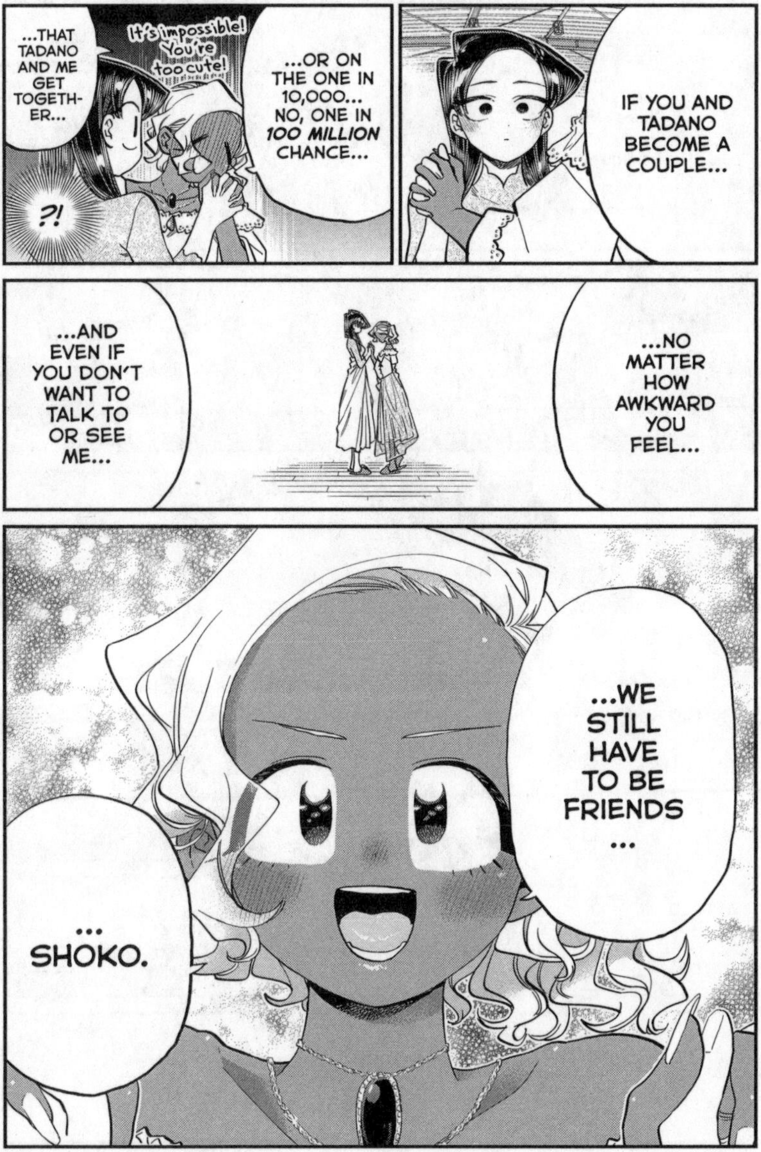
IF YOU AND TADANO BECOME A COUPLE...
...OR ON THE ONE IN 10,000... NO, ONE IN *100 MILLION* CHANCE...
It's impossible! You're too cute!
...THAT TADANO AND ME GET TOGETH-ER...
?!
...NO MATTER HOW AWKWARD YOU FEEL...
...AND EVEN IF YOU DON'T WANT TO TALK TO OR SEE ME...
...WE STILL HAVE TO BE FRIENDS ...
... SHOKO.

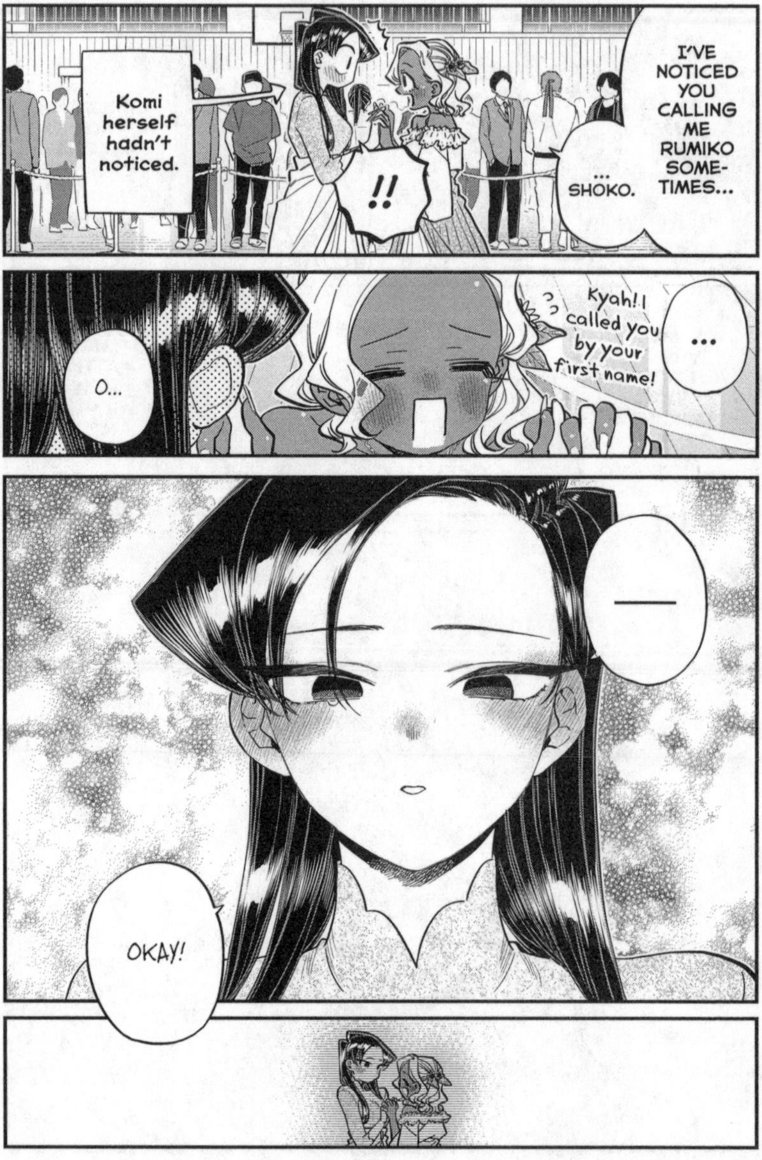
I'VE NOTICED YOU CALLING ME RUMIKO SOME-TIMES...
... SHOKO.
!!
Komi herself hadn't noticed.
...
Kyah!! I called you by your first name!
O...
—
OKAY!

Communication 234 — The End

Komi Can't Communicate

Komi Can't Communicate Bonus

The Former Student Council President Is...Weird

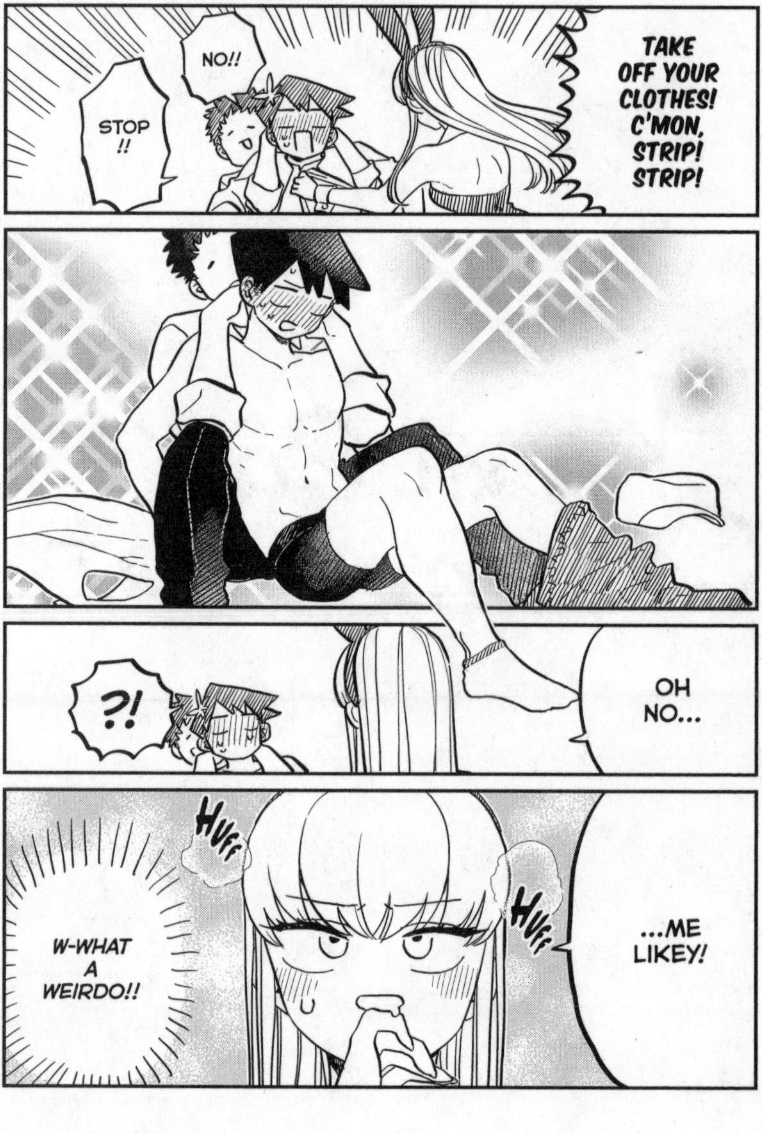
TAKE OFF YOUR CLOTHES! C'MON, STRIP! STRIP!
NO!!
STOP !!
OH NO...
?!
...ME LIKEY!
HUFF
HUFF
W-WHAT A WEIRDO!!

Komi Can't Communicate Bonus

Anujiru = A Popular Food in the Repupu Republic

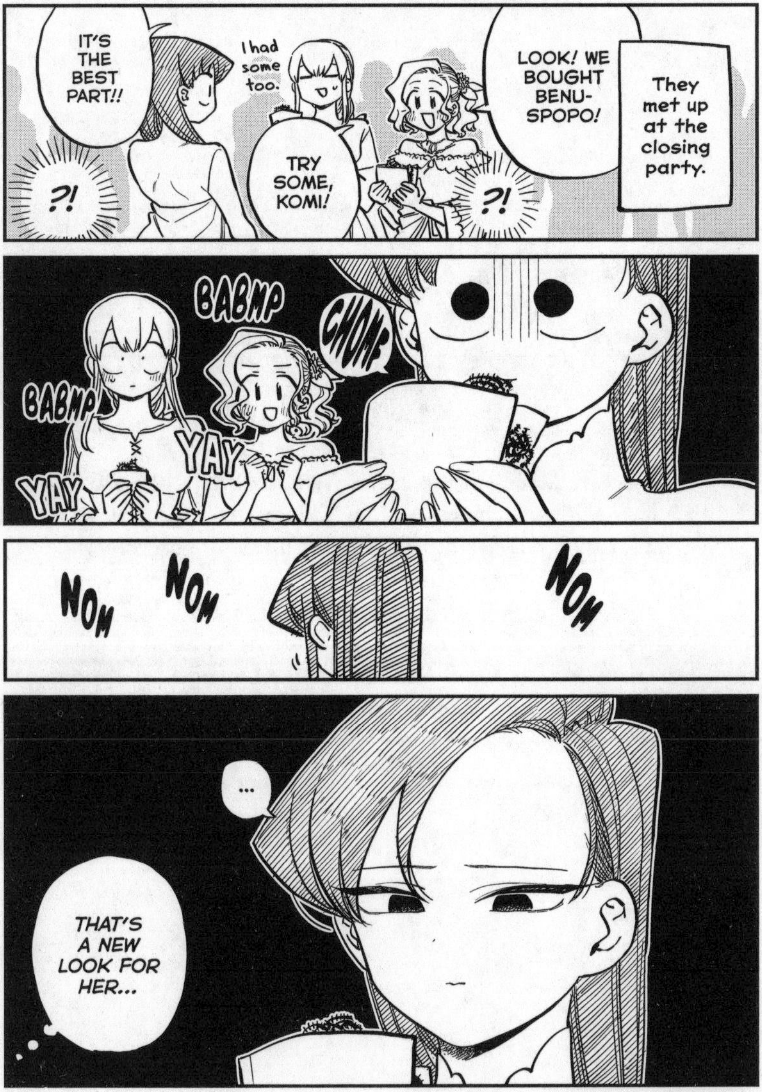
They met up at the closing party.
LOOK! WE BOUGHT BENU-SPOPO!
?!
I had some too.
TRY SOME, KOMI!
IT'S THE BEST PART!!
?!
CHOMP
BABMP
YAY
BABMP
YAY
NOM
NOM
NOM
...
THAT'S A NEW LOOK FOR HER...

Tomohito Oda won the grand prize for *World Worst One* in the 70th Shogakukan New Comic Artist Awards in 2012. Oda's series *Digicon*, about a tough high school girl who finds herself in control of an alien with plans for world domination, ran from 2014 to 2015. In 2015, *Komi Can't Communicate* debuted as a one-shot in *Weekly Shonen Sunday* and was picked up as a full series by the same magazine in 2016.

Komi Can't Communicate

VOL. 17
Shonen Sunday Edition

Story and Art by Tomohito Oda

English Translation & Adaptation/John Werry
Touch-Up Art & Lettering/Eve Grandt
Design/Julian [JR] Robinson
Editor/Pancha Diaz

COMI-SAN WA, COMYUSHO DESU. Vol. 17
by Tomohito ODA
© 2016 Tomohito ODA
All rights reserved.
Original Japanese edition published by SHOGAKUKAN.
English translation rights in the United States of America, Canada, the United
Kingdom, Ireland, Australia and New Zealand arranged with SHOGAKUKAN.

Original Cover Design/Masato ISHIZAWA + Bay Bridge Studio

Printed in the U.S.A.

Published by VIZ Media, LLC
P.O. Box 77010
San Francisco, CA 94107

10 9 8 7 6 5 4 3 2 1
First printing, February 2022

viz.com

shonensunday.com

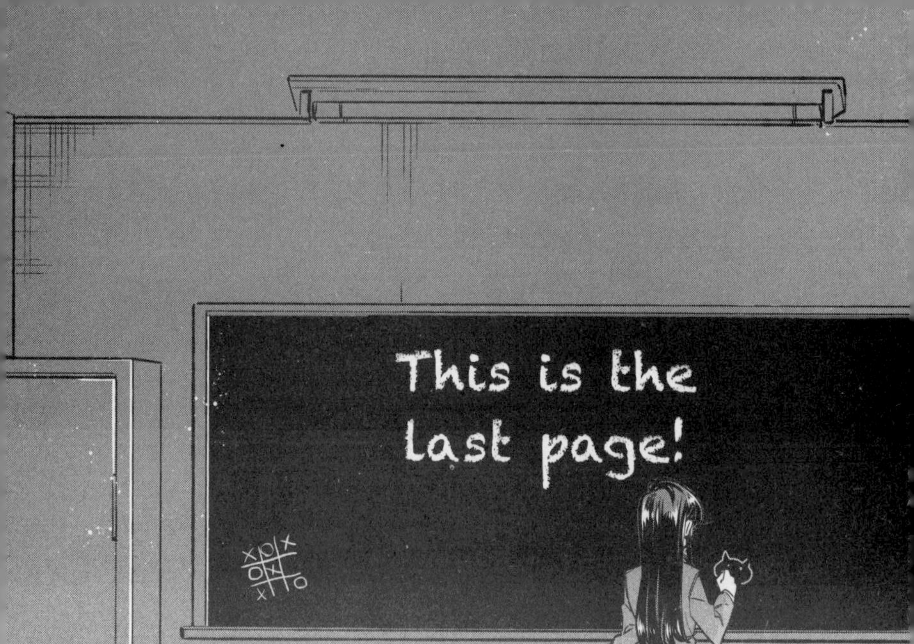
This is the last page!

Komi Can't Communicate has been printed in the original Japanese format to preserve the orientation of the artwork.

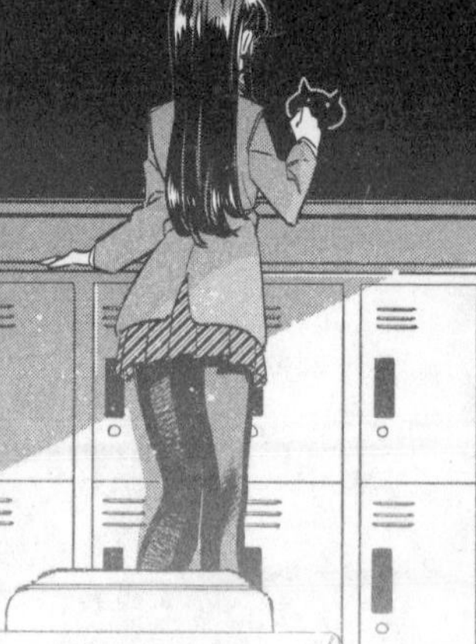

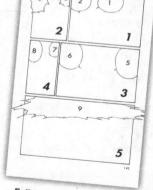

Follow the action this way.